IN THE HUNT

Other Titles in the Smart Pop Series

Taking the Red Pill
Seven Seasons of Buffy
Five Seasons of Angel
What Would Sipowicz Do?
Stepping through the Stargate
The Anthology at the End of the Universe
Finding Serenity
The War of the Worlds
Alias Assumed
Navigating the Golden Compass
Farscape Forever!
Flirting with Pride and Prejudice
Revisiting Narnia
Totally Charmed
King Kong Is Back!
Mapping the World of the Sorcerer's Apprentice
The Unauthorized X-Men
The Man from Krypton
Welcome to Wisteria Lane
Star Wars on Trial
The Battle for Azeroth
Boarding the Enterprise
Getting Lost
James Bond in the 21st Century
So Say We All
Investigating CSI
Literary Cash
Webslinger
Halo Effect
Neptune Noir
Coffee at Luke's
Perfectly Plum
Grey's Anatomy 101
Serenity Found
House Unauthorized
Batman Unauthorized

IN THE HUNT

Unauthorized Essays on *Supernatural*

Edited by Supernatural.tv
WITH LEAH WILSON

BENBELLA BOOKS, INC.
Dallas, Texas

BenBella Books, Inc.
6440 N. Central Expressway, Suite 503
Dallas, TX 75206
www.benbellabooks.com
Send feedback to feedback@benbellabooks.com

Printed in the United States of America
10 9 8 7 6 5 4 3 2 1

Library of Congress Cataloging-in-Publication Data

In the hunt : unauthorized essays on Supernatural / edited by Supernatural.tv with Leah Wilson.
p. cm.
ISBN 978-1-933771-63-2
1. Supernatural (Television program : 2005-) I. Wilson, Leah. II. Supernatural.tv (Online)

PN1992.77.S84I58 2009
791.45'72--dc22

2008045909

Proofreading by Stacia Seaman
Cover illustration by Ralph Voltz
Cover design by Laura Watkins
Text design and composition by Laura Watkins
Printed by Bang Printing

Distributed by Perseus Distribution
perseusdistribution.com

To place orders through Perseus Distribution:
Tel: (800) 343-4499
Fax: (800) 351-5073
E-mail: orderentry@perseusbooks.com

To the Reader

Because of the way the publishing industry works, the essays you're about to read were written after season three of *Supernatural* ended and before season four began. As is usually the case with any show worth its proverbial rock salt, a lot will have changed by the time you read this. In just the first three episodes of season four, the show had already radically revised both its cosmology and its backstory . . . and rendered half a dozen carefully crafted essays not just out of date, but borderline incorrect.

This leaves it to you, as the reader, to fill in the gaps: to take the theories and ideas we've compiled here and use them as a window through which to look at what's happened since the essays were written. We hope you'll read Avril Hannah-Jones's essay and ask whether the now-verified existence of the heavenly host alters her basic thesis that the Winchesters are the show's true angels; we want you to muse over what Jacob Clifton might have said about the timing of Dean and Sam discovering Mary's family background—is it indicative of the show's feminine Shadow finally coming to the fore?

We expect there are more surprises yet to come. Heck, we'd be disappointed if there weren't. And in the meantime? We hope *In the Hunt* helps you enjoy the ride.

—The Publisher

TABLE OF CONTENTS

Foreword
Not Just a Pretty Face (or Two) ix
KEITH R. A. DECANDIDO

Introduction xiii
SUPERNATURAL.TV

"We're Not Exactly the Bradys" 1
TANYA HUFF

The Burden of Being Sammy 11
DODGER WINSLOW

What's Supernatural About *Supernatural*? 27
RANDALL M. JENSEN

Horror, Humanity, and the Demon in the Mirror 39
GREGORY STEVENSON

Good and Evil in the World of *Supernatural* 53
AVRIL HANNAH-JONES

Sympathy for the Devils 67
ROBERT T. JESCHONEK

Dean Winchester: Bad-Ass . . . or Soccer Mom? 77
TANYA MICHAELS

"We've Got Work to Do" 87
AMY GARVEY

A Powerful Need 97
SHERYL A. RAKOWSKI

Buffy the Vampire Slayer, Jo the Monster Killer 107
MARY BORSELLINO

Spreading Disaster 119
JACOB CLIFTON

Who Threw Momma on the Ceiling? 143
CAROL POOLE

Scary Just Got Sexy 155
EMILY TURNER

Blue Collar Ghost Hunters 165
JAMIE CHAMBERS

A *Supernatural* Love Story 175
HEATHER SWAIN

Back in Black 197
JULES WILKINSON

Riding Down the Highway 209
MARY FECHTER

John Winchester and the Magic Bullet Theory 219
TRACY S. MORRIS

The Evils of Hating . . . Um, Evil 225
AMY BERNER

Another Roadside Attraction 237
MARIA LIMA

Keepers of the Lore 251
SHANNA SWENDSON

Ghouls in Cyberspace 263
LONDON E. BRICKLEY

Acknowledgments 275

Foreword

KEITH R. A. DECANDIDO

NOT JUST A PRETTY FACE (OR TWO)

Hello, my name is Keith, and I'm a heterosexual male who's also a *Supernatural* fan.

I realize that this may make me seem bizarre to some. If one wanders the Internet and peers at the audiences for *Supernatural* conventions, one observes a sea of female faces. Certainly most of the women I know who watch the show do so in part because they find Jensen Ackles and/or Jared Padalecki to be very easy on the eyes.

Only in part, though, and that's a critical aspect of *Supernatural*'s appeal: it's much, much better than it needs to be.

As a show on the CW, *Supernatural* could probably still be a successful fifth-network series if it just had two pretty men driving in a cool car, cracking wise and shooting demons in the head. And *Supernatural* does have all those things in abundance.

But it's got more besides. For starters, the show has a wonderful sense of family. And I don't mean so-called "family values," that rather nebulous attempt to revert to the nonexistent nuclear family exemplified by *Leave It to Beaver*, but rather the importance family has to a person. Family doesn't necessarily mean blood relatives—look at the characters of Bobby and Ellen, for example—but the show has excelled at showing those connections and what they mean. There aren't very many fictional siblings on television who cover all the aspects of that relationship the way Sam and Dean do: not just the love and affection and dedication, but also the near-telepathic bond, the arguing, the pranking, the affectionate abuse.

The show has often trotted out the cliché wherein the bad guys say that the brothers' bond is a weakness, and the heroes insist that it's a strength. But what *Supernatural* does so well is show that it's *both*. Heck, brotherly love has managed to get *both* brothers killed.

That complexity of family relationships also holds true with both father figures in the show: the boys' biological father, John Winchester, and their surrogate father, Bobby Singer. The search for the former informed the entire first season, and the character's death at the top of the second season in "In My Time of Dying" (2-1) has continued to resonate in the boys' lives since. John's relationship to his children could charitably be called complex (and perhaps more accurately, seriously messed up), as his influence has saved their lives and provided them with a source of love and comfort, but also left significant psychological scars on both boys that will probably never heal. (His last words to Dean sent him into a tizzy that lasted half the second season.)

As for Bobby, he himself said in the third-season finale, "No Rest for the Wicked" (3-16), how family goes beyond blood. Both that episode and "Dream a Little Dream of Me" (3-10), in which we learned some of Bobby's background, made it clear that Bobby is as much a father to Sam and Dean as John was (some could argue more so).

There are other aspects of the show that are immensely appealing. While *Supernatural* isn't as heavily serialized as, say, *Heroes* or *Lost*, the show is aggressively aware of its own continuity. When something is established in one episode, it remains true thenceforth. A prominent example: the Key of Solomon, introduced at the end of the first season in "Devil's Trap" (1-22), has remained a useful method of trapping demons in the two seasons since. Mystical creatures like reapers and demons and vampires have all remained consistent through multiple appearances.

The characters have grown and developed—not just Sam and Dean, but several of the supporting players as well. More importantly, the plots have moved forward. While the basic background of blowing into town and shooting demons in the head remains, the writers wisely didn't try to drag out the fight against Azazel, the demon who killed the boys' mother, longer than two seasons.

In addition, the show is hilariously funny. The best dramas are often the ones that make you laugh. I've probably chortled more at any random episode of *The West Wing* or *House* or *The Shield* or *Deadwood* or *Supernatural* than at any so-called comedy. From Dean's wiseass remarks and the brotherly banter to the general snottiness of the demons and "Don't play with my Jesus" ("Bad Day at Black Rock," 3-3), the show is always good for many a chuckle. Then again, the best horror always has you laughing just long enough for the laugh to catch in your throat when the icky stuff hits. And when the show does flat-out comedy, it's usually gold: the self-referential satire of "Hollywood Babylon" (2-18), the glorious slapstick of the bad-luck sufferers in "Bad Day at Black Rock," the tabloid-inspired goofiness of "Tall Tales" (2-15), the *Groundhog Day* riff in "Mystery Spot" (3-11), and the gleeful spoofs of supernatural reality shows and Web sites in "Hell House" (1-17) and "Ghostfacers" (3-13).

But perhaps what I personally find particularly appealing about *Supernatural* is their superlative use of music—compounded by the emphasis on classic rock, which is some of my favorite kind of music. But even if there wasn't a ton of overlap between Dean's tape collection and my iTunes library, I love how the show uses music to supplement and enhance what's happening on screen, mainly because it's something no other show on the air currently does (and too few have done in the past). The revelation that Sam and Dean were dealing with reapers in "Faith" (1-12) was made infinitely more satisfying by the use of Blue Öyster Cult's "(Don't Fear) The Reaper." The spellcasting in "Malleus Maleficarum" (3-9) was far cooler with the addition of Screamin' Jay Hawkins's "I Put a Spell on You." The tension of the "Hunted" (2-10) teaser was enhanced a thousandfold by the slow build of Jefferson

Airplane's "White Rabbit." The "Then"/"The Road So Far" scene selections in each of the season finales (as well as several late first-season and early second-season episodes) worked infinitely better with soundtracks ("Fight the Good Fight" by Triumph, "Time Has Come Today" by the Chambers Brothers, "Stranglehold" by Ted Nugent, "Wheel in the Sky" by Journey, and the incredibly apt "Carry on, Wayward Son" by Kansas). And rarely has a piece of music more perfectly suited a scene than "Renegade" by Styx at the conclusion of "Nightshifter" (2-12), especially with Dean uttering "We're so screwed" in the pause between the intro and when the main part of the song kicked in.

Plus, Sam and Dean singing "Wanted Dead or Alive" by Bon Jovi very, very, very badly in "No Rest for the Wicked" is perhaps one of the finest brother moments in the show's three seasons.

Finally, if *Supernatural* was just some show about two hot guys fighting demons, BenBella probably wouldn't have decided to do a Smart Pop book about it.

So bravo to Eric Kripke, Robert Singer, Ben Edlund, Sera Gamble, McG, and all the other folks involved in *Supernatural* for making it far more than just another CW show with good-looking young people in it.

Keith R. A. DeCandido is the author of two of the three *Supernatural* novels published by HarperEntertainment to date: *Nevermore* (2007) and *Bone Key* (2008). Those are but two of the forty-odd (some very odd) novels he's written, in addition to a mess of short stories, comic books, novellas, eBooks, and nonfiction. He has contributed to six previous Smart Pop volumes: *Webslinger*, *Star Wars on Trial*, *The Man from Krypton*, *The Unauthorized X-Men*, *Finding Serenity*, and *King Kong Is Back!* Find out less at Keith's Web site at DeCandido.net or read his inane ramblings at kradical.livejournal.com.

INTRODUCTION

When *Supernatural* first burst onto our screens in September 2005, no one could have imagined what an impact it would have on viewers. It was one of many similar genre shows to air that fall, and given the smaller WB network it aired on, it seemed doomed never to achieve a large audience.

And yet, despite its uphill battle, *Supernatural* was the only new genre show to survive when the following year's network schedules were announced. It may not have huge ratings, but it has grown a loyal fanbase that will stop at nothing to protect it.

So what makes *Supernatural* so different?

What makes ordinary people like myself turn into obsessed, overly passionate fans who think nothing of rearranging vacations, work plans, and much more just to fit the show into our lives?

Some might say it's the irresistible looks of *Supernatural*'s two main stars—and I will agree, Jensen and Jared are very appealing to the eye.

But there's so much more to it than that, so much more that we can learn about within the covers of this book.

Join me for a preview of what I know you will find some fascinating insights into the CW's best kept secret.

> *I think he wants us to pick up where he left off, you know, saving people, hunting things. The family business.*
>
> —DEAN WINCHESTER, "Wendigo" (1-2)

To embrace *Supernatural*, you first have to understand that, while *Supernatural*'s a show about heroism, heroism isn't always about fighting evil and saving the damsel in distress. While we all love to see Dean and Sam rock-salting a spirit or exorcizing a demon, those moments really only scrape the surface. Sometimes our hunters need saving too, and it's this element that grips fans, often to the point where we actually *don't want* to draw a line between fantasy and reality. When Jensen Ackles jokingly pleaded with viewers to write to Eric Kripke, the show's creator, and ask to save Dean from his demonic deal, you just knew that the CW's mailbox was going to be full for a few weeks to come.

We love to see the brothers' inner turmoil play out.

We love to see Dean and Sam struggling with their "inner demons."

Why?

Because heroism on this show is all about what the Winchester family will sacrifice for each other. It's about the unshakable faith they have in one another—a faith that carries them through possessions, near-death experiences, and ultimately the threat of Hell itself. This is the kind of family bond most people can only ever dream of. Would your father or brother die for you? Would they go to Hell for you, facing unimaginable pain and suffering?

These are the kind of heroics that attract us fans, just as much as the Winchesters battling rabid Rakshasas or soul-hungry demons.

> *When someone says a place is haunted, don't go in.*
>
> —DEAN WINCHESTER, "Asylum" (1-10)

We *Supernatural* fans like our heroes to be angsty, but we do still like them to be heroes. We like them to be fighting *external* demons, too. We still need our fix of all things freaky to get us through the night, after all.

And in this department, *Supernatural* excels, giving us a weekly mix of urban folklore and ancient legends played out in various backwater locations across the U.S. Usually, these myths have been tantalizingly re-imagined for our viewing delight by such talented writers as Sera Gamble and Jeremy Carver, to name but two. While some of these legends are eerily familiar to us, it's easily apparent that a massive amount of research goes into bringing us the more unheard of stories—stories that give the audience a chance to not only sink into the macabre plots but actually have fun with folklore that otherwise would have remained sunken in obscurity.

Forget history 101 and anthropology. It's much more fun to tag along with the Winchesters in the back seat of the Impala!

> *Hey, you better take care of that car, or I swear I'll haunt your ass.*
>
> —DEAN WINCHESTER, "Faith" (1-12)

And of course, speaking of the raven metal behemoth, the boys riding in the Impala is something we love to see on *Supernatural*. For true fans, the classic Chevy has become more than just an aging motor. Over three seasons, she has become a character in her own right, one we can't bear to see harmed any more than we can the Winchesters themselves. There was a time when most TV shows had a cool car, and Dean's "baby" is right up there with the best of them. Forget KITT and the General Lee—the Impala is big, she's black, and it appears she's more indestructible than Superman . . . at least if "In My Time of Dying" (2-1) is to be believed.

The fans apparently aren't the only ones who see the car as something more. In "Dead Man's Blood" (1-20), John chided Dean for not taking care of the Impala, and every time Dean's life hangs in the balance, she is his first thought after Sam. And in "Fresh Blood" (3-7), Sam even succumbed to his brother's wishes and began to learn how to fix his four-wheeled sibling.

Supernatural is as much about family values as hunting the unknown, and the Impala is 100 percent Winchester all the way!

> *I choose to go down swinging.*
>
> —DEAN WINCHESTER, "Jus in Bello" (3-12)

Whatever attracts each fan to *Supernatural*, one thing is a constant—we'll fight to the bitter end to keep the Winchesters on our screens. We're in love with each and every part of the show, from its production crew, writing staff, and stars, right on up to Master Kripke, who created all things Winchester. There's so much more depth to the show than I could ever bring to light in this introduction, but as fans, you don't need to take my word for it. If you're like me, you already live, breathe, and sometimes sleep *Supernatural*.

As Webmaster of one of the larger, if not largest, fan sites for the show, I've come to know firsthand the kind of people who tune in every week. Indeed, the chances are, I may even know you!

I've been the boss of other Web sites, and known many other fandoms in my many years, but one thing I have never seen before is the kind of devotion otherwise ordinary people give this show—and indeed, one another. We're not just fans, we're a community, a worldwide group of viewers who have also become *friends* because of one man's dream. The essays within these pages bear wonderful testament to our enthusiasm and zeal.

Eric Kripke once likened his vision to the epic *Star Wars*, and maybe he was right in more ways than even he knew. *Supernatural* may not be a journey to a galaxy far, far away, but it does explore the depths of the human mind, pushing its characters to the brink and beyond, and we the obsessed viewers are right there along with them.

I suspect that, long after its demise, *Supernatural* will still be seen in countless countries via countless reruns, and may one day reach the same level of cult "status" as the likes of *Star Trek* and the U.K.'s *Doctor Who*.

Until then, may *Supernatural* stay "in the hunt" for many years to come!

Dawn (Kittsbud)
Webmaster, Supernatural.tv

One of Supernatural's *greatest enigmas—and most controversial discussion points—isn't a demon or a monster, an urban legend or a twisted folktale, but John Winchester, the patriarch of the show and, arguably, the catalyst behind the Winchester boys' story. Often described as controlling and strict, hard and obsessive, John is also repeatedly depicted as self-sacrificing and loving, devoted to his boys and desperate to protect them from the evil he knows is out there stalking his family—a "hero" in every sense of the word. It is this dichotomy that makes John Winchester so intriguing. Good father or bad father? Benevolent teacher or drill sergeant? Hero or villain? Success or failure? Tanya Huff investigates.*

TANYA HUFF

"We're Not Exactly the Bradys"

Just to get one thing out of the way up front—I do not have kids. What's more, there's no chance of my ever having kids. Therefore, my discussing John Winchester's parenting choices and the results of same could be considered marital advice from yet another unmarried marriage counselor. On the other hand, I never had a wife be eviscerated by a demon and pinned to the ceiling to burn, nor have I ever owned a '67 Impala. It's unlikely that the lack of either will weigh against me during any evaluation of my scholarship on the topic, so perhaps we can ignore the lack of kids thing as well.

It is therefore my opinion that John Winchester, for all his flaws as a father—and they were legion—was not, as it happens, a bad father. He was not, by any means, a good father ("So, somewhere along the line, I stopped being your father. And I became your drill sergeant" ["Dead Man's Blood," 1-20]), but he had to have done something right. He must have because his sons, for all *their* flaws—and those flaws are also legion—are good men.

Dean Winchester, tired of the fight and wanting nothing more than a chance to live happily ever after, is so much a good man that his subconscious refuses to let him rest. His mother was alive, Sam had Jess back, he had a beautiful woman who loved him, and yet he sacrificed happiness because strangers needed him, and there was a job that only he could do. He didn't want to and he trembled on the edge of screaming that it wasn't fair but he did it anyway—took the hard road because it was the right thing to do.

Sam Winchester, tainted by demon blood and intended to lead the armies of Hell, refused to hit his enemy when he was down. Refused to end it by killing a helpless man despite that man having done his best to kill him. It wasn't the smart thing to do when you consider the way things turned out, but it was the right thing to do.

Good men don't just happen, they're made—and to see how we have to go back to the beginning.

John Winchester, an ex-Marine who saw combat in Vietnam, married to Mary, a woman he loves desperately, settles down in Lawrence, Kansas. There's nothing in the evidence to suggest that the town was home to either of them—there's a definite lack of family around when the shit hits the fan—but maybe they're there because John had a chance to buy into a friend's garage. He's a good mechanic and this is the kind of chance a man can build a life on.

John and Mary buy a house and have two sons—Dean, and then when Dean is almost four and a half years old, Samuel. Sam. Sammy, although, later, only Dean gets to call him that. John's a hands-on father. Not only does he put his four–year-old to bed, Mary expects him to answer when Sam is heard crying over the baby monitor. This is worth noting because twenty-odd years ago this was even less the default behavior for fathers than it is now.

He has a little trouble sleeping sometimes, but hey, that happens. Given what he chooses to watch on this particular night, he's probably not suffering from Post Traumatic Stress Disorder because of his time in combat. Guys with combat-induced PTSD don't watch war movies—as a general rule, they can't handle the sound of gunfire. Among other things.

It's fairly safe then to say that on the night Mary is killed, John is about as happy and as emotionally stable as it's possible to get.

And then his wife starts screaming, jerking him out of sleep. There's a moment of calm when he reaches Sam's nursery and sees the baby safe. But then he sees blood drip from the ceiling. When he looks up, Mary, pinned to the ceiling, belly cut open, bursts into flame. John is horrified and no one would blame him if he froze, unable to cope with what he sees. But he doesn't freeze—his wife may be dying in a horrible and bizarre way but she's not his only responsibility and before he attempts to save her, he grabs his younger son and runs from the room. Had Dean not met him in the hall, his next stop would probably have been Dean's room, but the boy is right there. He places the baby in Dean's arms and says, "Take your brother outside as fast as you can. Don't look back. Now, Dean, go!" ("Pilot," 1-1).

He trusts a four-year-old with a baby. He knows Dean will do exactly as he said. Why? Because his father asked him to. Four-year-olds who obey instantly, who have their entirely justifiable fears calmed by their father giving them a job and trusting them to do it, are rare. This indicates a level of trust already in place because that sort of thing doesn't spontaneously appear in emergencies. John had to have already been giving Dean tasks, trusting him to complete them and making it worth his while to do so—children being selfish little beasts—and given what we've seen of them together so far, it's a fair guess to say that John's reward for this behavior was nothing more than his love and approval.

Only when the boys are on the way out of the house does John go back to help Mary, only to find that she's beyond help. Even in his shock and terror and grief, he doesn't stay, futilely (metaphorically) throwing himself onto the pyre with his wife—he races outside and grabs up both boys, carrying them to further safety as the house blows. Inarguably, John Winchester loved his wife but he lived for his sons.

The official explanation is that it was an electrical fire. In the first flush of grief, John's allowed to be a little crazy, so probably no one takes his raving about what actually happened very seriously. But John knows what he saw. It would be so much easier to deny his memory, to believe the sight of Mary dying on the ceiling was a construct of his grief, but he's not that kind of a man and he goes looking for answers.

In the unincorporated area of Stull, Kansas, which lies just west of Lawrence across Clinton Lake, there's a cemetery that a popular local urban legend claims is a "gateway to hell."[1] So it's not entirely surprising that Missouri Mosely, the psychic John consults, is actually, well, psychic, and as she tells Sam and Dean later, "I just told him what was really out there in the dark. I guess you could say . . . I drew back the curtains for him" ("Home," 1-9). She didn't know exactly what had killed Mary but she knew it was something evil.

Now as much as he may have wanted to, it seems John didn't go off hunting this evil right away. Even if we assume the "friend" who'd owned the garage with him is a little dicey on dates ("Matter of fact, it must be, uh . . . twenty years since John disappeared" ["Home"]), later evidence makes it clear John isn't the kind of man who just charges in. He researches first. Not only that but he has a six-month-old baby he has to learn to be the sole parent of—and if Sam was nursing, that's going to be a steep learning curve—and a traumatized four-year-old. ("See, when I was your age, I saw something real bad happen to my mom, and I was scared, too. I didn't feel like talking, just like you" [Dean to Lucas in "Dead in the Water" (1-3)]).

They clearly have some kind of a support system in place—Missouri knew the boys as children and she didn't meet John until after the fire. So how do John and Sam and Dean end up on the road?

It happens when John sells his interest in the garage and buys guns—and his garage-owning "friend" calls Children's Aid (deleted scene from "Home").

John packs his whole life into a '67 Impala rather than lose his sons. He's not going to stop hunting for whatever it was that killed Mary and he's not going to give up his boys—he's not left with much of a choice.

And here's where we need to pause for a moment because, seriously, what kind of a father thinks life on the road is a good choice? If he gave the boys up, he could keep hunting and they could have a life worth living—without him, granted, but safe and normal. Bit of a selfish bastard, wasn't he? His need to keep his sons with him is more important than

[1] "Lawrence, Kansas." Wikipedia. 21 July 2008. <http://en.wikipedia.org/wiki/Lawrence,_Kansas>

their well-being.

Except . . .

He knows his family has been touched by evil, knows it because he saw it with his own eyes. If he leaves his sons behind, how will people who don't believe in this evil protect them? He has to take them with him; it's the only way to keep them safe ("After your mother passed, all I saw was evil, everywhere. And all I cared about was keeping you boys alive" ["Dead Man's Blood" 1-20]). Well, Missouri believes in the evil but, if asked, she'd probably say—given that she doesn't seem willing to lie to him—that she couldn't stop it.

He wants a normal, safe life for his boys but they can't have that until this thing is dead. He couldn't possibly have expected the hunt to last as long as it did.

The odds are good that during those first few years before he considered Dean old enough to leave in charge of Sam—and we know they were only a *few* years—John had to have wished he could go after this evil without the boys. Anyone who's ever travelled for any distance with two young kids in the car has thought about leaving them with Child Protective Services. Or by the side of the road. Or in one of those charity drop boxes. Car companies put those DVD players in there for a reason. John couldn't give up the hunt and he wouldn't give up his boys, so he found a way to make it work.

What kind of life did they have? Evidence suggests they didn't live in motels. To begin with, the boys were in school (Sam could actually be a genius, and given the number of times it seemed they moved he probably is, but you don't get a full ride to Stanford being home-schooled by John Winchester), and schools require a home address. Living in a motel with kids is one of the fastest ways to have questions asked about how things are at home. Granted, most child welfare services are overworked but John wouldn't risk that. They likely stayed in motels for specific hunts on weekends ("It was the third night in this crap room. . . ." ["Something Wicked," 1-18]) and over holidays ("A Very Supernatural Christmas," 3-8) and in the cheapest housing John could find otherwise. John and Dean seem to have kept what John was actually doing from Sam until Sam was nine, and that would have required at least a certain level of normal.

So you're a father and you're raising your sons on your own knowing that something out there is after them and the only person you have to turn to, the only person who knows what it is to lose what you've lost, is your oldest boy. The older sibling raising the younger and being the support to the surviving parent isn't unusual in single parent households—in allowing Dean to become his support staff, John is doing nothing that's unusual or horrible or abusive. The only thing different here than in a thousand other households is the degree. John doesn't hide things from Dean. He can't. Dean has to know about the dangers in order to protect himself and his younger brother. They are, after all, living in a war zone.

We only have a few actual glimpses of their lives growing up. We're given only three pieces of primary source material, unfiltered by other characters' perceptions, where we can come to our own conclusions about what's going on.

There's the photograph that Sam found in John's hotel room of the three of them ("Pilot"). John had Sam on his lap, safe in the circle of his arms, and Dean was by his side (echoing their positions the night Mary died). All three of them looked happy. And the thing about kids is, if they're unhappy it shows, so it's safe to say that they were happy.

There's the weekend they were left alone when John went to hunt the shtriga. John was quiet and calm while going over his instructions with Dean. He praised him ("That's my man" ["Something Wicked"]), clearly expected him to succeed (and kids will rise or fall to meet expectation), and while they were a bit beyond hugging (not unusual for nine-/ten-year-old boys) there was the manly clasp of the shoulder that said touch was still a part of Dean's life. When Dean actually acted like a nine-/ten-year-old and disobeyed, putting Sam in danger, John, in spite of his terror, didn't lash out at Dean. He was angry, yes, but *all* he said was, "I told you not to leave the room. I told you not to let him out of your sight" ("Something Wicked"). There was a distinct lack of the sort of accusation that many fathers would have thrown. Accusations like, "How could you be so stupid?!" or "Are you trying to get your brother killed?!" Terror did not make John mean. Nor did a belief in his own machismo keep him from showing emotions; both his fear for Sammy and his relief that his younger son was safe were right there on his face.

There's the Christmas he missed. . . . Okay, it's hard to put a positive spin on that beyond the fact he's not the only father who's missed Christmas in the midst of fighting a war.

Everything else about the way John Winchester raised his sons we have to piece together, extrapolate from secondary sources.

We can assume that since he kept Sam's soccer trophy and Dean's first shotgun ("Bad Day at Black Rock," 3-3) he was proud of them when they were young. And we know he was proud of them when they were adults—he told other people how proud he was of Sam and he showed his pride in Dean when he sent people to him for help ("Phantom Traveler," 1-4). Granted, he didn't seem to tell *them* as often as he should have, but you find me a dad who says exactly the right thing every damn time and we can have him cloned and make a fortune. He was willing to hug his adult sons, which is pretty solid evidence that hugs happened all their lives—maybe not frequently, but you don't take that kind of comfort from physical contact if you've never had it. His reaction to Sam's fear of "the thing in the closet" was peculiar by any other than Winchester standards ("Yeah, when I told Dad I was scared of the thing in my closet, he gave me a .45" ["Pilot"]), but since we know John had to have checked the closet and found nothing there, he gets points for taking his son's fear seriously and giving him a way to defeat it. We know he argued with other Hunters, and since he kept the boys away from what little community the Hunters had it's not a huge stretch to assume the boys were at least one of the reasons why. Those few friends John had, had to be worried about both the kids and John—even the demons knew, "He lets his guard down around his boys, lets his emotions cloud his judgment" ("Shadow," 1-16). But he was not compromising about his boys—they were all he had left of Mary and he was going to keep them safe. The physical evidence suggests neither boy grew up undernourished so John must've kept them fed. He drank but since he also excelled at a dangerous, physical . . . uh, obsession . . . he couldn't have drunk to the extent Sam's resentment suggests, and since even at his most pissy Sam never mentions any physical abuse when John was drunk, it's a good bet it never happened.

Actually, there's one more thing we *know* happened.

We know that when Sam told John he wanted to go to college, John lost his temper. We also know that Sam lost his temper back at him (the fact that Sam fought with John his whole life tells us that John did not maintain discipline through fear). Sam was having a fairly typical teenage rebellion (Sam would have seen John as the one who kept him from a normal life. Dean didn't have that rebellion because he'd had normal and lost it the same time his father had). Sam wanted to live his own life, and he said some things. John, having realized from the night Sam was six months old that he was the only one who could keep his boys safe from the evil that had touched their lives and killed their mother, was experiencing the ramped-up Winchester version of not wanting to let his child go, and so *he* said some things.

Oh yeah, things were definitely said.

Among them, "If you go, don't come back."

John Winchester is not the first father to ever say this.

Sam Winchester is not the first son to ever throw his clothes and his big curved knives into a duffle bag and stomp out. Okay, maybe the knife thing is unique, but the rest, not so much.

Dean stood by his father, if only by his silence, because he'd been taught his whole life that was the best way to keep Sam safe. But Dean's twists and turns are a whole different road trip and, here and now, we're not going there.

A little less usual: John doesn't see his younger son, except at a distance ("But even when you two weren't talkin' . . . he used to swing by Stanford whenever" ["Bugs," 1-8]), for four and a half years.

Here's where we pause again because if John was afraid of what would happen to Sam out on his own, away from the protection of his family, and since it's clear he didn't stay mad for that entire time, why didn't he come up with a compromise? A way for Sam to still be a part of the family?

He could have sent Dean to be with his brother and keep an eye on him. John didn't need Dean to be a part of finding the thing that killed Mary; they were already hunting separately and, what's more, as soon as he got a good lead, he ditched Dean for Dean's own safety.

Sam could have hunted during the holidays. He'd have had access to new research materials that could have helped with John's primary hunt. Later, it certainly wouldn't hurt, all things considered, to have a lawyer on the team.

John admitted he wanted more for his boys than the obsession that ruled his life. I think he saw college as Sam's chance to get out. To have the kind of life his mother would have wanted for him. It's the only logical reason why John kept his distance all those years.

Why didn't Sam pick up the phone? Well, we're not taking the road trip through Sam's psyche right now either.

And when they finally got back together again? John knew what Sam was—or more accurately, could be. His younger son could be or become the kind of evil John had been hunting obsessively for twenty-three years and yet this knowledge, while it might have been breaking his heart, didn't change his feelings toward Sam—the love, the pride, it was all still very evident.

And for Dean? John was not only willing to give up his life—and again, not the first father willing to do this—he was willing to give up the thing that had defined him since Mary's death: the chance to destroy the thing that killed her. He'd always expected to die on this hunt; he'd long since come to terms with his own death. Given that he knew Hell existed, and given the things he'd done, he'd likely also come to terms with ending up somewhere that had turned out to be less metaphorical than most people think. But he had never even considered that he wouldn't, someday, take out the thing that killed his wife . . .

. . . until he offered the Yellow-Eyed Demon the Colt in exchange for Dean's life.

In the end, when it comes right down to the bottom line regarding both his boys, John Winchester is a father first.

Not a great father.

Not without flaws.

But he taught his sons how to be strong, how to fight for what they believed in, and how to stand up for people who couldn't fight for themselves. There was gentleness and laughter when they were adults and that says that, as well as the fight, there was gentleness and laughter when they were children.

He loved them and, more importantly, in spite of all the other things he couldn't say, they knew that.

It wasn't the life he wanted for them, but when circumstances gave him no choice in the matter, he did his best.

> SAM: Well, I'll tell you one thing—we're lucky we had Dad.
> DEAN: (surprised) I never thought I'd hear you say that.
> SAM: Well, he could've gone a whole 'nother way after Mom. A little more tequila, a little less demon-hunting, and we would've had Max's childhood. All things considered, we turned out okay—thanks to him.
> DEAN: (pause) All things considered. (He gets in the car.) ("Nightmare," 1-14)

TANYA HUFF lives and writes in rural Ontario with her partner Fiona Patton, seven cats, and an incontinent Chihuahua. Her twenty-third novel and the fourth Torin Kerr book, *Valor's Trial*, came out in June 2008 from DAW. She'd give a kidney to write for *Supernatural*, mostly because that'd be easier than what she'd have to do to actually get a shot at it.

While upbringing, shared experiences, and a common goal ensure the characters of Dean and Sam Winchester are similar in many ways, much of Supernatural's *drama stems from the brothers' essential differences: the nonconformist and the conformist, the hunter and the would-be student; one embracing the fantastical while the other clings to the everyday.*

But that's not the only dichotomy the boys represent. Dodger Winslow examines how Supernatural's *chalk and cheese brothers can be seen to symbolize these two extremes of perception: the fantasy of how we'd like others to see us versus the reality of how we're actually seen; the fantasy of who we'd like to be versus the reality of who we actually are. Do we think it's all about Dean when really it's all about Sam? Is Dean the fantasy and Sam the reality?*

DODGER WINSLOW

The Burden of Being Sammy

(A Parenthetical Discussion of Self-Perception Versus Reality)

He's kind of like the cute chick on *The Munsters*, only taller and with better hair. Or in Kripke world, he's Luke Skywalker to Dean's Han Solo in the far, far away of rural America as the two of them tool down Route 66 through infamous hives of scum and villainy in the coolest landspeeder *ever*.

He's the Holy Grail, the vessel, the hero, the point. He's clearly John's favorite. He's an emo bitch and a spoiled brat who throws selfish tantrums and stomps away in guy-like hissy fits. He's the prodigal son, the rebel without a cause, the journey that matters, the poster child of him and all the children like him. He's Captain Obvious and Geek Boy. He likes anemic pop crap and won't shut his cake hole; he's a pain-in-the-ass kid brother who's too smart, always cautious, usually right, and still manages to need saving on a regular basis. He's a pudgy twelve-year-old, the teen who left home in a stomp, the guy who fights with his dad because they're too much alike to ever get along, and the man who grieves the murder of his lover by developing a bit of an unholy thirst for vengeance. He's the one with plans, dreams, hopes for the future. He's the one looking for love, willing to show love, striving to be normal, wanting to fit in, bonded to his family, but also independent of his family.

He is Sammy; and he is Us.

Oh come on. Admit it. We all *want* to be Dean. But the truth of the matter is, we're all much closer to being Sammy, aren't we?

Yes, we'd love to say we'd fall on our swords for the sake of family. But if they told us we couldn't move out of the house when we hit age, we'd still go, wouldn't we? Yes, we'd all love to be preternaturally smooth and successful with the opposite sex. But really, aren't most of us just a little insecure and more looking to bunk up with someone we like, rather than just someone with qualifying equipment?

And yes, absolutely, every one of us would want to be Dean cool, wouldn't we? Look Dean good in a leather jacket? Have a Dean swagger vibe that owns any room into which we walk? Be Dean bold and Dean rebellious in the face of all authority figures? Be Dean tortured to the roots of our very souls . . . something we'd hide with Dean wit and Dean stoic forbearance and just enough Dean attitude so everyone loves us Deanly because they can't ever really touch us, we're just that Dean special and that Dean aloof and that oh-so-Deanishly Dean?

But the truth of the world we live in is never quite the way we'd write it if we were Kripke and in charge of creating our own state of being.

The truth of who we are is Sammy. It's Sammy sorta-smooth and kinda-smart but just a bit geeky for it. It's Sammy in baggy clothes with an occasional opportunity to look really hot in nothing but a towel . . . if we stand just the right way, in just the right light, and if whoever is looking isn't so singularly Dean-struck they don't even freaking notice us. It's Sammy normally abnormal, Sammy I-can-fit-in-but-I-have-to-be-nice-and-polite-and-work-at-it-a-bit. It's Sammy "yes, sir" to the cops, and Sammy "are you sure we should be doing this?" to any overt breaking of the rules that holds the potential to get us busted big time.

And most of all, it's Sammy hurt-us-and-we-cry, Sammy cut-us-and-we-bleed, Sammy feel-the-love-and-we-hug.

Give it up, girlfriends. We're all Sammys, we just want to see ourselves as Deans.

And oh, the burden of being Sammy. The burden of being the center of the universe upon which every story ever told turns. The burden of being the fulcrum of your family, to whom the others must connect in order to make you a family. The burden of being the one who is always, at the very foundation of it, to blame for every tragedy that has ever befallen those you love.

Oh, wait . . . isn't that *Dean*?

And herein lies the gold of self-perception. And equally, the gold of a storyteller who tells his story not only in terms of how we perceive ourselves to be, but also in terms of who we actually are.

Perception first. From our perspective (the viewer perspective), we perceive these to all be things more truly said of Dean than of Sam. Why? Because they are all things said of self in the worldview of self-perception, and because we want to see ourselves as Dean instead of Sammy.

In this way, we see it oh so clearly: Every story is about Dean, no matter who it is really about (because our lives are about us, no matter who else might star in them on occasion). Sam and John can only connect through the midpoint of Dean. for he is the glue who holds the family together (because we are all the most important cog in our own family dynamics, whether the rest of those yahoo relatives realize it or not). And Dean, in failing to save those he loves from inevitable tragedy, will always wrongfully blame himself for the pain they feel, even if he was only four years old and couldn't possibly have saved his mother (because we all blame ourselves for the things that happen to those we love—for our failure to see it coming, or our failure to be hero enough to stand in front of it when it arrives—even when we can see how wrongful that blame is in the logic of what actually happened).

But from the storyteller's (external) perspective, is that person Dean or is it Sam?

Ah, now *there's* the rub. The storyteller is telling the hero's (your) story. He's just telling it in such a way as to allow you (the viewer) to experience yourself both as you are perceived by others (Sammy) and as you aspire to be perceived by others (Dean). Or, perhaps more germanely, how you actually are (Sammy) and how you think you are (Dean) or wish you were (again, Dean).

So to adjust an aspirational self-perception to a more accurate external perspective, every story is about Sammy (you) even though it really *should* be about Dean (not really you) because he's way more cool and interesting and good-looking than Sammy (the real you), mostly because he is too Dean to be anyone other than Dean (not really you).

Likewise, Dean (the way you want to be seen) and John (your family who knows you too well to fall for that crap; and who is, by the way, just like you even though neither one of you will admit it, because you both want to think you're much more like Dean than that selfish, emo bitch Sammy) can only really connect through the midpoint of Sammy (the you they know, emo bitch that you've always been since the day you were born) for Sammy (you) is the glue who holds the family together (because you are the most important cog in your own family dynamic, whether the rest of those yahoo relatives realize it or not; all of them wanting to come off like a bunch of Deans, even though they are really just a bunch of Johns, which is nothing but another way of saying they're just a bunch of Sammys).

And lastly, in failing to save those he (you) loves (John the family, Jess the love) from inevitable evisceration and ceiling pyrotechnics (loss, either of life or love, and the subsequent pain of that loss) by a Demon (events outside your control) either known (should have seen it coming) or unknown (should have been able to stop it when it arrived even if you didn't see it coming), Sammy (you, again) will always rightfully (because the world turns around you, thus the *self* aspect of the concept *self*ish) blame himself (yourself) for the pain they (those you love, including yourself) feel, even if it wasn't him (you) who actually caused the tragedy (because, hello? event outside your control) so much as simply Sammy (you) being the reason the Demon (tragic events outside your control) came after his (your) family in the first place (because the world turns around you, and every story told in the context of your life is about you, no matter who else might star in them on occasion).

So self-perception and external perspective: Who is the hero and who is the star? Logical assumption to the contrary, in *Supernatural*, they are not one and the same. The hero is who the story is about. In the case of *Supernatural*, that would be Sammy (you). But the star . . . ah, the star.

The star is whom the viewer *perceives* the story to be about. And in the case of *Supernatural*, that is almost universally Dean (not really you).

As Kripke says: Luke Skywalker to Han Solo.

So how can the hero not be the star? It's not that hard when self-perception and external perspective share the stage in individualist form to put to flesh the storyteller's agenda of making a statement on the difference between the way we want to see ourselves and the way we actually are.

Huh? you ask. In answer, I give you Sam and Dean. I give you Luke and Han. I give you yourself and who you would like to be. One is life; one is larger than life; but both are storyteller turns on the subject of self-perception versus external perspective. With this as the context for discussion, let's look at season one in terms of Sammy, love, and family . . . and how the burden of being Sammy is very much the burden of not being Dean.

On the subject of Sammy and love, let's talk Jess.

By talking Dean. (Because you can't talk Sammy without talking Dean.)

You realize Dean (not really you) would have been *way* cooler than to actually fall for Jess (love, as in romantic love, as in the love of your life, not just a one-night stand) in such a way that her loss could cripple him, right? That's one of the whole points of Dean (not really you). He's wounded by life. He's emotionally distant because that's the heroic way he deals with his pain. He lives the emo life inside, where it belongs, rather than outside, where it can embarrass him or make him vulnerable. And he does it because he is just that strong and just that stoic and just that much the hero (and just that much Not Really You).

Not to put too fine a point on it, but Dean (not really you) is the antithesis of Sammy (you) when it comes to the subject of love. Why? Because on no subject are our own self-perceptions more reflective of our desire to be stronger (better, faster) than we actually are than when the subject of love is put on the table.

As an aspirational reflection of our desire to be strong, in control, and above the emo bitchness that defines the very essence of our human nature, Dean (not really you) doesn't really fall in love so much as drift in and out of lust (emotionally distant). Such is the life of the mythic hero (and the perception of self that prefers to be in control of love rather than controlled by it, and to leave rather than be left). Yet still, there is always hope (hope springs eternal, thus fanfic) that the hero (you perceive yourself to be) will find true love (usually on a white steed from across a crowded room); and if he (not really you) did, he (not really you) would fall (in a manly, heroic way; though not incestuously or slashily so) in love.

This is not how Sam (you) loved Jess. To show the contrast, let's walk Dean (not really you) a mile in Sammy's (your) shoes on the road of Jess (love). Because again, to speak of Sammy (you), we must speak of Dean (not really you) and how the difference between these two perceptions-put-to-flesh-as-individuals plays to the storyteller's agenda to speak to the differences between who we (the viewer) are and who we—rightfully or otherwise—aspire to be.

So for the sake of that contrast, if Dean (not really you) actually *did* fall in love with Jess (love, as in the love of your life, not just a one-night stand), he (not really you) would do so in such a way that if she (love) did die (was lost), it wouldn't cripple him. At least, not the way it would cripple Sammy (you).

Everyone knows Jess (love) could die (be lost) at any time (it's happened before, when you were younger, through no fault of your own). Because to be perfectly honest (get a clue), although inarguably tragic to those involved, love (Jess) crashes and burns and bleeds from the ceiling (dies due to events beyond your control) every day all over the world. All of which begs the wise viewer to realize that Sammy (you) being in Jess (love . . . get your mind out of the gutter) means that Jess (love) might die (be lost) because a Demon (events beyond your control) targets her (love) for death (loss) for no other reason than being with Sammy (you, because every story is all about you, no matter who else stars in them on occasion). So this is a life fact (love hurts) of which both Sam (you) and Dean (not really you) are aware; but it is a life fact only one of them (you and not really you) will heed (emotionally available versus emotionally unavailable).

We all aspire to learn from the lessons of love, but few of us really do.

Heeding the warning of the impermanent nature of love (he's older, wiser, cooler, and wounded by the world enough to know), Dean (not really you) would be smart enough (having already experienced this at least once, and having learned from that experience) not to invest himself emotionally (love, as compared to lust) to such a degree that losing Jess (love) would put him to his knees (make him cry like a baby in front of the girl he is trying to impress). Sammy (you) on the other hand—being the selfish (real), emo bitch (human as compared to heroic) that he is (you are)—*does* fall for Jess (love) hook, line, and sinker (emotionally committed to the nines). So when she (love) dies (is lost), as so often happens (life sucks), he's (you are) crippled by it.

We aspire to be savvy about the dangers of love, but few of us really are. We aspire to control love rather than let love control us, but we seldom do.

Dean (not really you) would have seen it coming. Dean (not really you) would have either walked away from Jess (love) to keep from getting her (again, love) killed (losing her), or he (not really you) would have saved her (love) because Dean (not really you) is just that strong, cool, and heroic a guy. And because he (not really you) would have been willing to walk away (punk out), if she (love) were to die anyway (get lost), Dean (not really you) would have no doubt blamed himself for that loss (because he's wounded by life, and he suffers those wounds in silence, locking his pain inside where no one else will see it, even if they know it must be there because he's emotionally distant, not emotionally absent), but it would be a wrongful blame (just a hero being heroically tragic), because Dean did everything right (he's Dean [not really you]).

He (not really you) is slick and witty and heroic and strong and incredibly hot and just the right mix of vulnerability and invulnerability (he was Dean). Because Dean (not really you) is all these things and more, it follows that if he (not really you) lost Jess (love), it would be the Demon's (events beyond your control's) fault. Yes, he (not really you) would likely take the blame because he's the hero (as compared to human) and heroes (and children) blame themselves for failures beyond their capacity to prevent. But while Dean (not really you) would blame himself, he (not really you) wouldn't let Jess's (love's) death (loss) break him, because he (not really you) would never let Jess (love) get to him that way (emotionally distant, anyone?). He's stronger (emotionally unavailable) than that. Better (emotionally unavailable) than that.

Cooler (emotionally unavailable) than that.

He's Dean (who you wish you could be).

He's not Sammy (who you really are).

On the other hand, Sammy (you) totally deserves the blame (illogical guilt) he (you) takes as his own for Jess's (love's) death (loss) for a variety of reasons, all of which are self-imposed (guilt) and none of which are valid (Guilt with a capital G).

First and foremost, Sammy deserves the blame (guilt) because he (you) should have seen it coming (it's happened before, damnit!). Sammy should have walked away (punked out) from Jess (love) to save her (can't lose what you don't have). But he (you) was too much of a selfish (real), emo bitch (human) to do that, justifying (reasoning) his selfishness (emotional needs) with the idea that just because it (losing love) happened once in his life (life) doesn't mean it will happen every time (logic, faith, emotional availability). What a selfish (real), emo bitch (human) Sammy is (you are) to take such a foolish (faith-based) risk (get back on the horse that threw you) with Jess's life (love) and his (your) heart (heart). So Sammy (you) should have seen it coming (the fact that it *could* happen), and he (you) should have been willing to walk away (punk out) based on the fact that it (losing love) has happened to him (you) in the past (life) so it might happen to him (you) again in the future (life).

We don't learn not to risk love when we get our hearts broken. We learn to try again and hope for a different result. It's called faith in the future, and it is one of the fundamental foundations of human nature.

Secondly, Sammy deserves the blame (guilt) because he lied to Jess (love). He wasn't completely truthful (human nature) about everything he is (human nature) and everything that has ever happened to him (human nature) in his past (life). He (you) didn't warn Jess (love) that she could die (be lost) because he's (you've) had that happen (losing love) before (life). Sammy (you) didn't save her (love) because he (you) isn't Dean (who you wish you were, how you would like to see yourself as being) enough to walk away from (punk out on) Jess (love) just because something bad (life) might (could, maybe, perhaps) happen.

While we may aspire to avoid risking the kind of pain losing love brings by being strong enough to avoid the emotional entanglements that physical intimacy breeds, by being emotionally distant enough to get what we need from the physical intimacy alone, we can't really do that. To love and be loved requires risking pain and loss. Anything less is just sex.

And lastly, Sammy deserves the blame (guilt) because he (you) needed Jess (love). He (you) needed her (love) more than he should have (emo bitch that you are). And because the Demon (events beyond your control) is after Sammy (you), not Jess (love) . . . because every story told is all about Sammy (you) even if other people star in them on occasion.

On an essential human level, in the real world rather than the theoretical world of poets and romance novels, love is about what we get, not what we give. And even in the giving, love is about what we get from the giving. Losing love is about what we lose getting, not what we lose giving.

So Jess (love) only died (was lost) because the Demon (events beyond your control) was after Sammy (you). And Sammy (you), being the selfish (real), emo bitch (human) that he is, wasn't Dean (not really you) enough to walk away (punk out) when he should have (before you became emotionally entangled). So he (you) deserves the blame (guilt). And he's (you are) emo bitch (human) enough to show his pain (feel) all over the place (visibly) instead of bearing it (hiding it) in silence (heroically) like Dean (not really you) would do if he (who you want to be seen as) were in Sammy's (who you are's) place (loving and losing as compared to refusing to love so you won't lose).

Safety is in emotional distance. Love is in emotional risk. We aspire to be safe. We invariably fail at being safe in failing to resist the urge to risk. Emo bitches that all humans are, we fail at being strong enough to walk away from emotional risk for our own good, or for the good of others.

On the subject of love, we most often aspire to be Dean: in control, mitigating risk, managing collateral damage. We most often are, however, Sam: out of control, neck deep in risk taken in faith of greater reward, and vulnerable to the full agony of every wound inflicted by love lost, by Jess put to the match by the Demon of events beyond our control.

On the subject of Sammy and family, let's talk John.

Again, by talking Dean (yada, yada, yada, no Sammy without Dean, yada).

This one thing we take to be self-evident: Dean (not really you) loves John (the family) without question. He follows John's (the family's) directives without argument, and always puts John's (the family's) needs above any need or desire Dean (not really you) might have or wish to have. In return, John (the family) takes Dean (not really you) for granted, an untenable situation Dean (not really you) bears in long-suffering silence, a wound the pain of which he (not really you) will never show (emotionally distant).

We aspire to be self-sacrificing and heroic to a degree that the needs of those we love always come before our own. Very few of us actually are either that self-sacrificing or heroic, be the stakes life and death or just who gets the extra cookie.

Sammy (you), on the other hand, is clearly John's (the family's) favorite. And yet Sammy (you) is a bit of a selfish (real), emo bitch (human) rebel (individual), especially compared to Dean (self-sacrificial not really you). Sammy (you) puts what he (you) wants at least equal to, if not above, what John (the family) wants. Beyond that, Sammy (you) categorically refuses to follow John's (the family's) directives blindly, although he (you) will go along with John's (the family's) plan if he (you) agrees with it (get something out of it, too) and John (the family) doesn't treat him (you) like a child (member of lesser standing).

All of which is not to say that Sammy (you) loves John (the family) any less than Dean (not really you) does. In fact, all evidence in play suggests Sammy (you) loves John (the family) fiercely and is willing to sacrifice and die for John (the family) if necessary. That being said, he (you) still won't sublimate his desires or identity to John's (the family's) control, because he (you) is still primarily an individual (you) first and John's son (a member of the family) second, as he (you) should be. Furthermore, Sammy (you) doesn't exist only as an extension of John (the family), nor will he toe the line John (the family) consistently tries to pressure him (you) into toeing, not because it is best for Sammy (you), but rather because John (the family) is all about John (the family), even if he (the family) does love his sons (all the members of the family).

It also bears pointing out that, in contrast to Dean (not really you), if John (the family) presumes upon Sammy's (your) individuality, or if John (the family) presumes to take Sammy's (your) commitment to John (the family) for granted, Sammy (you) rails at the heavens (emo bitch that you are), shouts his protest (selfish individual that you are), and tells John (the family) exactly where he (again, the family) can shove his bull hockey (lack of appreciation for sacrifices made) and how far up it should go (what a rebel).

And Sammy does this because he (you) is an individual. He (you) is someone with hopes and dreams and a future of his own (normal), not only hopes and dreams and a future that revolves only around John (the family). Yes, Sammy (you) is John's son (a member of the family); but he (you) is not *only* John's son (a member of the family).

Family is our identity, but it is not our *only* identity. Though we may aspire to (and even perceive ourselves to) put the needs and/or wants of our families (or others we love) before our own, the reality of human nature is that we are individuals first, and members of a group second. What the group wants or needs may harmonize with what we, as individuals, want or need, but it rarely supersedes those wants or needs except in the most atypical of circumstances (Dean's going to die and Sammy can save him) or the most extreme cases of an imbalance of need (Dean is starving to death and Sammy just wants the last cookie).

But even as an individual, fiercely independent and determined to be his own person (again, normal), Sammy (you) and John (the family) are so much alike in so many ways that everyone but he (you) and John (the family) can see the resemblance as clear as day. Which, of course, is why Sammy (you) and John (the family) fight like cats and dogs, usually within minutes of finding each other again and having a happy reunion full of hugs and professions of undying loyalty, fidelity, and love, love, love.

Love doesn't mean compatibility. We aspire to dovetail perfectly with those we love, working together like well-oiled machines. Far more often, though, we dovetail with those we love like oil and water to the end of enormous conflict and/or a fine vinaigrette dressing. But that doesn't mean we love them any less, or don't miss them when they aren't making us crazy with how much they make us crazy.

All that touchy-feely (emotionally available), chick-flicky (emotionally available), huggy crap (emotionally available, expressing feelings), of course, isn't something in which Dean (not really you) would indulge. He's too cool (emotionally unavailable). He's too strong (emotionally unavailable). He's too Dean (not really you.)

Sure, there's always a hug there for John (family) in a quick, guy-hug kind of way (I love you, man. . . . Can I have your beer?), as well as an obvious allegiance (love) for John (the family) that Dean (not really you) is more than willing to express/show (even tough guys love their daddies). And beyond that, Dean's (not really you's) love for John (the family) actually supersedes all else (not really you's individuality) in how obviously Dean (not really you) defines himself as John's son (a member of the family) first and an individual second.

But even so (being Daddy's boy instead of your own man), Dean (not really you) wouldn't get all emo bitch (human) about that emotion all the time (emotionally unavailable). He (not really you) wouldn't fret (actively) about whether or not John (the family) loves him. He (not really you) would never think John (the family) would turn away from (abandon) him, or not want to see (stop loving) him. Yes, those are his (not really you's) greatest fears, but he won't indulge them (show them) because he is too strong (emotionally unavailable). He is too cool (emotionally unavailable). He is too Dean (not really you).

In contrast, Sammy (you) will actively fret (emotionally available) over whether or not John loves him (emo bitch that you are), wants to see him (petulant grudge-holding bitch that you are), or is angry with him (Daddy's boy that you are, even while being your own man). But unlike Dean (not really you), Sammy (you) won't fear those things to an unnatural (emotionally constipating) degree. To the contrary, despite all his (your) apparent emo bitchness (human insecurity) on the subject of John (the family), Sammy (you) is quite confident (normal) that as his father (blood of your blood), John (the family) will always love him (you), even if John (the family) is mad at him (petulant grudge-holding bitches that they are) and a real pain in the ass (too much like you to ever not piss you off) when y'all get together on holidays.

We aspire to be the way we want our families to see us when we are with them. Invariably, they see us exactly as we are anyway.

Thanksgiving is particularly good for both hugs and fistfights, regardless of what level of emotional unavailability you aspire to maintain right up until you ring the doorbell with pie in hand.

But despite Dean's (not really you's) self-sacrificial (abnormal) loyalty and obedience to (dependence on) John (the family), and despite Sammy's (your) more selfish (real), emo bitch (human) antagonism (unrelenting individualism) when it comes to John (the family), Sammy (you) is clearly John's (the family's) favorite. But Dean (not really you) doesn't resent it (because he's the self-sacrificing hero). In fact, Dean (not really you) takes great pride and satisfaction in seeing how much John (the family) loves Sammy (you). And while this might smack (to the uninitiated) of self-sacrifice on Dean's (not really you's) part, it is actually Dean's (not really you's) true and deep understanding that, no matter how different they (you and your family) may look on the outside (to others), it is really John (the family) and Sammy (you) who are just alike (cut from the same bolt of genetic cloth, as it were).

Regardless of what we aspire to be, we can usually see who we really are if we stop to look into the eyes of those who love us enough to know us as we are. And to prefer that reality over the more heroic and/or cooler individual we might aspire to be. Even if the other guy does drive a '67 Chevy Impala.

Because all overt surface detail (clone-ish similarities) to the contrary, Dean (not really you) and John (the family) only *look* alike. And they do (look alike) because John (the family), like Sammy (you), wants to see himself as something he (the family) really isn't: Dean (not really you). Cool, witty, heroic, self-sacrificing, wounded to the soul yet still emotionally distant Dean (again, not really you. And not really them either).

So John (the family) is no more Dean (not really you) than Sammy (you) is. In fact, truth be told, John (the family) is also a bit of a selfish (real), emo bitch (human) who puts his own (the family's) needs above Dean's (not really you's) and Sammy's (yours) by doing things like trying to sacrifice himself (shoot me in the heart, son!) for a freaking cause (it's more important than me, it's more important than anything) on the altar of Mary's (love) death (loss)—a death (loss) at the hand of a Demon (events beyond their control), but for which John (the family) inexplicably (but you understand it, don't you?) blames himself (because every story told is all about the family even if other people star in them on occasion), the same way Sammy (you) blames himself (because every story told is all about you even if other people star in them on occasion) for Jess's (love's) death (loss) at the hand of that same Demon (events beyond your control).

People are actually very much alike in how they really are. Likewise, self-perception is invariably aspirational to very similar states of heroic being. We call these aspirational states of being archetypes. We also call them stars. We occasionally call them Dean.

Yeah. Sammy (you) and John (the family) are two peas in a pod. And Dean (not really you) is actually—despite surface similarities (the way both you and your family want to see themselves, but not the way either you or your family actually is) to the contrary—the odd man out, if only in the fact that he (not really you) isn't the selfish (real) emo bitch (human) he would have to be to qualify as that third pea in the peapod. So the whole three Deans (Sammy [you selfish emo bitch you]-wants-to-be-Dean, John [those selfish emo bitches, too]-wants-to-be-Dean, Dean [not really you or anyone else, just an aspirational state of being]-is-Dean) in a peapod thing? Not gonna happen. Because while three Deans in a peapod is every fangirl's fantasy, that just ain't the way real life works (thus fanfic).

In real life, the heroes are never the cool, witty, selfless, swaggering, smooth, ridiculously handsome, rebellious, emotionally distant, stoic, strong, wounded-to-the-soul-but-suffering-it-all-in-silence-with-only-an-occasional-tear-shed-to-tell-the-tale guys. Rather, they are invariably sorta-smooth but still-a-bit-geeky dorks with floppy hair, dressed in somewhat baggy clothes with an occasional opportunity to look really hot in just a towel, smart, nice, mostly respectful, more-or-less law abiding, selfish, emo bitches who cry when they're hurt, bleed when they're cut, and get all chick-flicky when they really, really, *really* need to get or give a hug.

All of which is to say: Dean is an aspirational state of being. He's not really you. Nor anybody else, for that matter.

In real life, the heroes need their hollyhocks (asses) saved by someone else every once in a while, too. They fight with those they love, and in those fights, they're wrong (I am not!) as often as they're right. They have just enough fumble with the opposite sex to make them accessible, and without fail—*without freaking fail*—they put what they need and/or want above what others need and/or want all the time (the same way every other real human being on the planet does). Where their heroism kicks in, then, isn't in the day-to-day of living life; it's in the extreme situation, the rare occurrence, the event outside our normal capacity to control. That's when heroes (storytelling or otherwise) can, *and will*, rise above the failings of our shared human nature to heed the call of extraordinary action, even when that call requires sacrificing themselves for the good of someone else.

And Sammy is that hero, even when he's also being a selfish, emo bitch. Whether he's shooting Dean in the chest with rock salt (bitch) or using his own body as a flesh-and-bone shield between relative strangers and a Wendigo (hero); whether he's in a nose-to-nose shouting match with John (bitch) or shooting John in the leg instead of the head, thus sacrificing his shot at revenge (literally) in lieu of saving his father's life (hero, not that John will appreciate it, because family never appreciates your sacrifices the way they should, do they?). Sammy is human. Sammy is *not* an aspirational state of being. Sammy is you.

So to the point of it all: real heroes (again, storytelling or otherwise) are just selfish, emo bitches like the rest of us. They're people on a journey, doing the best they can to overcome their own flaws and failings, trying to survive their losses and mitigate the damage done by events beyond their control to the end of maybe finding a Jess (or a Mary) along the way to keep them warm on cold nights and take their turn doing the dishes.

Sammy is one of those guys. That's the burden of being Sammy: being real.

And not being Dean.

Dean is who we want to be; Sammy is who we are. Dean is our self-perception; Sammy is our self-reality. Dean is a storyteller's hero myth; Sammy is the reality about which every story is told, even if other people star in them on occasion to the perception that it's all about Dean, when it's really all about the burden of being Sammy.

Dodger Winslow is an enigma wrapped in a riddle dressed in a conundrum. When she's not being evasive or mysterious, she's usually writing or rattling on about the much maligned and dramatically misunderstood John Winchester.

Few of us out in the "real world" are likely to begin a conversation, "So this killer truck . . ." as Dean does in the season one episode "Route 666." Even Sam comments, "Our lives are weird, man," in season two's "Children Shouldn't Play with Dead Things." But while killer trucks, demons, werewolves, reapers, and death omens are just another day at the office for our heroes, Sam and Dean's lives are full of things we ordinary folk would term "supernatural."

Randall M. Jensen takes a look at horror and the supernatural in Supernatural *and how the Winchesters' perceptions differ from those of us who remain blissfully unaware of what's really out there in the dark.*

RANDALL M. JENSEN

WHAT'S SUPERNATURAL ABOUT *SUPERNATURAL*?

Supernatural begins like any number of horror stories. Once upon a time, not too long ago, an ordinary family lived in an ordinary house on an ordinary street somewhere in Kansas. John and Mary and their two boys, Dean and Sam. Very ordinary names. But then, one night, something extraordinary happens. In the dark, with the lights flickering, and with building tension and slightly spooky music playing in the background, we glimpse a shadowy figure, we hear a bloodcurdling scream, and then, as we watch with John, we see something impossible: Mary sprawls on the ceiling, bleeding, and she spontaneously bursts into flames. The ordinary is gone forever and life for the Winchesters will never be the same.

Although it would be difficult (and pointless) to try to give a precise and universal definition of horror, it's worth recalling Freud's observation in his essay "The Uncanny" that "the uncanny is that class of the frightening which leads back to what is known of old and long familiar."

If we make the plausible assumption that Freud's notion of the uncanny lies somewhere near the heart of horror fiction, we may think of horror as *what happens when the familiar meets or becomes the unfamiliar*. Horror stories involve something strange, out of place, unseen or unknown, something that makes our skin crawl and our spines tingle. We all know the delicious dread good horror can provoke in us. But it's also significant that this thing, this disturbing anomaly, is an unexpected intrusion into our everyday world. Horror *needs* the familiar as well as the unfamiliar. Now, the horrific element doesn't have to be something supernatural, since even something perfectly natural can be uncanny. Think of what a good storyteller or filmmaker can do with something as simple as the dark. However, perhaps unfairly, the books and movies most of us call to mind if we're asked to list well-known horror stories probably do involve the supernatural. And since our show's very title is *Supernatural*, we're especially interested in horror that contains a healthy dose of the supernatural. So let's spend some time thinking about the way the supernatural functions in our favorite show and perhaps we'll learn something about the distinctive nature of the show's stories as horror.

SUPERNATURAL AND THE SUPERNATURAL

Supernatural depicts a world that's very different from the real one. The most glaring difference is the world's *population*: demons, ghosts, vampires, werewolves, shapeshifters, reapers, and other strange creatures roam the planet with us. But there's an even deeper difference, because the Winchesters' world runs by a different set of *rules*, too. Dead isn't dead, not really: you can bring the dead back to life, if you know how. And corpses can move around by themselves, even when they're so decrepit they've got no earthly right to do so. Magic works. Lines of chalk on the floor have incredible causal influence over unimaginably powerful beings. Salt isn't just something you put in your soup. And so on. The world of *Supernatural* is, well, supernatural. But what exactly do Sam and Dean *mean* when they call something supernatural? How do they *know* whether or not they're dealing with something supernatural? Let's hunt down the answers to these questions.

Nearly every episode of *Supernatural* is jam-packed full of supernatural entities and events, whether they're puzzling, frightening, gruesome, thrilling, humorous, friendly, or just downright weird. The one exception seems to be the first season's "The Benders" (1-15), in which Sam and Dean come up against a sadistic backwoods family who are, in Sam's words, "just people." There's nothing supernatural—in a certain sense—about them, but no doubt we'd agree with Sam that there's something decidedly *un*natural about human beings that live as they do. Other than this standout episode, it's wall-to-wall demons, monsters, and spirits. Of course, this is because Sam and Dean are constantly on the lookout for their kind of prey, whether by scanning the papers for bizarre stories, talking to Bobby or Ellen or Ash or the other hunters at the Roadhouse, or trying to decipher their dad's journal. What exactly are they looking for? To begin with, something that's odd, unusual, apparently inexplicable. Someone has seen something that's literally unbelievable. Or somebody winds up dead and it just isn't clear how. This might be a job for the Winchesters! But then again, it might not be.

What counts as supernatural in our show's world? The answer to this question turns out to be surprisingly interesting. When Sam and Dean are searching for a potential hunt, they often use the label "supernatural" to characterize what they're after. They don't want to cross state lines only to find out that a story is based on some really bizarre coincidence and there's no quarry for them to hunt down. They're after something that's genuinely supernatural, not just something strange or freaky. Yet vampire nests and demon possessions are very much a part of the world they inhabit. They're not unusual at all in their lives, and in that sense, they're perfectly natural—at least for the Winchester family. But in this sense, what's natural to you and me and what's natural to Sam and Dean aren't the same thing, not by a long shot.

For example, is a haunting a natural or supernatural phenomenon? To us, the answer's clear: What could be more supernatural than that? (I'll assume that, like me, you haven't had an encounter with Casper.) However, what if we were to experience hauntings on a regular basis as Sam and Dean do? At some point, wouldn't we come to regard hauntings as *natural* in some important respect? And maybe we would come to think that formerly we were mistaken to see them as supernatural. If so, we'd be guided by the thought that what's supernatural is simply *what doesn't or can't happen in nature.* In *An Enquiry Concerning Human Understanding*, the philosopher David Hume defines a miracle as "a violation of the laws of nature," and this seems to be close to the idea we're after in defining the supernatural. Now, maybe a miracle is a *good* supernatural event. Not too many people would cry miracle upon seeing a scary, fugly, god-animated scarecrow, but they would definitely think that something supernatural was going on. In our world, creatures such as pagan gods are the stuff of imagination rather than creatures that are found out there in the biosphere. That's why, by our account, they're supernatural beings. But in *Supernatural*, they are presented as if they're normal residents of the world, even if such beings tend to keep it on the down-low, sometimes pretending to be just another particularly annoying suburban couple who are just a bit too happy about the holidays. In the world Eric Kripke has created, there just *are* demons, ghosts, and so on, even if most folks aren't in the know about this. Such creatures are rather like the bizarre species that live deep in caves, on the ocean floor, or in some forgotten jungle: they're unknown to most of us, but they're out there and we can learn about their characteristic traits. What we regard as the supernatural realm is for Sam and Dean a part of nature. The supernatural has thus been "naturalized."

After all, Sam and Dean enter many haunted houses and meet and dispose of many spooky "supernatural" creatures. It's precisely this piling up of experiences of the (formerly) supernatural realm that leads them to alter their picture of the world. Whereas a single monster is a horrifying and seemingly impossible interruption of our reality, thousands of monsters belonging to dozens of species show that we're dealing with a new reality. Not only do Sam and Dean see the world differently than most everyone around them, but in an important way, they even live in a different world, a world with a different nature. If they were to think and act as they do without having had such ample experience of ghosts, demons, and the like, they'd simply be screwballs, out of touch with the real world, rather like the two guys who eventually become the "Ghostfacers." At first, those losers believed in ghosts without any experience at all to confirm their beliefs. But since even idiots can get lucky, they just happened to be right! Sam and Dean are different. For them, the appearance of a ghost is not at all something that goes against everything they've experienced in their lives. Quite the opposite, really. Again, the supernatural has become the natural.

Why then do Sam and Dean use the label "supernatural" in the way they do? What's going on here, I think, is that Sam and Dean are using "supernatural" in our sense, or more precisely, in the sense assumed by most people in the alternate universe that is the world of *Supernatural*. It means "something the uninitiated think isn't 'real,' i.e., isn't part of nature." We (and most of the folks in Sam and Dean's world) don't believe in ghosts. And so we regard them as supernatural. Sam and Dean simply agree to talk as most people do because it's easier to talk that way. As the eighteenth-century British philosopher George Berkeley once said in a different context (in *A Treatise Concerning the Principles of Human Knowledge*), we can "speak with the vulgar, but think with the learned." We do still talk about the sun rising and setting, after all, even though we realize that isn't what is actually happening. And even the most reductionistic neuroscientist might ask you what's on your mind or talk about finding a kindred spirit, even though she doesn't for a second believe in immaterial minds or spirits. In much that way, Sam and Dean call a lot of what they encounter supernatural even though it plainly isn't, not in their world. Such ambiguities are fairly common in language; sometimes it avoids confusion to sort them out.

On a few occasions, however, the Winchester brothers run into something that seems to be supernatural *from their own point of view*. Here I'm thinking of two episodes in particular, "Faith" (1-12) and "Houses of the Holy" (2-13). In these storylines, Sam and Dean find themselves faced with something that simply doesn't fit into their view of things, wondering whether to believe in something they haven't ever seen before. A mere man who has the power to heal? Or, even more dramatically, an angel? As far as Sam and Dean know, in spite of all they've seen, things like this just don't happen, and thus they don't fit into their view of the world. From all the time they've spent hunting, from all the knowledge they've gained from their dad's journal and from other hunters, Sam and Dean have put together a kind of "science" of hunting, a kind of expanded "biology," I suppose, with demonology and the like in addition to entomology, zoology, botany, etc. It's sketchy, to be sure, and focused pretty intently on figuring out how to *kill* the species they study. But this quasi-scientific picture of the world gives them a conception of what is natural—what follows the rules—and what doesn't. And angels don't have a place in their expanded science, at least not so far. They aren't excluded by definition, either, of course. Sam and Dean might "discover" angels—or some other hitherto unknown variety of creature—much as a field biologist might discover a new species. Perhaps someday they will need to add some chapters to the John Winchester journal, or even to expand it into an introductory demonology text. For now, however, the "bright side" of what we think of as the supernatural realm just isn't part of Sam and Dean's world. For them, the unknown and the genuinely supernatural are to be found here. Demons, unfortunately, are as natural as can be. Angels? Well, the jury is still out.

Interestingly, our two heroes react differently when confronted with the possibility of something that's truly supernatural. Sam seems quite ready to flirt with belief in angels, as he began to do in "Houses of the Holy." Dean, on the other hand, infamously remarked that he'd just as soon believe in unicorns that ride silver moonbeams and shoot rainbows out of their asses. Dean believes in what he can see—in what he has seen. And he hasn't seen any angels, or even met anyone else who claims to have seen one. His view is that angels are on his "bull-crap list" and that this so-called angel was just another demon—a vengeful spirit, to be precise. The real explanation of this supposed "supernatural" happening (i.e., an angelic manifestation) was a perfectly natural one within Dean's 'verse: it's just another damned demon. Of course, as we know, he was right.

Since Sam and Dean are different in so many ways—musical tastes, dating habits, vocabulary, life ambitions, and so on—it's no big surprise that they reacted differently on this score. But why, exactly? Dean resists believing in angels (or in God) because of all the horror he's seen, and in particular because his mother believed that guardian angels watch over us and yet nothing protected her from the Yellow-Eyed Demon. As a result, Dean is angry and bitter. To believe in some supernatural force of good is to believe in something that let his mother die a horrible death. Dean is the kind of conflicted agnostic who doubts God's existence and yet at the same time is pissed off at him for not existing. If evidence of angelic activity started to appear, at this point Dean seems like he'd be pretty committed to explaining it away. Or he'd *claim* to be rejecting it, that is, both to himself and to others. But sometimes loud and angry denials indicate that someone actually believes what he is denying, even though he doesn't want to. Whatever the case may be, it would take a lot to overcome Dean's resistance. For him, it isn't just a matter of following the evidence trail, whatever he might say to the contrary. He's going to stick like glue to his current picture of the world, and not just because he's a die-hard rationalist.

Sam, on the other hand, wants so much to believe at least in part because he hopes he can be saved from his own dark destiny. He needs help, so he hopes there is someone out there who can help him. And sometimes he wants to believe because it means he might be able to save Dean, whether from his heart problems in "Faith" or from his impending doom in season three. Sam seems to believe even when the evidence is pretty flimsy, like he's desperately searching for a sign. There was no good reason for him to buy the angel story in "Houses of the Holy," when there was a perfectly ordinary and natural (for Sam and Dean!) explanation of what was going on. Whereas Dean's mind is closed a bit *too* tight, perhaps Sam's view of the world is a bit too open. If Dean's too cynical at times, Sam is a bit too gullible.

Of course, Sam and Dean's attitudes on this aren't static. At times Sam has seemed to lose any faith or hope he might have had, especially when it seemed his fate—or Dean's—was inevitable. Dean has doubted his skepticism at times, too, although not because he got touched by an angel. On one occasion, it was simply a piece of steel that landed in the right place at the right time, fortuitously impaling a bad guy (in "Houses of the Holy" again). An incredible coincidence, and it could be just that: odd, really serendipitous, but not supernatural. Yet surprisingly it made Dean wonder if there was some providential hand behind it all. Objectively speaking, the impaling wasn't any more compelling as evidence than the angelic manifestations were. Yet Dean began to believe in something beyond what he's seen, something that's actually supernatural. Why? Perhaps because he finally wanted to. We got another look at this more hopeful side of Dean in "Long-Distance Call" (3-14), when he was the one who was too quick to believe something that he probably shouldn't have believed: that his dead dad was on the phone.

No matter how weird a world might be, conceptually there will always be room for something that defies its limits, something that's truly supernatural. We can learn some pretty interesting things about people—about Sam and Dean, for example—by examining their attitudes toward this supernatural realm. It's also worth pondering how different kinds of horror stories depict the supernatural.

Supernatural as Horror

Supernatural seems to be part of what we might think of as a new trend in horror fiction. Classic horror tales describe how something strange and forbidding breaks into our everyday world. As Noel Carroll puts it in "The Nature of Horror," characters in horror tales "regard the monsters that they encounter as abnormal, as disturbances of the natural order." Notice how this definition seems to tie the horror genre to the supernatural, as defined above. Some particular thing shows up that just doesn't obey the rules; it defies our categories and so we don't know how to think about it. In fact, this is one way of thinking about what a monster is: something *singular* that doesn't fit our view of the world. A number of more recent horror narratives, including *Supernatural*, seem importantly different. These stories *naturalize* their horrific elements, making them familiar and, at least in some sense, normal and natural, so that horror somehow becomes part of the mundane world. Although we should be wary of offering exact classifications here, and there is certainly room for a more detailed analysis, we can divide such stories into two broad categories without exercising too much force.

The first kind of story re-conceives a supernatural creature as a natural one: the monster isn't from the pit of Hell, or animated by an amalgam of magic and science; he's just a human being who's been infected by a virus, not really "supernatural" at all. A scientific monstrosity, not a supernatural one. Think of the undead creatures from *28 Days Later* or the recent film version of Richard Matheson's *I Am Legend*. Or consider Ridley Scott's *Alien*. These stories locate a horror story inside the natural world as we understand it; they work without any intervention from the outside. Unforeseen events give rise to something that *looks* supernatural, but really isn't. This kind of story eliminates the supernatural piece by piece, showing how what looked like magic or mystery can be explained in scientific terms. Although this kind of horror has been flourishing fairly recently, thereby earning the title of a recent trend, it's not really a new phenomenon. In fact, Mary Shelley's *Frankenstein* (1818) is perhaps the quintessential scientific horror tale. And, more generally, a lot of science fiction stories can be classified as belonging to the horror genre, too. It's no surprise that a modernist sensibility would favor reducing the magical to the scientific, the inexplicable to the explicable. But this isn't how *Supernatural* rolls at all; our show isn't into reductionism.

The second kind of story involves expanding or altering our conception of nature. Such horror stories have a lot in common with fantasy, because they take up the project of building another world, an alternate reality. They're extended exercises in wondering "What if?" In such a story, vampires are magical creatures, perhaps, but then the world of the narrative is a magical world! Consider two of be best known instances of this kind of story: Laurell K. Hamilton's Anita Blake series and Charlaine Harris's Sookie Stackhouse books. In these popular story arcs, vampires and werewolves are just part of American society. They have jobs and they have to pay the rent. They even have their own bars and nightclubs to frequent. Laws have to be written to handle their special circumstances, maybe even some anti-discrimination legislation. And, of course, they're potential dates for whoever is our current protagonist. Here, too, the presence of a monster requires no incursion from the outside—there need be nothing supernatural in that sense. It's just that the inside of these storied worlds is a lot bigger than the inside of our world (and, as we've seen, that creates an ambiguity in what it means for something to be supernatural). Joss Whedon's endearing and enduring Buffyverse is one of the earliest and most formative examples of this kind of story in television. Buffy goes to class, chats with her friends, and stakes a vampire in the cemetery. As I've characterized it in this essay, "the Winchesterverse" is this same kind of place, although sadly it makes for a much less graceful moniker.

This second kind of horror story may in some ways not be a horror story at all. Or maybe what makes it horror isn't necessarily what one might think. Remember that horror is the intrusion of the unfamiliar into the familiar. If a vampire is depicted as familiar in a story, as part of the story's backdrop, then it isn't going to be a source of horror. A related point is that a story's genre isn't merely a matter of its setting. Even though a story has vampires in it, it might be more a romance or a detective novel than a horror novel. It might make you laugh or work hard at solving a mystery without arousing any dread whatsoever. So what is horror and what isn't? Must horror be about the supernatural? Is *Supernatural* horror? Once we discern the ambiguity in the concepts of horror and the supernatural and the ways in which these two concepts can come apart, it becomes really hard to identify horror's boundaries. Yet some boundaries simply are fuzzy, and it's a mistake to try to make something clear when it's not. In the end, arriving at a decisive conclusion that something does or doesn't count as horror is only important to the people who have to decide where to shelve books or DVDs. Those of us who want to think about stories do better if we have a conversation, even a debate, about how and in what ways something does or doesn't look and feel like horror.

As a television show with an ongoing but serialized storyline, *Supernatural* has the opportunity to blend genres. (Thankfully, we haven't had to endure a musical theatre episode.) Overall, the show is a mix of classic and new horror. Sometimes, we're asked to see through the eyes of the uninitiated, for whom the world is empty of monsters. A guy picks up a sexy hitchhiker in a white dress and we're with him when she disappears and reappears. That can't happen! Other times we're inside Sam and Dean's perspective and the creatures are expected. They're dangerous, of course, but not uncanny. We may feel fear and tension, as we would while watching people we care about putting themselves at risk, but we don't feel dread. Still other times even our two heroes face something they just don't understand, something they'd rather look away from. A new monster they don't yet understand, perhaps. Or an angel. From story to story, the border between the familiar and the unfamiliar shifts, and the locus of horror shifts with it. Often, even though Sam and Dean spend most of their time hunting monsters that would frighten us out of our wits, the things that really fill them with horror and dread aren't so different from what horrifies us. They grapple with the questions of whether there's something that transcends human experience, whether the universe is ultimately friendly or hostile, and whether life is meaningful or empty. And what really frightens each of them is the doom looming over the other. *Supernatural*'s horror is most effective when its source is the love of two brothers. Dean can face off with any hellish creature you like, but he can't face a world without Sammy or a world where Sam has become the thing they fight. Likewise, Sam is most haunted by Dean's recurring death in "Mystery Spot" (3-11) and by Dean's all too rapidly approaching damnation. This dread of the death and destruction of those we love is all too tragically familiar and its invocation is what makes *Supernatural* most moving, most frightening, and most horrifying.

RANDALL M. JENSEN is Associate Professor of Philosophy at Northwestern College in Orange City, Iowa. He has contributed chapters to several books on philosophy and popular culture, including most recently *Batman and Philosophy* and *Battlestar Galactica and Philosophy*. Given his longstanding fascination with horror, fantasy, science fiction, comics, and so on, he's delighted that he has finally found a way to make it part of his day job.

Humans like to be frightened. At least, we like to be frightened from the safety of our living room or the comfort of our couch. Be it in slasher flicks or fairy tales or TV shows like Supernatural, *we prove time and again that we enjoy having the pants scared off of us. Why? What is it about a show like* Supernatural *that is so compelling? Is it the scare that keeps us coming back for more? Or, as Dr. Gregory Stevenson suggests, do the supernatural trials and tribulations of the Winchesters appeal because they merely hold a mirror to the more mundane terrors we all face every day?*

GREGORY STEVENSON

HORROR, HUMANITY, AND THE DEMON IN THE MIRROR

One night I was putting my then four-year-old daughter Alexandra to bed. As I was tucking her in, she looked up at me with the kind of sweet, innocent eyes that belong to four-year-old girls and said, "Daddy, tell me a scary story." There is something deeply ingrained within us that seeks out the frightening amidst the comfortable, the bizarre amidst the normal, and the supernatural amidst the natural. Is that not why children love fairy tales? I'm not talking about the sanitized fairy tales we force-feed children today in which the three little pigs reconcile their differences with the big bad wolf. I'm talking about the original fairy tales in the Brothers Grimm tradition—fairy tales in which people's eyes get poked out, grandmothers get eaten by wolves, and fee-fi-fo-fumming giants meet a grisly end. Real fairy tales are dark stories that tap into that part of us that finds a strange form of comfort in the encounter with things that frighten us. What could be scarier than to be lost in a strange wood only to come upon a kindly old lady in a candy house? The promise of sweets quickly turns sour as you find yourself locked in a cage and staring at an oven, knowing that it's not a Honey Baked Ham the old lady is planning to slide in there. My mother read that story to me as a child. It was terrifying . . . and I loved it!

That's the reason I began to watch *Supernatural*. I wanted to hear a scary story. When I speak of scary stories, I am not particularly interested in the kind of horror shows that try to shock the audience through gross-out displays of blood and gore or by having monsters jump out from unexpected places at unexpected moments. No, the kind of scary stories I'm talking about are the kind that make the hair stand up on your forearms—those creepy kinds of tales that generate bone-tingling shivers and spark the kinds of irrational thoughts ("I think there is a monster in my closet") that make you afraid to get up to go to the bathroom in the middle of the night. Those are the tales that *Supernatural* tells.

Yet a strange thing happened to me over the course of this show's first three seasons. The episodes no longer scare me as they once did. As I look back, I recall the episodes of season one being scarier than those of season two, and the episodes of season two being scarier than those of season three. Has the show lost its touch? Have the writers gone soft? I don't think so. I think I've simply become conditioned to the show, desensitized if you will, like the time I listened to Pearl Jam's version of "Last Kiss" so many times that it eventually stopped having the same jolting impact. So one might expect that I have become bored with *Supernatural*. Not at all. If anything, I've enjoyed the third season most of all. This is a curious thing. If the show no longer scares me to the degree it once did, then why do I keep watching? Why do any of this show's viewers keep coming back week after week? Is it simply the promise of cheap thrills or the presence of two hot guys (I exclude myself from this motivation)? Or is it something deeper? As with the little old lady in the gingerbread house, might our fascination with scary stories involve more than meets the eye?

Monsters and Metaphors

The best horror stories are about much more than making one's date cling a little tighter. They are like a funhouse mirror held up to our darkest fears and deepest insecurities. They take those fears and reshape them into something monstrous. Renowned psychologist Bruno Bettleheim suggested that children need fairy tales for this very reason. In fairy tales, the abstract and intangible fears that children have difficulty wrapping their minds around (like the fear of abandonment) become embodied as witches and wolves that can be fought against and vanquished.[1] The monsters, in other words, are metaphors for what truly frightens them. Adults have fears too and these fears are often much darker and more real than the terrors that children face. This is why some of our most noted writers of fairy tales, J. R. R. Tolkien (The Lord of the Rings) and C. S. Lewis (The Chronicles of Narnia), have said that fairy tales function best for adults.[2,3] In the horror stories we tell each other, the monsters often represent adult fears. Frankenstein's monster represents the horror of science run amok without ethical guidelines. Jekyll and Hyde remind us of the potential for both good and evil within each human being. The Wolfman represents the constant struggle against our own animalistic urges. Count Dracula serves as a metaphor for the powerful elite who feed off the poor and vulnerable. Vampires boast a long tradition of standing in for our social ills and anxieties, whether plague, racism, or the AIDS virus. With the rapid rise of the technological age, we become anxious about the potential impact of computers on our society and fear that they might one day prove to be our downfall. So, when the machine in *The Terminator* is finally stripped of its human façade and pursues Sarah Connor as a monstrous mixture of metal and computer chips, with fire-red eyes radiating artificial intelligence, we never look at our PCs the same way again.

Why are we drawn to such horror stories? We should not discount the adrenaline rush of a good fright or the numerous benefits of having one's date grab on more tightly, but perhaps it's something deeper that keeps us coming back time and again. Perhaps we keep watching

[1] Bettleheim, Bruno. *The Uses of Enchantment: The Meaning and Importance of Fairy Tales*. New York: Knopf, 1976. Pages 120–122.

[2] Tolkien, J. R. R. "On Fairy Stories." In *Poems and Stories*, 116–154. Boston: Houghton Mifflin, 1994. Pages 143–145, 154.

[3] Lewis, C. S. "Sometimes Fairy Stories May Say Best What's to Be Said." In *On Stories and Other Essays on Literature*, edited by Walter Hooper, 45–48. New York: Harcourt Brace Jovanovich, 1982. Page 47.

because we see ourselves and our own struggles reflected back to us. When the monsters are defeated, we cheer—not just because the bad guy has fallen, but because we witness the defeat of our own anxieties. Ultimately, horror stories are less about the world outside us than they are the world inside us.

Is *Supernatural* Atheistic?

At Christmas time one year, a young Dean Winchester informed his little brother Sam that monsters were real, but Santa wasn't ("A Very Supernatural Christmas," 3-8). In other words, evil's afoot, but goodness is a little harder to find. For a show called *Supernatural*, this show has a rather one-sided view of the supernatural. Demons and other dark entities abound, yet benevolent supernatural beings are scarce. Some would suggest that, by definition, evil requires the existence of good; that if Hell exists, so must Heaven. Yet in *Supernatural*'s world, there are no angels, no assertions of God's existence, no Santa, not even a harmless Easter bunny. There are pagan "gods," but essentially they function as little more than amped-up demons. One might think that a *Supernatural* Christmas episode would bring a little good cheer. Instead, the episode revolved around an evil Santa-like figure who turned out to be a pair of cannibalistic pagan gods. At least in keeping with the holiday spirit, these gods were impaled by a Christmas tree branch ("A Very Supernatural Christmas").

Why call a show *Supernatural* and then exclude half of the supernatural realm? The mundane answer might be because benevolent supernatural beings aren't nearly as frightening. (I say this despite the fact that the thought of an old guy wearing bright red clothing with bells on it and sneaking into my house in the middle of the night to eat my milk and cookies is a tad creepy.) There is, however, a deeper answer. To have God or angels make an appearance would make the story more about the cosmic war between good and evil than the human war between the good and evil impulses within ourselves.

By keeping God in the shadows, *Supernatural* shifts the focus to the human struggle. In fact, God is not the only one absent on *Supernatural*. Satan has also left the building. Dean, who despite his experience with all kinds of demonic entities remained doubtful about the existence of God, was similarly quite surprised to learn that many demons believe the devil is real. A demon informed him that many demons are true believers in a higher (lower?) power they call Lucifer. Though no demon has ever seen Lucifer, they believe in him, that he made them, and that one day he will return for them. As the demon said, "I've got faith. So you see, is my kind really all that different from yours?" ("Sin City," 3-4). The answer, though, is yes. What distinguishes their faith is its object. The demons trust in the power of evil; Sam and Dean trust in the potential of humanity for goodness.

Although God does not show up in the credits at the end of any episode, the idea of God is a recurring character on this show. The concept of God's will and who precisely is carrying out that will is a common theme. Several characters on the show, from the prostitute who murdered a churchgoer to the preacher's wife who summoned a reaper against her enemies to the demon hunters who tried to kill Sam, believed that they were called to do God's will, prompting Dean to counter: "God save us from half the people who think they're doing God's work" ("Faith," 1-12). The irony is that Sam and Dean may be the people doing God's work. In the episode "Faith," Layla suggested to Dean, "Maybe God works in mysterious ways." When the faith healer Roy then selected Dean out of the crowd and healed him, Roy said it was due to what he saw in Dean's heart: "A young man with an important purpose. A job to do. And it isn't finished." In another episode, a man told a priest just before committing suicide in the church, "Father, God's not with us. Not anymore. . . . He can't help us. And if he can, he won't" ("Sin City"). Of course, Sam and Dean then rode into town and defeated the demonic presence there. Perhaps God helped out after all.

If God is not completely absent on *Supernatural*, neither are His presence or will obvious. Much like in real life. And *Supernatural* is very much about real life. By keeping both God and Satan at a distance, potentially there but always in the background, *Supernatural* becomes a show about how human beings conduct themselves in the shadows of good and evil.

The Demon in the Mirror

If monsters are metaphors in the best horror traditions, then what do the monsters on *Supernatural* represent? In one third season episode, Ruby, a somewhat repentant demon, informed Dean that all demons were once human. What Hell does, she helpfully related, is burn away all traces of humanity from a person ("Malleus Maleficarum," 3-9). The demon is what's left. Thus, in the world as imagined by *Supernatural*, the demons are metaphors of the human potential for evil. In fact, they represent the fulfillment of that potential. Whereas the first two seasons of *Supernatural* had Sam and Dean fighting battles against a variety of supernatural foes, the third season shifted gears into an all-out war between the Winchester brothers and the demonic forces. What made this so engaging to watch was the nagging sense that the battle depicted on the screen was just as much about the battle raging within ourselves—the constant tug-of-war between good and evil.

Consider the episode "Sin City," in which a Rockwellian small town in Ohio was transformed into a den of iniquity. Sam and Dean, of course, attributed this to demonic presence in the town. There were demons there, all right, but demons weren't the problem. When confronted, a rather attractive demon confessed that all she did was point people in the right direction. She had lunch with a mover and shaker named Trotter and simply hinted about some businesses through which profit could be made by catering to vice. The result? As she put it, "Supposedly God-fearing folk waist-deep in booze, sex, gambling. I barely lifted a finger. . . . All you gotta do is nudge humans in the right direction . . . and they'll walk right into Hell with big fat smiles on their faces." The human potential for evil and sin is unlimited and the evidence is abundant. The comely demon noted, "War, genocide. It's only getting worse. I mean, this past century you people racked up a body count that amazed even us." That potential for evil, she claimed, was why the demons would win the war, or in other words, why the darker side of our human nature often triumphs. The line between demon and human was awfully blurred in this episode, so much so that when Dean attempted to defend humanity by asserting that demons are evil, it rang a little hollow. So even though Sam and Dean defeated the demons in this town, they belatedly realized that the human businessman Trotter was still alive and well and thus wondered whether they had accomplished anything at all.

If, according to *Supernatural*, a demon is what one would see in the mirror once all pretensions of humanity were stripped away, then what exactly defines humanity on this show? Was Bela correct when she accused Sam and Dean of being merely a stone's throw away from serial killers ("Red Sky at Morning," 3-6)? Since the line between demon and human is so finely drawn, what is it that keeps that line in place? In one episode, the Trickster analyzed Sam and Dean from the demon perspective and told them that their weakness was that they kept sacrificing themselves for each other ("Mystery Spot," 3-11). On this, he was quite wrong. Demons serve only themselves and their own interests, so they can only see the selflessness of the Winchester brothers as moral failure. Yet what looks like weakness from the demon perspective is in fact Sam and Dean's greatest strength, because it is precisely that ability to act in the interests of others, to sacrifice oneself for another, that defines the essence of the human potential for good. It is the antidote to the poison of demon self-interestedness. It is what makes one human. This principle is best represented in the characters of Bela and Ruby.

The third season of *Supernatural* saw the introduction of two female characters who, at first, appeared to be little more than potential love interests for Sam and Dean, but who quickly revealed themselves to be far more complex and interesting because they represented two separate paths: one moving toward humanity and one moving away from it. Bela is human, but you can't always tell. She is a hunter like the Winchester brothers, but it's not demons she hunts. She hunts treasure—artifacts and objects of supernatural significance that fetch a high price on some kind of supernatural eBay. Like the demons Sam and Dean hunt, Bela acts only in her own self-interest. She is a constant thorn in the side of Sam and Dean as she frequently steals out from under their noses the very item they need to save themselves or others. In "Red Sky at Morning," individuals who saw a ghost ship on the water inevitably died shortly thereafter. When Sam and Dean attempted to save a man who'd seen the ship, Bela questioned why they would bother. Dean replied, "Yeah, well, see, we have souls so we're gonna try." Dean's comment, for all its throw-away sarcasm, hinted at a deeper truth. By her lack of concern for others, Bela showed herself to have more in common with the demons than with her own kind. Of course once Bela herself saw the ghost ship, she quickly sang a different tune and selfishly begged Sam and Dean to save *her*. Eventually we learned that Bela had once made a deal with a demon to kill her parents. In order to get out of the deal, she then tried to kill Sam and Dean ("Time Is On My Side," 3-15). Although Bela may have been human, she was certainly in touch with her inner demon. At the end of season three, Bela's deal ran out and she seemingly met her fate, sent to Hell to become the demon she had essentially been living as anyway ("Time Is On My Side," 3-15).

In contrast Ruby, the self-professed "little fallen angel" on Sam's shoulder, is a demon. She is, however, the only demon who wants Sam and Dean to win. She fights alongside them and aids them in their war against her own kind. Why?

> RUBY: Isn't it obvious? I'm not like them. I don't know why. I wish I was, but I'm not. I remember what it's like.
> DEAN: What what's like?
> RUBY: Being human. ("Malleus Maleficarum," 3-9)

If acting in the interests of others is a mark of humanity, then Ruby certainly has not forgotten what it's like. Whereas Bela frequently ran from danger and had no interest in the Winchester brothers' war against evil beyond how she could profit from it, Ruby regularly put herself in the line of fire in order to help Sam and Dean. When Sam and Dean found themselves trapped inside a police station and under siege by a horde of demons, Ruby came to the rescue by offering to perform a spell that would kill all demons within a mile radius. The catch? It would, of course, kill her as well. Her willingness to sacrifice herself for others betrayed her growing humanity—to a point. She failed to reveal, at first, that the spell would also require the sacrifice of a virgin, an act she was perfectly willing to perform (she is still a demon, after all) ("Jus in Bello," 3-12). The characters of Bela and Ruby remind us of the dueling temptations within us all: to become more human or less human, to embrace the demon within or to fight against it.

"NOBODY'S KILLING ANY VIRGINS!"

Sam and Dean are brothers, but in some ways, they couldn't be more different. During the first two seasons of the show, the contrast is starkly drawn. Sam is the stoic, quintessential good guy. Dean is the fun-loving bad boy who likes to live on the edge. Sam operates on faith that there is a force for good greater than himself. Consequently, he prays to God every day ("Houses of the Holy," 2-13). Dean is a thorough-going skeptic with respect to any outside force for good. Despite all his experience with the supernatural, he refuses to believe in anything that he himself has not personally encountered. He has no faith, whether in God or in humanity. Whereas Sam always sees the potential for goodness in others, Dean is more likely to envision their potential for evil. These differences manifest in conflicting attitudes toward the killing of human beings. Sam is adamant that the killing of a human being is wrong in any and every circumstance. It is a violation of his moral code. Dean, however, is a pragmatist. He sees no moral dilemma in killing human beings if the situation calls for it, either because a person has devoted himself or herself to evil or because it will serve a greater good.

But a funny thing happened over the course of this show's first three seasons. Sam and Dean gradually swapped places, each becoming more like the other. That Sam has been devolving has long been recognized by fans. The Sam of season three is a darker, more corrupted version of season one Sam. One could perhaps attribute this to the common assertion that the Sam who returned from death at the end of season two came back different, that he brought a touch of the demonic back with him. Perhaps, but Sam's devolution began earlier than that. By season two, Sam's experiences were increasingly leaving him disillusioned. In season one, Sam counseled Dean about the importance of having faith ("Faith"). Then in season two, when Sam discovered that what he had thought was a real angel was in fact a vengeful spirit, he adopted Dean's view that it is better to operate on sight rather than faith ("Houses of the Holy"). By season three, the Sam who always argued strongly against the killing of humans for any reason adopted an us-or-them mentality in the war against demons and a willingness to accept human collateral damage if necessary. He suggested killing fellow demon-hunter Gordon when he turned against them ("Fresh Blood," 3-7) and murdering a coven of humans dabbling in witchcraft ("Malleus Maleficarum"). Likewise, when Ruby offered to perform the spell that required the sacrifice of a virgin, Sam sided with her, coming to the conclusion that the death of one innocent girl was worth it to save the lives of other innocents ("Jus in Bello"). To put it bluntly, the Sam of season one would have a hard time recognizing the Sam of season three. Sam is a man of faith who wants to believe in the goodness of others, but life experiences, such as confrontations with the human potential for evil and situations that call into question the existence of a supernatural force for good, keep getting in his way.

Dean, on the other hand, has the opposite problem. What is often overlooked is that, just as Sam is devolving, Dean is *e*volving. As one goes down, the other goes up. At first, Dean is a religious skeptic with a faith in nothing beyond himself, yet life experiences keep getting in his way too. Dean's evolution can best be charted by a close look at three episodes, one from each season. In the first season episode "Faith," Sam and Dean investigated a faith healer named Roy. Sam was characteristically open to the possibility that the man was genuine, while Dean was characteristically dismissive.

> SAM: Maybe it's time to have a little faith, Dean.
> DEAN: You know what I got faith in? Reality. Knowin' what's really going on.
> SAM: How can you be a skeptic with the things we see every day?
> DEAN: Exactly. We *see* them. We know they're real.

Once Sam and Dean realized that for every person Roy healed, another person died at the exact same moment, Dean suggested that they kill Roy. The murder of a human being was a viable option for Dean because human evil could be seen and thus definitively dealt with. Roy, however, turned out to be innocent. What Dean saw had deceived him. That message was hammered home to him through the character of Layla, a young woman who was dying and had faith that Roy could heal her. When it became clear that her healing would not happen, Dean believed she would become as disillusioned as he was. Layla, however, informed him that faith is about believing not only when miracles happen, but even when they don't. The episode concluded with the following exchange:

> DEAN: So, what now?
> LAYLA: (*smiling*) God works in mysterious ways.
> DEAN: I'm not much of a prayin' type, but I'm gonna pray for you.
> LAYLA: Well, there's a miracle right there.

It's a small step for Dean and one that initially does not seem to have moved him very far.

By the time we come to the second season episode "Houses of the Holy," Dean appears to have changed little. When individuals began killing seemingly upstanding citizens and claiming that angels ordered them to do it, Dean reiterated his belief that relying on anything other than what one could see was irrational and futile. Although he was willing to accept that this was the work of a demon or spirit, he found the suggestion of angels to be ludicrous, no more persuasive than arguments for unicorns. The reason Dean gave was that he had never seen one; yet, in a moment of uncharacteristic openness, Dean revealed that the truth of his anger and skepticism cut much deeper. The last thing his mother said to him before she was killed by a demon was that angels were watching over him. No angels protected her, however, so Dean concluded, "There is no higher power. There is no God. I mean, there's just chaos and violence. Random, unpredictable evil that comes out of nowhere and rips you to shreds. So you want me to believe in this stuff? I'm gonna need to see some hard proof."

What Dean failed to recognize was that faith is a different kind of seeing. The killers in this episode were killing people like Carl Gulley who, based on sight, appeared to be an upstanding citizen. But when Sam and Dean entered his basement, they found the remains of murdered college students. The other victims likewise harbored similarly dark secrets. The message to Dean was clear: one's eyes do not always point to the reality of things.

Dean, still adamant that God and angels are not in the picture, especially after they proved that the "angel" ordering these murders was merely the spirit of a deceased priest, pursued a man whom the deceased priest ordered killed. When the man attempted to murder a girl, Dean intervened and saved her. The woman responded by saying, "Thank God," *not* "Thank you." What normally might seem a perfunctory exclamation of relief here took on a deeper meaning. Was Dean unwittingly acting as an agent of the divine? When a freak accident then caused the improbable death of the attempted murderer, Dean, who witnessed the event, responded with his own, albeit less noble, exclamation: "Holy—" Dean did not finish the exclamation, and that was just as well, because by tossing out the word "Holy," Dean unknowingly acknowledged that what he just saw with his eyes betrayed a larger vision of reality than he was perhaps ready to accept. Shaken by the experience, Dean made a startling confession:

> DEAN: The way he died, if I hadn't seen it with my own two eyes, I never would have believed it. I mean, I don't know what to call it.
>
> SAM: What? Dean, what'd you see?
>
> DEAN: Maybe (*pause*) God's will.

Dean's experiences in "Faith" and "Houses of the Holy" shaped his evolution. In the season three episode "Sin City," Dean made a proclamation that would have shamed the Dean of season one. A demon asked him, "Do you believe in God, Dean?" Dean sincerely answered, "I don't know. I'd like to." It's not a ringing endorsement, but for one so initially antagonistic to the very idea of faith, Dean's come a long way. Whereas the Sam of season three began to act a lot more like Dean, the Dean of season three began to act more like Sam. In an exact role reversal near the end of season three, we actually heard *Sam* demanding "hard proof," while accusing Dean of operating on "blind faith" ("Long-Distance Call," 3-14). Likewise, when Dean told Gordon that it was an inviolate rule that demon hunters do not kill innocent people, we viewers had to do a double-take to make sure that wasn't Sam talking ("Fresh Blood"). When Sam wanted to kill the coven of witches, it was Dean who protested that they couldn't kill humans despite whatever evil actions they may have committed ("Malleus Maleficarum"). Similarly, when Sam and Ruby were willing to sacrifice an innocent girl to save the lives of many others, it was Dean who shouted out, "Stop! Stop! Nobody's killing any virgins!" The pragmatist Dean who was always willing to bend any rule in the interest of victory now proclaimed, "It doesn't mean that we throw away the rule book and stop acting like humans. . . . I mean, look, if that's how you win wars, then I don't want to win" ("Jus in Bello"). Because of Dean's refusal to let them sacrifice the virgin, several innocent people died, including the virgin girl herself. The demon Ruby threw this back in Dean's face as proof that he in fact did not know how to win a war. But Dean won the battle that mattered most. By refusing to sacrifice the girl, he refused to sacrifice his humanity.

These opposite journeys of Sam and Dean are about more than just the evolution or devolution of a character. They are about the potential for such a journey being taken by each one of us. Sam and Dean are fighting a war against demons, but it's a war that's really being waged within themselves. Sam is fighting against his own potential for evil, while Dean fights for something to believe in beyond himself and what he can see. As such, Sam and Dean represent the never-ending war that all humans fight as we battle for and against the competing impulses to better ourselves or to give in to our darker side. For all its supernatural bluster, the show *Supernatural* is ultimately more about the natural.

Supernatural stands within the grand tradition of horror shows that hold a mirror to ourselves and our world. Sam and Dean may face off against vampires, angry spirits, and demonic Santa clones, but that's nothing compared to the evil that human beings perpetuate against themselves: terrorism, child predators, children shooting up middle schools. That is the real horror show. By taking our society's horrors and reflecting them back to us as demons and monsters, what *Supernatural* does is remind us of humanity's potential to act in demonic and monstrous ways. But it also reminds us of our potential to fight against the demons within. Like Sam and Dean, we all have to decide how to take up that battle. I, for one, think it's best if we don't kill any virgins.

Dr. Gregory Stevenson is Professor of Religion and Greek at Rochester College in Michigan, although his favorite classes to teach are those on religion and popular culture because he gets to watch television and call it research. His current "research" project is an article on the influence of the Book of Revelation on comic books. Some of his musings on popular culture can be found at http://caritas2.blogspot.com.

Supernatural is a dark show, in both tone and content. Much of it is shot at night, using muted colors and moody lighting, and the heroes travel to dark places, both physically and emotionally, to investigate evil things that should never see the light of day.

So in all this darkness, in all this evil, where can we find the light? Evil exists in the Supernatural world as a matter of fact, but can we say the same of good?

Avril Hannah-Jones looks at the origins of good and evil in the Supernatural world, at choice and at destiny, at demons and at angels.

AVRIL HANNAH-JONES

GOOD AND EVIL IN THE WORLD OF *SUPERNATURAL*

One of the roles of religion is to answer questions: Where did we come from? Where are we going? How should we behave on the journey? And among the most troubling and significant, how can evil exist in a world created and loved by a benevolent God? Classical Judeo-Christian answers have relied on free will; God gave humans the gift of choice, and sometimes human choices lead to evil.[1]

Popular culture, too, can offer answers to questions about the meaning of life. Alongside all the action and emotion and fun of *Supernatural* are a suggested explanation for the existence of evil and a proposal for how humanity should respond to it. At the core of *Supernatural* is the belief that good and evil are both profoundly "natural," the result of human choice. The philosophy of *Supernatural* agrees with Judeo-Christian theology that the line between good and evil lies within the human heart.

[1] See, for example, the *Catechism of the Catholic Church* (Strathfield: St Pauls, 2004), sections 309–24.

"Of Course You Should Be Afraid of the Dark": Evil on *Supernatural*

> *"Don't be afraid of the dark?" What, are you kidding me? Of course you should be afraid of the dark. You know what's out there! ("Pilot")*
>
> —Dean Winchester, "Pilot"

From the first episode of *Supernatural* one thing is clear: evil is real. A shadowy figure stands over a baby's crib; a young mother is pinned, bleeding, to the ceiling; a fire erupts and destroys a home; and a previously ordinary family takes to the road to fight "what's out there." In the world of *Supernatural*, evil is no mere illusion, not simply the absence or distortion of good. As Missouri Mosley told the adult Sam and Dean Winchester, "All those years ago, real evil came to you. It walked this house" ("Home," 1-9).

While it might be expected that in a show called *Supernatural* this real evil would be just that—supernatural—the philosophy behind the show is that evil is caused by human choice. This is most obvious when the beings committing acts of evil are human: Ansem Weems, Gordon Walker, Ava Wilson, Jake Talley. But it is equally true when the being perpetrating evil is supernatural.

The pilot sets up one of the show's constants: angry spirits are created by violent death. The angry spirits are responding to violence done to them—as with Peter Sweeney, haunting the men who accidentally drowned him ("Dead in the Water," 1-3)—or are continuing in death violence committed in life—as with both Preacher Jacob Karns ("Hook Man," 1-7) and Dr. Ellicott ("Asylum," 1-10). As Dean says of Nurse Glockner, "In life, she's a vigilante. In death, the same thing" ("Folsom Prison Blues," 2-19). Sometimes the spirit is more confused than angry, and can be convinced to let go of life and move on, as with Molly ("Roadkill," 2-16) and Father Thomas Gregory ("Houses of the Holy," 2-13).[2] Dean was himself once in

---

[2] Such spirits also provide the clearest evidence offered of the existence of a "Heaven" to match *Supernatural*'s well-mapped Hell, as they disappear into blinding white light. While Hell is a matter of record, colorfully described by "Meg" as "a prison made of bone and flesh and blood and fear" ("Born Under a Bad Sign," 2-14), the existence of Heaven remains a matter of hope. As Sam tells Dean, "Doesn't really matter, Dean. Hope's kind of the whole point" ("Roadkill").

danger of becoming an angry spirit, having to choose between accepting his death and moving on, or continuing to fight death and haunt the hospital ("In My Time of Dying," 2-1).

Other supernatural evil is also the result of human activity. Wendigos are created when a human turns cannibal ("Wendigo," 1-2). The curse on Oasis Plains, Oklahoma, is a response to the slaughter of the Euchee Tribe ("Bugs," 1-8). The "ghost" of Mordechai Murdock, and the deaths he caused, was created by a group of students who made up a ghost story and posted it online, after painting a Tibetan spirit sigil on the wall of an abandoned house ("Hell House," 1-17). The "overnight successes" killed by Hell Hounds were slaughtered because they had made deals with a demon ("Crossroad Blues," 2-8), and Ruby became a demon because as a witch she had also sold her soul ("Malleus Maleficarum," 3-9). Most of the evil the Winchesters fight, no matter how supernatural its presentation, is the result of a human choice. And that evil is defeated only when other humans make a choice to fight it.

"THEY'RE EVERYWHERE": AZAZEL, LILITH, AND OTHER DEMONS

> NANCY: When I was little I would come home from church and talk about the devil. My parents would tell me to stop being so literal. I guess I showed them, huh? ("Jus in Bello," 3-12).

The one exception to this explanation for evil appeared to be demons. When demons possess humans whatever havoc is subsequently wreaked is the fault of the demonic possessor rather than the human possessed ("Born Under a Bad Sign," 2-14). Yet as the Winchesters have fought their personal nemeses—two named demons with definite Judeo-Christian roots[3]—it has become evident that demons, too, are beings whose evil results from

[3] *Supernatural* creator Eric Kripke has denied that there is anything particularly Christian about the show's demonology (TV.com Q&A: *Supernatural* creator Eric Kripke. http://www.tv.com/supernatural/show/30144/story/10682.html, January 10, 2008, accessed on March 31, 2008). However, he has also described *Supernatural* as "Star Wars in truck-stop America" (Commentary on "Pilot"), and "truck-stop America" has Judeo-Christian roots. It is a world dotted by small towns called Jericho, Nazareth, and Salvation; Christian churches are apparently the only places of worship; and the only visible religious professionals are Christian clergy.

human choice.

The Winchesters' quest, and thus the impetus for the series, was initiated by an evil that attacked their family and killed the mother, Mary. We, together with the remaining Winchesters, gradually learned more about that evil, until the father, John, came face to face with the demon who murdered his wife by summoning him with the sigil of Azazel, the first hint of who this demon truly was ("In My Time of Dying"). Finally, Dean discovered the demon's name: Azazel. As a possessed Casey asked Dean, "What, you think his friends just called him Yellow Eyes?" ("Sin City," 3-4).

Azazel is mentioned in Leviticus as a wilderness-dwelling being.[4] There is no other mention of him in the Bible, but in the apocalyptic book *1 Enoch*, written between 200 and 60 B.C.E., Azazel is one of the two hundred angels who saw and lusted after the beautiful daughters of men and as a result fell from Heaven. It was Azazel who taught humanity to make swords, daggers, shields, breastplates, bracelets, and ornaments. Azazel also taught humanity about cosmetics.[5] In *The Apocalypse of Abraham* (circa second century C.E.) Azazel is described as the fire of Hell and apparently carries Hell about with him. He is also identified with the serpent that tempted Eve, and is described as a great dragon that devours the wicked.[6]

While Azazel was the Winchesters' adversary for over twenty years, and the repercussions of his actions still affect them, after his death their more immediate problem became a new power ("Malleus Maleficarum"). This power is named, by the demon Ruby, as Lilith; she typically manifests herself as a rather frightening little girl who can apparently vaporize a police station and everyone in it with her glowing

[4] "Aaron shall cast lots on the two goats, one lot for the Lord and the other lot for Azazel. Aaron shall present the goat on which the lot fell for the Lord, and offer it as a sin-offering; but the goat on which the lot fell for Azazel shall be presented alive before the Lord to make atonement over it, so that it may be sent away into the wilderness to Azazel." Leviticus 16:8-10. All biblical quotes are from the New Revised Standard Version, unless otherwise noted.

[5] "1 Enoch" in H. F. D. Sparks (ed.), *The Apocryphal Old Testament* (Oxford; Clarendon Press, 1984), pp. 190–199.

[6] Edward Langton, *Essentials of Demonology: A Study of Jewish and Christian Doctrine, Its Origin and Development* (London: The Epworth Press, 1949), pp. 130–132.

white eyes and a wave of her hand ("Jus In Bello"). Like Azazel, Lilith comes from Judeo-Christian mythology. She is a night demon, referenced in the biblical book of Isaiah,[7] and she is possibly also the "terror by night" mentioned in the Psalms.[8] Again, like Azazel, she has a much more detailed history in apocryphal literature. In Jewish Aggadah, Lilith was Adam's first wife. Made, as Adam was, from the dust of the ground, she demanded to be equal to her husband and flew away from him when it was denied her. In punishment three angels killed her demon children, and in revenge Lilith injures babies—boys until they are circumcised at eight days old and girls until they are twenty days old.[9] Like Azazel, Lilith then developed a fascinating mythology in post-biblical literature. Also like Azazel, Lilith was once good, and chose her evil path.

In Judeo-Christian myth most demons are fallen angels.[10] They were not created evil, they "fell." While *Supernatural* is a world without "angels,"[11] its demons are also fallen beings. To Dean's surprise and horror, Ruby revealed to him that demons, "every one I've ever met," were all themselves once human. Going to Hell literally causes humans to forget who they once were as the torments of Hell burn away their humanity ("Malleus Malficarum"). The suggestion that *Supernatural*'s demons are fallen humans is worrying not only for Dean, who has sold his soul and at the end of season three was dragged to Hell, but for Sam, who may also have a demonic future.

"Lucifer Actually Means Light Bringer": Sam Winchester as the Morning Star

> *How art thou fallen from Heaven, O Lucifer, son of the morning! (Isaiah 14:12, KJV)*

---

[7] "Wildcats shall meet with hyenas, goat-demons shall call to each other; there too Lilith shall repose, and find a place to rest." Isaiah 34:14.

[8] Psalm 91:5.

[9] Louis Ginzberg, *The Legends of the Jews: Volume 1 From the Creation to Jacob* (Baltimore and London: The John Hopkins University Press, 1998), pp. 65–66.

[10] *Catechism of the Catholic Church*, sections 391–394.

[11] Don Williams, "'Supernatural' Creator Nixes Divine Intervention." BuddyTv.com. 31 March 2008. <http://www.buddytv.com/articles/supernatural/supernatural-creator-nixes-div-14351.aspx>

Trapped in a basement in "Sin City," Dean found himself having a surprisingly civil and informative conversation with a demon. "Casey" tells Dean the legend of Lucifer, once the most beautiful of all God's angels. "Casey" has faith in Lucifer, the "higher power" that "they say" made demons what they are and will one day return to them.

Throughout the series there have been hints that Sam Winchester might be the being in whom Lucifer will be incarnated. Meeting Sam in a dream at Cold Oak, Azazel explained that he was looking for the best and brightest of the psychic children of Sam's generation to lead Hell's army and showed Sam a vision of an infant Sammy being fed Azazel's blood ("All Hell Breaks Loose [Part 1]," 2-21). As the possessed Casey herself told Dean, "Sam was supposed to be the Grand Poobah and lead the big army, but he hasn't exactly stepped up to the plate, has he?" Other demons have also recognized in "little Sammy Winchester" a potentially powerful evil being: the prodigy, the boy-king, the Antichrist. Sam was shown that Mary knew Azazel ("All Hell Breaks Loose [Part 1]") and Ruby went even further, revealing that everyone who had ever known Mary had been "systematically wiped off the map" to cover up what Azazel had done to Sam ("The Kids Are Alright," 3-2). There is something "special" about Sam, beyond his psychic abilities; Dean's conversation with "Casey" gave an explanation.

According to legend, it was pride that caused Lucifer's fall.[12] Demons think pride is Sam's weakness, too. In "The Magnificent Seven" (3-1) it was Pride who led the attack on Sam. Similarly, "Father Gil" told Sam that, "Somehow I see you out in front of the pack. You could do some great things" ("Sin City"). While demons have tried to tempt Dean into the sin of despair by suggesting that his family doesn't need him,[13] they have tried to tempt Sam into the sin of pride by suggesting that he doesn't need his

---

[12] Henry Ansgar Kelly, *Satan: A Biography* (Cambridge: Cambridge University Press, 2006), pp. 194–199.

[13] Meg ("Shadow," 1-16) and Azazel ("Devil's Trap," 1-22). In his conversation with Bobby after bringing Sam back it appeared that Dean agreed with them. He believed his life would only have meaning if he sacrificed it to save Sam ("All Hell Breaks Loose [Part 2]," 2-22). But after a confrontation with a demonic version of himself saying exactly the same thing, Dean finally asserted that he did not deserve to go to Hell and refused to give in to the self-hatred and despair with which demons had tempted him ("Dream a Little Dream of Me," 3-10).

family. The Crossroads Demon suggested that Sam would be relieved when he no longer had to take care of "desperate, sloppy, needy Dean" ("Bedtime Stories," 3-5). The Trickster told Sam that Dean was his weakness ("Mystery Spot," 3-11).

The possibility that Sam might be Lucifer does not make his fall inevitable. Lucifer, the Light Bringer, the Morning Star, is not simply a demonic figure. The Morning Star is also a title for Jesus.[14] Thus if Sam is a "Lucifer" figure, he could just as easily be a Christ-figure as he could be an Antichrist. One (human) attacker even pinned Sam to the ground in the position of crucifixion, nails restraining his hands, providing a visual representation of Sam as Christ ("Dream a Little Dream of Me," 3-10). Sam is an unfallen Lucifer-figure, and he has the potential to choose either good or evil.

Yet Dean is also a Christ-figure. In the alternate world created by the djinn, in a graveyard at night, Dean asked his absent yet intimately present father, "Why is it my job to save these people? Why do I have to be some kind of hero?" Dean echoes the questions Christ asked his Father in the Garden of Gethsemane. And Dean ends his dialogue by accepting the need for sacrifice, just as Jesus did: "My Father, if this cannot pass unless I drink it, your will be done" (Matthew 26:42) Dean then goes to kill the djinn with a silver knife dipped in lamb's blood, further hinting at a connection between Dean and Jesus, the Lamb of God ("What Is and What Should Never Be," 2-20).

Sam and Dean have the option of choosing between good and evil because, while *Supernatural* is unambiguous about the existence of evil, it nevertheless hints at the existence of good. Supernatural good is as much a part of the world of the Winchesters as supernatural evil. And like evil, it is a result of human choice.

"IF YOU *KNOW* EVIL'S OUT THERE, HOW CAN YOU NOT BELIEVE GOOD'S OUT THERE, TOO?"

> SAM: [I]f you *know* evil's out there, how can you not believe good's out there, too?
>
> DEAN: Because I've seen what evil does to good people. ("Faith," 1-12)

[14] 2 Peter 1:19; Revelation 22:16.

The theology of *Supernatural* is the reverse of popular religion, which postulates the idea of "the Devil" as a way of explaining the existence of evil in a world created by a supposedly all-powerful, all-good God.[15] In the *Supernatural* universe, the tangible presence of demons is not matched by the equally discernible presence of angels, and a higher power of good can only be hypothesized. Evil is a matter of empirical knowledge, of what Sam and Dean can see with their own two eyes; good is a matter of hope, a possibility that keeps them fighting.

The first episode of *Supernatural* hinted at the existence of good. Sam told a girl wearing a pentagram necklace, "A pentagram is a protection against evil. Really powerful. I mean, if you believe in that kind of thing" ("Pilot"). Since Sam obviously knows supernatural lore, the implication is that pentagrams work. There are other hints that there is a higher power of good that cooperates with humanity in hunting evil as well. The demons the Winchesters hunt all flinch at "Christo,"[16] are burnt by holy water,[17] and can be exorcised by the Latin *Rituale Romanum* ("Phantom Traveler," 1-4), while evil spirits cannot cross the hallowed ground of a church ("Route 666," 1-13).[18]

There are the events that might have been coincidence, were it not that, as Bobby Singer says, "I believe in a lot of things. Coincidence ain't one of them" ("The Magnificent Seven"). In the Winchesters' hometown of Lawrence, for example, little Sari was scared by a figure of fire in her closet—at the exact moment that her mother Jenny found a collection of Winchester family photographs in the basement. When Sam and Dean turned up on Jenny's doorstep and Sam used their real names, Jenny responded, "That is so funny. You know, I think I found some of your photos the other night" ("Home"). She then invited them in, two

[15] T. J. Wray and Gregory Mobley, *The Birth of Satan: Tracing the Devil's Biblical Roots* (New York: Palgrave Macmillan, 2005), p. 39.

[16] Sam describes "Christo" as the name of God in Latin. It actually translates as "by Christ." Presumably John Winchester taught his sons this handy demon-detecting device when they were too young to worry about exact translations, and so simplified it for them. While "Christo" works on demons, Ed yelling "The power of Christ compels you!" had absolutely no effect on Mordecai Murdock. Then again, Murdock was a special case; Dean was outraged to find that rock salt did not work on him either ("Hell House").

[17] Except for Azazel, who is apparently immune to holy water ("Devil's Trap," 1-22).

[18] However, hallowed ground only works on minor league demons ("Salvation").

strangers who just happened to be able to protect her family. That the figure of fire Sari feared in fact turned out to be Mary Winchester demonstrated that the sequence of events was more than just a coincidence.

Another such "coincidence" was Roy Le Grange's decision to heal Dean because he looked into Dean's heart and saw a young man with an important purpose, an unfinished job. While Roy's ability to heal came, without his knowledge, from his wife's maleficent binding of a reaper, again it seemed to be more than just coincidence that Roy chose Dean, a young man with a destiny ("Faith").

The life and work of Pastor Jim Murphy was also a hint that good might be tangible. An old friend of John Winchester ("Asylum"; "Something Wicked," 1-18), Pastor Jim was first seen standing in his church, leafing through a Bible, a chalice at his hand. A young woman entered, looking for help, and Jim offered it: "I like to say, salvation was created for sinners" ("Salvation," 1-21). Sadly, the young woman was Meg, a woman possessed by the daughter of a powerful demon. Undeterred by the church being on hallowed ground, "Meg" killed Pastor Jim to send a message to John Winchester. The very fact that Jim Murphy was both hunter and pastor, someone who knew exactly what was out there, had the weapons to dispatch it, and yet still apparently believed in good, offers hope for the existence of supernatural good as well as supernatural evil.

As with evil, the power of supernatural good comes from human choice. Exorcisms work, pentagrams act as protection, holy water hurts demons, and salt repels evil—if a human chooses to use them. *Supernatural* even postulates that human choice can lead to the existence of angels, holy forces against evil.

"ANY FLUFFY WHITE WING FEATHERS?": THE EXISTENCE OF ANGELS

> FATHER REYNOLDS: The Archangel Michael. With the flaming sword. The fighter of demons. Holy force against evil. . . . I like to think of them as more loving than wrathful, but, yes, a lot of Scripture paints angels as God's warriors. ("Houses of the Holy")

In the world the Winchesters inhabit, demons exist, are everywhere, and can possess anyone. Angels, on the other hand, have never appeared in supernatural form on *Supernatural*. Dean does not believe in them; Sam only hopes they exist. The only time the Winchesters encountered an apparently supernatural angel, it turned out to be the confused spirit of a Catholic priest who needed help to rest in peace.

This does not mean that there are no angels on *Supernatural*. At the beginning of "Something Wicked" a little girl prayed, "Now I lay me down to sleep. I pray the Lord my soul to keep. Thy angels watch me through the night. And keep me safe till morning light." Several days later Dean and Sam worked through the night to kill a shtriga, saving the little girl and every other child the shtriga attacked. When morning light came, and the children recovered, the mother of one described it as a miracle. The little girl's prayer was answered—"angels" came.

In the oldest Biblical stories of angels there is no mention of fluffy white wing feathers.[19] Angels, as the Hebrew *malakh* and the Greek *angelos* indicate, were simply God's messengers. Biblical angels were more likely to carry a sword than a harp; many appeared as warriors.[20] They wore no special clothing and appeared in no special way. Those they visited thought that they were human until, having accomplished God's work, the angels departed.[21] They symbolized the fact that humans were not alone, that God's help was close at hand.

Sam and Dean Winchester resemble these early biblical angels. In "What Is and What Should Never Be" we saw a world in which the Winchesters did not hunt evil, and it was one in which hundreds of people died prematurely. In the "real world" where Sam and Dean do save people and hunt things, armed with extra-ordinary knowledge, they often appear without warning, protecting the innocent, acting with courage that seems superhuman. Because of their intervention, children are not orphaned and parents are able to see their children grow up.

Sam and Dean bring help and hope to everyone they save, including each other. Immediately after Jessica's death, it was Dean who gave Sam a

---

[19] Claus Westermann, *God's Angels Need No Wings* (Philadelphia: Fortress Press, 1979), p. 96.

[20] See, for example, Joshua 5:13-15.

[21] See, for example, Genesis 18, Numbers 22:22-35, and Judges 6:11-24.

way not to descend into a pit of anger and sorrow and revenge: "[S]aving people, hunting things. The family business" ("Wendigo"). It was also Dean who convinced Sam that all humans are worthy of protection, that not even prisoners deserve to die at the hands of a vengeful spirit ("Folsom Prison Blues"). Even when John made Dean pledge to kill Sam should it become necessary, Dean refused to believe that Sam was destined to turn evil ("Hunted," 2-10) and swore that, if it was the last thing he did, he would save Sam ("Born Under a Bad Sign"). It was Dean who promised Sam that Sam would never turn evil: "As long as I'm around, nothing bad is going to happen to you" ("Nightmare," 1-14), a promise renewed again and again. While at times Sam has wished that something else was watching out for him ("Houses of the Holy"), so far Dean has done everything necessary to keep Sam alive and prevent him from turning evil. No supernatural angel could have done a better job.

Similarly, at least until the end of season two, Sam acted as Dean's good angel by opening his eyes to shades of gray and always, always arguing against killing humans. While Dean saw in Max Miller someone "no different from anything else we've hunted," Sam saw a person with whom they could talk ("Nightmare"). It was Sam who pointed out to Dean that their job was hunting evil, not merely anything supernatural ("Bloodlust," 2-3). Sam reminded Dean of the need to struggle with shades of gray and thus keep their consciences clear even when they were forced to kill ("Croatoan," 2-9).

Without the other acting as their angel, Dean and Sam would journey down dark paths. Dean without Sam would resemble Gordon Walker, living in a world of black and white and enjoying the infliction of pain ("Bloodlust"). One of the tragedies of Dean's deal was that, to Dean's horror, it changed Sam. As he prepared to live without his brother, Sam no longer argued with Dean about "the sanctity of life and all that crap" ("Malleus Maleficarum"). We have been shown a glimpse of what Sam might be like with Dean gone, and it is a frightening prospect ("Mystery Spot"). Because Sam and Dean are each other's only angels, because they can only hear God's message of faith, hope, and love from each other; one without the other is less than human. Angels are vulnerable to falling, and Sam and Dean are no exception.

Dean has no faith in angels because he says he has never seen one. If he wants to see an angel with his "own two eyes" all he needs to do is look at his brother. Or look in a mirror.

Conclusion

> DEAN: I think the world's going to end bloody. But it doesn't mean we shouldn't fight. We do have choices. I choose to go down swinging. ("Jus in Bello")

Humanity's ability to make the wrong choices is balanced by our ability to make the right choices. Humans can choose to do good, to act courageously, to fight when fighting is necessary. Faced with the choice of becoming an angry spirit or moving on, humans can choose to let go and face the unknown ("Roadkill"). Ava Wilson believed that she had no choice but to embrace evil: "It's me or them" ("All Hell Breaks Loose [Part 1]"). But Madison's willingness to die rather than hurt others shows that there is always a choice: "This is the way you can save me. Please. I'm asking you to save me" ("Heart," 2-17). The choice may be self-sacrifice, but *Supernatural* argues that humans always have a choice.

Supernatural, like other forms of pop culture that deal with themes of good and evil, offers its viewers the hope that evil can be defeated by humans taking responsibility for their own actions and working together for good. In their choice to hunt things and save people, Dean and Sam Winchester are God's warriors. Angels and occasional Christ-figures, Sam and Dean are also profoundly human. They make mistakes, and the occasional incredibly stupid decision, but in their determination not to allow evil to win they act as role models for all those who watch them.

I would like to thank Wendy Crawford, Carol Davis, and especially Jennifer Dowling for commenting on earlier drafts of this essay. They also did their best to turn my Australian English into good American—any remaining mistakes are mine.

REV. DR. AVRIL HANNAH-JONES was recently ordained by the Uniting Church in Australia and is Minister to four small congregations in rural Victoria. Her worldview is the mirror image of Dean Winchester's: she believes absolutely in God and the powers of good; disbelieves completely in demons and personified evil; and is agnostic on the subject of angels. After hard days at work Avril has been known to console herself with the thought that at least she hasn't had her throat cut in her own church by a demon she was trying to counsel.

Supernatural *is rife with demons, vampires, evil entities of all kinds:* monsters. *But who, exactly, are the monsters in this story? What gives the Winchester boys the right to kill, banish, exorcise, and indiscriminately slaughter the world's supernatural minority? Are they themselves so much different from the things they hunt to near extinction?*

Robert T. Jeschonek examines Sam and Dean Winchester from the point of view of society's victimized supernatural community and asks the question: Are the Winchesters slowly becoming more like the things they hunt . . . ?

ROBERT T. JESCHONEK

Sympathy for the Devils

What makes *Supernatural* so special? Here's a clue: it's the same thing that pumped up *Kolchak: The Night Stalker* and *The X-Files*.

It's the *monsters*, of course. The colorful villains who kick-start the action, chew the scenery to pieces, and threaten our way of life. They're so scary and cool, their names are burned forever into our memories . . . the names of some of the wildest monsters in TV history:

Carl Kolchak.

Fox Mulder and Dana Scully.

Sam and Dean Winchester.

These are the monsters who haunt the TV screens and nightmares of viewers like us—viewers who just happen to be vampires, demons, and other creatures. Monsters like Sam and Dean would be our natural enemies if we ever met them in real life, yet we're drawn to watch them on TV. They make for great drama, serve up metaphors for our common struggles, and reenact blasts from the past. We might even identify with them a little . . . and as the show goes on, *they* begin to identify with *us*.

All About the Drama

Real life wouldn't make much of a TV show, would it? Who wants to watch people like us—vampires, demons, changelings, ghosts, and ghouls—going about our daily business—sucking blood, possessing housewives, shifting shapes, haunting houses, and slaughtering innocents? In other words, *the same old same old*? Let's face it: even the wickedest ways can become kind of humdrum if they're repeated day in and day out.

When we watch *Supernatural*, we want the opposite. We want thrills and chills and drama as our TV creature counterparts fight for their lives against seemingly insurmountable odds.

Which is where the monsters come in—monsters by the name of Sam and Dean Winchester. Starting with the first episode of the series, they cut a murderous swath across America. When it comes to paranormal creatures, they kill whatever they cross paths with, from Bloody Mary to the Hook Man to the Shtriga to the Rakshasa and the Crocatta. They execute a werewolf, a djinn, pagan gods, and of course any number of demons, vampires, and ghosts.

The crimes of Sam and Dean flood *Supernatural* with crackling intensity. They raise the stakes in every story, as we watch their victims—our bloodsucking, hellraising kin—struggle to survive. It makes for truly operatic escapism.

And yet, *Supernatural* lacks the one key element we hunger for in any good story: it almost never has a happy ending for *our* heroes. Each episode ends with Sam and Dean riding off down the road in their Chevy Impala, alive and well, leaving a trail of vampire dust-heaps, dead demons, or sliced and diced creatures behind them. Over and over, our own dark-side heroes lose, and the deluded "do-gooder" monsters win, charting a vicious circle of misery and injustice.

It's a bold choice by the show's writers and producers, and it works. We keep coming back for more. But how can this TV series still be popular with viewers like us? How can we bear to tune in, week after week, to see *our* kind of people annihilated by despicable *human scum*? By the very prey we were born or summoned or conjured to feed on, torture, haunt, and possess?

Maybe it's because there's more going on in these stories than meets the eye.

METAPHORICALLY SPOOKING

Supernatural episodes are more than pointless, lurid crime fiction. Creatures we care about perish—staked through the heart or exorcised or gunned down with a mystic Colt firearm—but always in service to metaphors that address thought-provoking themes.

In *Supernatural*, we see demons, vampires, ghosts, gods, and ghouls face attacks by the agents of a world that doesn't understand or appreciate them. The monsters, Sam and Dean, are enforcers representing the power elite . . . spreading fear, crushing dissent, and culling oppressed minorities wherever they go. Again and again, our heroes are punished by an empowered, conformist majority that infringes on their basic rights and denies them a productive role in society. Thus, *Supernatural* stands as a metaphor for racism, sexism, and creaturism—for oppression in all its forms. It makes us think about the discrimination we all face as minorities in a world that hates and fears us . . . a world that fails to recognize our cultural contributions, socioeconomic value, and importance as predators in the food chain.

Like the most enlightening literature and entertainment, *Supernatural* uses metaphor to shine a light on the injustices and inequalities of our world. This adds another layer to the show's storytelling, amplifying its power as a modern-day fable to move and inspire us.

Supernatural also spotlights a broad canvas of universal themes. The *Supernatural* episode "Houses of the Holy" (2-13), in which angelic beings triggered a series of murders (talk about true-to-life *monsters*), spotlighted the destructive effects of misplaced faith. "Sin City" (3-4) explored the nature of sin, as Sam and Dean visited a town where demonic influence had dramatically loosened inhibitions (and made the town a better place, if you ask me). "What Is and What Should Never Be" (2-20) looked at the nature of reality itself, as Dean was tempted to live happily ever after in a wish-fulfilling alternate world conjured by a djinn (who ended up slaughtered for his trouble, of course).

When it comes to themes and metaphors, *Supernatural* shares the spirit of many other series . . . but one other layer of the show is absolutely unique. How many other television series can say they reenact *the greatest story ever told* on a regular basis? How many do it *in every single episode*?

Lucifer's Fallen, and He Can't Get Up

Every episode of *Supernatural* reenacts what we of the vampire/demon/creature community consider the greatest story ever told: the Fall of Lucifer Morningstar, the angel who rebelled against God Himself and ended up banished to Hell, which he promptly turned into his own personal kingdom: "Once he was the most beautiful of all God's angels, but God demanded that he bow down before man, and when he refused, God banished him" ("Sin City").

Like the rebellious Fallen Angel Lucifer, *Supernatural*'s sympathetic demons, vampires, ghosts, ghouls, and creatures strive to thrive and evolve. They repeatedly challenge the authority of society, only to be put down again and again by the ruthless Winchesters, just as God cast Lucifer out of Heaven.

By retelling the story of the Fall of Lucifer so many times in so many ways, *Supernatural* reminds us of the story's relevance to our lives today. It also reinforces the importance of hope in a hostile universe. Each week, God's strong-arm agents, the brothers Winchester, cast out another "devil" with violent finality . . . but, like Lucifer, the "devils" always embrace their fate defiantly, going down fighting every time. As in *Paradise Lost*, they never waver in their conviction that it is "Better to reign in Hell than serve in Heaven."[1]

And there's always another "devil" next week. Comrades of the same courageous stripe rise to pick up the gauntlet and continue the struggle. This is the bright heart of the series, which keeps us coming back for more: *Supernatural* gives us hope that no matter how outnumbered and outgunned we might be by the human vermin infesting the world, we

---

[1] Milton, John. *Paradise Lost*. Project Gutenberg, 1992. 10 June 2008. <http://www.gutenberg.org/files/26/26.txt>

will never stop rising up with dignity and defiance against the forces that seek to oppose us.

If that alone isn't enough to inspire us, we can find even more hope in another aspect of *Supernatural*. We can find it in—of all places—the monsters themselves.

REHAB FOR MONSTERS

In the course of *Supernatural*, the monsters—Sam and Dean—undergo a dramatic rehabilitation. Over time, they adopt a new outlook that brings them closer to our way of thinking.

In the beginning, the Winchesters didn't pull any punches when it came to the supernatural. Their policy toward vampires, demons, and all such like-minded heroes of darkness was zero tolerance. Make that *sub-zero* tolerance.

Then, a change came upon them. In "Bloodlust" (2-3), Sam and Dean encountered a colony of pacifist vampires. These vampires, led by a woman named Lenore, were committed to drinking the blood of animals instead of the blood of humans. A gung-ho hunter, Gordon Walker, wanted to kill the vampires anyway . . . but Sam and Dean wouldn't let him. Instead of murdering the peace-loving vampire clan, the Winchesters protected them and helped them escape.

It was a mind-blowing turning point in the series. Instead of blindly attacking and killing vampires, Sam and Dean actually *sympathized* with them. They *rescued* our bloodsucking heroes from the same breed of hunter scum that they themselves have been from the start. They even questioned past killings they'd committed:

> DEAN: Think about all the hunts we went on, Sammy, our whole lives.
> SAM: Okay.
> DEAN: What if we killed things that didn't deserve killing? You know?

These two seemingly heartless monsters actually felt remorse and uncertainty about their crimes . . . and that was only the beginning. From that moment on, the monsters—and *Supernatural*—were never the same.

Though the Winchesters went on killing our kind, they experienced flashes of sympathy . . . even *love*. In "Heart" (2-17) Sam actually *fell in love with a werewolf*. That's right: a *werewolf*. Of course, Sam *did* end up *killing* her . . . but only after she begged him to do it. When the deed was done, he felt misery and remorse, which aren't his *usual* reactions to killing paranormal prey.

Another supernatural character also offers the Winchester monsters a new point of view. Ruby, a demon, helped Sam and Dean on several occasions, giving them advice and fighting alongside them with an enchanted knife that killed her demonic brethren. She helped Sam and Dean's ally, Bobby, rebuild the mystic Colt ("Sin City") and tried to help Sam use his dormant psychic powers to save Dean from going to Hell ("No Rest for the Wicked," 3-16). She also changed Sam and Dean's understanding of demons when she told them she was once *human* . . . and explained that the same applies to *all* demons ("Malleus Maleficarum," 3-9). Sam and Dean still couldn't bring themselves to trust her, but they did at least realize that demons were complex creatures with souls that were once as human as their own.

What a change! In the early days, Sam and Dean looked at the world in black and white; they saw everything in terms of absolutes, of "good" and "evil." It's to be expected, perhaps, given their lifelong training as hunters and the loss of their mother to a supernatural threat; they had to boil the world down to clearly defined opposites just to survive. Over time, though, Sam and Dean have developed a more nuanced perspective. They have come to see that paranormal beings and creatures can have many facets, not all of them destructive. They have realized, as we of the alternate morality set have always known, that the world is painted in shades of gray rather than stark black and white.

It's a mature worldview, and it's more than just a new way of looking at the enemy. It's a new way for Sam and Dean to look at *themselves* . . . because ultimately, the two of them are becoming as supernatural as the creatures they hunt.

SUPERNATURAL EVOLUTION

Supernatural doesn't stop with Sam and Dean feeling sympathetic toward vampires, werewolves, demons, and creatures. The show actually makes Sam and Dean *more like them*.

Sam was the first to take this step up the evolutionary ladder. Beginning in season one of the show, he manifested psychic powers—precognition and telekinesis. In effect, he became a *supernatural* being, no longer purely human . . . and his link to the supernatural continues to intensify.

In season two, the pace of Sam's evolution accelerated. His powers grew stronger and more active, and he discovered he was part of a group of paranormally endowed humans. Sam was drawn to these kindred spirits and eventually pitted against them—his nemesis, the Yellow-Eyed Demon Azazel, wanted the last man or woman standing to lead his doomsday army. Azazel, it turned out, was behind Sam's change all along.

And this is the greatest irony. Not only is Sam touched by the supernatural. Not only has he gradually become more like the paranormally empowered creatures he and his brother routinely murder. It turns out *he was supernatural all along*.

Azazel dosed Sam with his hellish blood when he was a baby. That means the blood of a demon runs in Sam's veins and has been there since *Supernatural*'s start. From Sam's first scene in episode one of the series, *he has been part-demon*.

So one of the Winchesters, at least, is more closely connected to the supernatural than he, or we, ever imagined. Sam's psychic powers fell dormant until the very end of season three, but he still can't reverse his fundamental link to demonkind. He is a product of supernatural evolution.

And soon enough, his brother, Dean, changed too.

Dean's evolution happened more slowly but was no less profound. It started in season two's "All Hell Breaks Loose (Part 2)" (2-22) when Sam was killed by one of his paranormal brethren and Dean sold his own soul—and all but one year of his life—to the Crossroads Demon in exchange for Sam's resurrection.

In the year of life that Dean had left, he faced growing dread at the prospect of going to Hell. Various demons told him what to expect, and he didn't like what he heard . . . especially from Ruby. Anyone who spends enough time in Hell will become a demon, she said . . . and Dean could be no exception.

> Ruby: It might take centuries, but sooner or later Hell will burn away your humanity. Every hellbound soul, every *one*, turns into something else. Turns you into us. So yeah, yeah, you can count on it.

When the deal came due, a Hell Hound dragged Dean into Hell itself ("No Rest for the Wicked"), where, according to Ruby, he would eventually be transformed into a demon. Once again, a Winchester has taken a personal evolutionary leap into the supernatural. Dean, like his brother, will be infused with demonic influence. A monster will be reborn as *one of us*.

It's a beautiful twist. It's the full flower of *Supernatural*'s promise, the ultimate expression of hope in what at first appears to be a grim and hopeless show. If monstrous, murderous humans like Sam and Dean can become demons, maybe there is hope that *everyone* can find enlightenment and redemption on the dark side.

Friends of the Devils

Clearly, when it comes to *Supernatural*, the monsters—Sam and Dean Winchester—make the show. They give *Supernatural* the high-octane drama that thrills us, fuel metaphors that enlighten us, and reenact historic touchstones that inspire us. In spite of the evil they do, they develop a more nuanced, balanced outlook toward our kind and come to see the world in shades of gray instead of unrealistic black and white. They become more like us all the time, more like the supernatural creatures they've been hunting, making us—against our better judgment—care about what happens to them. Sam and Dean go from being two-dimensional, unsympathetic menaces to fully realized, multidimensional characters who intrigue us on multiple levels. They are characters we might not mind sharing a full-moon rampage or a goblet of blood or a damned soul or a haunch of human flesh with.

Does this mean we care too much about these characters? Does their appeal foster an unhealthy interest in villains . . . characters who still, for all their sympathetic qualities, wallow in violence and antisocial behavior toward the demons, vampires, witches, werewolves, shapeshifters, tricksters, and other creatures who make up our community?

Maybe. But maybe that's the point of the whole damned show.

Think about it. In *Supernatural*, we have antiheroes (Sam and Dean Winchester) who commit crimes against society (in this case, *our* society of supernaturally oriented beings). We have misunderstood opponents of a social order who pay a heavy price for their rebelliousness (though a heavy price for *them*—unleashing an increasingly demonic nature or going to Hell—would be a sweet reward for *us*).

Haven't we seen that somewhere before? Haven't *we* embraced a similar figure whose rebelliousness laid him low? And hasn't *he* been considered a monster, too? Don't *his* enemies see him as such, the same way we see Sam and Dean?

In the end, aren't we all devils to someone?

And don't we all deserve a little sympathy?

ROBERT T. JESCHONEK wrote *Mad Scientist Meets Cannibal*, a collection of science fiction and fantasy stories from PS Publishing. Robert's work has been featured in Smart Pop's *House Unauthorized* and in publications including *Postscripts*, *Helix*, and *Abyss & Apex*. He has also written Star Trek fiction, including *New Frontier*, *Voyager*, and Starfleet Corps of Engineers adventures. His prize-winning stories, "Our Million-Year Mission" and "Whatever You Do, Don't Read This Story," appeared in *Star Trek: Strange New Worlds*. Visit him online at www.robertjeschonek.com.

"There's no place like home," a famous Kansas resident once said. For Dean Winchester, "home" might have burned to the ground back in Lawrence, along with Mom and any shred of normality he could have hoped for, but family is forever as far as he is concerned, and taking care of his family, specifically taking care of his "pain in the ass little brother" Sam, is his job, his purpose, what makes him who he is. His home.

Does this make Dean more of a care-giver than an ass-kicker? Tanya Michaels investigates whether the two roles are mutually exclusive.

TANYA MICHAELS

Dean Winchester: Bad-Ass . . . or Soccer Mom?

> *This is humiliating. [I] feel like a freaking soccer mom.*
> —Dean (driving a minivan), "Everybody Loves a Clown," 2-2

Even casual viewers of *Supernatural* are familiar with Dean Winchester's black Chevy Impala, a classic car he loves that was given to him by his father. Symbolic of Dean's life and how he sees himself, the Impala is practically a character in the show. However, after the car was nearly destroyed in the first season finale, a subsequent episode found Dean temporarily—and hilariously—behind the wheel of a minivan. While we equate Dean with his Impala and the classic metal rock always blaring from its cassette deck, the incongruous minivan is surprisingly reflective of who he is deep down.

Deep, *deep* down. But trust me: it's there.

When grown brothers Sam and Dean Winchester were introduced in the pilot episode, the audience was clearly meant to accept that Sam is the good brother and that Dean is the rebel/screw-up. Within minutes of meeting

Sam, we knew that he had a steady girlfriend and that he was a successful Stanford student with an important law school interview scheduled. Our first look at adult Dean? He broke into Sam's apartment in the middle of the night, making a wiseass quip about looking for beer, and stopped just shy of hitting on his brother's girlfriend. (In the later "What Is and What Should Never Be" (2-20), which imagined an alternate reality for the brothers, Sam accused Dean of hooking up with "my prom date . . . on prom night." Dean admitted, "Yeah, that does kinda sound like me.")

Dean's seeming disregard for authority is peppered throughout the series, starting in the pilot, when he told Sam to "blow off" his interview and when he was rude to the police, which drew righteous indignation from Sam. Dean's full of attitude and smart-aleck comebacks when he's arrested midway through the episode—and again when he's arrested in "The Usual Suspects" (2-7), and in "Folsom Prison Blues" (2-19), and in "Jus In Bello" (3-12). Although little brother Sam was along for most of these bookings, he wasn't the one cracking jokes and being a generally uncooperative pain in the butt. Where Sam is more likely to follow rules and question the ethics of their actions, especially in the first season, Dean seems untroubled by a conscience:

> DEAN: Well, let's see. . . . Honest. (weighs imaginary scales with his hands) Fun and easy. No contest. ("Bugs," 1-8)

In the two brothers' habitual squabbles, Dean derides Sam's attempts to be Joe Normal. During the pilot episode, they fought on a bridge after Dean countered that Sam was not born to be a lawyer and marry his girl—that, sooner or later, Sam will have to admit he's "one of them." Meaning, a Winchester. Dean sneers at normalcy in general, claiming in "Bugs" that a typical suburban existence would be intolerable.

> DEAN: Manicured lawns. How was your day, honey? I'd blow my brains out.
> SAM: There's nothing wrong with normal.
> DEAN: I'd take our family over normal any day.

(Liar! But we'll get back to that momentarily.)

On the surface, this exchange seems to cement the idea that Sam is the Boy Scout while Dean is happily bent. Dean himself buys into his role as the Bad Boy and Sam's as the Sensitive One, prone to "touchy-feely, self-help yoga crap" ("Phantom Traveler," 1-4) as well as "angst, more droopy music, and staring out the rainy windows" ("Playthings," 2-11). When Sam began behaving out of character in "Born Under a Bad Sign" (2-14), Dean protested that "smoking, throwing bottles at people . . . sounds more like me than you." Thankfully, the Winchester brothers aren't simply the Bad Boy and the Sensitive One. Were that the case, the show wouldn't be nearly as compelling and both brothers would be as one-dimensional as their parodied caricatures of themselves in "Tall Tales" (2-15).

Seemingly insubordinate Dean Winchester, with a quip for every occasion and a questionable moral compass, is far from the family rebel. Instead, the son who has repeatedly proven his disdain for authority is militaristic in his devotion to their father John. It was Sam, erstwhile do-gooder, who defied their father's wishes, took off on his own, and metaphorically (and perhaps literally) told John to go stick it:

> DEAN: I remember that fight. In fact, I seem to recall a few choice phrases coming out of your mouth. ("Bugs")

Throughout the first season, Sam expressed frustration with their impossible-to-find father, challenging the absent John's actions and motives, while Dean continued to follow orders without question, the good son. (This specific tension outlives John himself. Dean snapped in "Long Distance Call" (3-14) that even with their dad dead, Sam's still butting heads with him. And Sam countered that Dean was still following their late father with blind faith.) When Sam assured a sixteen-year-old boy in "Bugs" who didn't get along with his own father that it would all be okay once the teen could escape to college, just as Sam did, Dean was appalled. In a following scene, Dean took on the more traditional, rule-abiding role when demanding to know how Sam could tell the kid to "ditch his family":

> DEAN: How 'bout telling him to respect his old man? How's that for advice?

The undercurrent while they searched for John wasn't merely that Dean wanted to find their father, but that he also wanted them to be a family again. After they finally did catch up to John, Sam wasn't shy about challenging his father directly. In "Dead Man's Blood" (1-20), *Sam* was driving the Impala—the symbolic bad-boy-mobile—when he decided he'd had enough of taking orders, swerved off the road, and nearly came to blows with their dad. Edgier than Sam's status as black sheep of the family was the emergence of his psychic powers and their connection to the Yellow-Eyed Demon Azazel. By the halfway point of the second season, both Sam and his brother feared that he would "go Dark Side" ("Hunted," 2-10). And there were still lingering questions at the end of the third season about whether or not Sam, brought back from the dead, is entirely human—especially given the power he demonstrated in the finale. (In "Fresh Blood" [3-7], fellow demon hunter Gordon Walker went so far as to proclaim Sam "the Antichrist." But given that Gordon was a vindictive nut-job, we'll overlook that assessment.)

From season to season, no matter what Sam is ultimately proven to be or not be, there is one unwavering constant in his life—Dean Winchester. Earlier, I mentioned our first look at adult Dean, which also included his trademark smirking and a physical scuffle between brothers. But that "introduction" is far less crucial than the one we received in the pilot's prologue, where we saw Sam as an infant and Dean as a child himself, the night Mary Winchester died in a demon-conjured fire. While his home burned around him, young Dean was charged with getting baby Sam out of the house and keeping him safe. It was a task he took to heart.

In many ways, Dean became the mother in the Winchester family dynamic. (Okay, a completely sarcastic mother, but even the *best* moms can be real smartasses. So I've heard.) Sure, upon first glance, lascivious, pool-hustling, credit-card-fraud-perpetrating Dean doesn't seem like someone you would entrust so much as a goldfish to. It was punch-line fodder in "Dead in the Water" (1-3) when he tried to hit on a single mom by saying he liked kids:

SAM: Name three children that you even *know*.

Yet Dean is the one who went on to form a breakthrough bond with the mute boy in the episode; even after Dean and Sam left town the first time, Dean was troubled enough to go back and check on Lucas, which resulted in their saving Lucas's mother. Then there was the connection between Dean and the boy Michael in "Something Wicked" (1-18). And again with Ben, the eight-year-old in "The Kids Are Alright" (3-2). In that particular episode, Dean had reason to wonder if the child he was getting along with so well was actually his son. When Dean's former lover assured him that he wasn't the father, she noted that he looked "disappointed"— an uncharacteristic reaction from the person Dean is usually portrayed as.

Are Dean's sometimes funny, sometimes poignant scenes with kids simply a contrivance designed to melt fangirl hearts? No. (Frankly, it doesn't take much more than Jensen Ackles's eyes to melt fangirl hearts. So I've heard.) The truth is, Dean is a nurturer.

He defends Sam physically, of course, as any lethal mama-bear would. But he also tries to shield Sam emotionally, as we saw in flashback in "A Very Supernatural Christmas" (3-8), when Dean refused to answer Sam's childhood questions about their father's work. Dean referenced occasions like these in "All Hell Breaks Loose (Part 2)" (2-22) when he said Sam used to ask questions Dean begged him not to ask, because Dean wanted to keep him a kid for a while longer. In the pilot episode, Sam criticized their father for giving him a gun instead of telling him not to be afraid of the dark; while Dean dutifully stood up for John in that conversation, Dean himself tried to give Sam a normal childhood:

> SAM: Sometimes I wish I could have that kind of innocence.
> DEAN: If it means anything, sometimes I wish you could, too.
> ("Something Wicked")

The above is an interesting exchange because both brothers so readily accept Dean's parental role. Forget how whacked out it is that a small boy was conditioned to believe himself the liable caretaker for his even smaller brother (John Winchester, you kinda suck), but how is it that Sensitive Sammy has overlooked Dean's right to innocence? In point of fact, Dean lost more the night of Mary's death than Sam did since, as Sam says in the pilot, Sam wouldn't even know what their mom looked like without pictures. She was never part of his life, so how can he miss her—how can he miss having a family—as keenly as his older brother?

In Mary's absence, can there be any doubt that Dean was the most nurturing influence in Sam's early life? That role certainly wouldn't fall to John. What does it say about your parenting skills when your kid only realizes you're demonically possessed because you finally told him he did a good job? That's essentially what happened in the first season finale ("Devil's Trap," 1-22), when John praised Dean for always looking out for their family. Dean contended that his actual father would be furious that Dean had wasted a necessary bullet, no matter the reason, and would "tear me a new one."

In the subsequent "In My Time of Dying" (2-1), John *did* praise Dean (this time not because he was possessed but because he was dying). John's own recollections of the past further prove that Dean was the de facto mother-hen in the testosterone-fueled Winchester family:

> JOHN: I'd come home from a hunt, and after what I'd seen, I'd be wrecked. . . . [You'd] put your hand on my shoulder and look me in the eye and say, "It's okay, Dad." Dean, I'm sorry. You shouldn't have had to say that to me. I should have been saying that to you.

Well, duh. And John lost any points he won with me by finally giving his kid kudos because he immediately followed it with the caution that Sammy might, um, become a demon and that it was Dean's responsibility to save Sam, even if that meant destroying him. Frankly, it's a shock that Dean didn't snap under pressure and resentment and shove his kid brother under a bus years ago. But the strongest indication the viewers—or Sam himself—ever get of Dean's discontent is in "Skin" (1-6). Though the episode opens with Dean scoffing at Sam staying in touch with his college buddies ("A job like this, you can't get close to people"), the shapeshifter who later inhabits Dean's skin tells us that Dean's not as nonchalant about his loner persona as he would like others to believe. After proving that it has access to Dean's thoughts and memories, the not-quite-Dean shares a few revelations with Sam:

SHAPESHIFTER DEAN: He's sure got issues with you. You got to go to college. He had to stay home. I mean, *I* had to stay home. With Dad. You don't think I had dreams of my own? But Dad needed me. Where the hell were you? . . . Deep down, I'm just jealous. You got friends, you could have a life. Me, I know I'm a freak and sooner or later everyone's gonna leave me. You left. Hell, I did everything Dad asked me to and he ditched me, too. No explanation, nothing.

This expresses not only Dean's sense of familial obligation but his fear of being alone, his desire for relationships in his life. For all that Dean projects a love-'em-and-leave-'em image, giving the impression he would break out in hives at the very mention of meaningful commitment, we find out in "Route 666" (1-13) that he previously had a very serious girlfriend, Cassie, a woman in whom he was so emotionally invested that he told her about his real job—prompting her to freak out and abandon him (ouch).

He and Cassie were reunited in "Route 666" when she contacted him to ask for help with paranormal murders. During the episode, she slept with him but made it clear, after Dean saved her butt from a homicidal spirit, that it was a one-time thing. When they exchanged their goodbyes (again), even though she'd hurt him before and in spite of his usual aversion to sentiment, Dean voiced the hope that maybe this farewell would be "less permanent." Cassie effectively squashed that, choosing to be a "realist" about their situation.

Normally Sam encourages his brother to share his feelings (and gets a sarcastic retort for his troubles), but it's Dean who made himself vulnerable by breaking Winchester Rule #1 and confiding in Cassie. Even Sam, who we are led to believe would have proposed to Jessica, never told her the truth about how his mom died or what's really out there.

Don't be fooled by the blaring Metallica or the fact that Dean's nickname for his brother is "bitch"—Dean Winchester is a big softie. Despite his abilities to kick ass and his contention that the dark job is full of "perks" ("Skin"), what he really craves is home and hearth—that which the yellow-eyed demon stole from him decades ago.

Perhaps the most telling episode is the second season's "What Is and What Should Never Be," in which Dean was attacked by a djinn/genie, a creature whose fabled wish-granting powers are actually a method of subduing prey inside a dream world while the djinn feeds off the person for the next few days (resulting in the victim's eventual death).

In Dean's dream world, was he a heavy metal superstar dating half a dozen lingerie models? No, he worked at an auto-garage back home in Lawrence, Kansas . . . where his mother still lived. Though his father was dead in this alternate reality, Dean was thrilled to learn that Dad died in his sleep, after watching his sons grow up and spending his spare time on prosaic pastimes like softball. Included in a set of family photos was a delightfully clichéd Christmas picture where all four Winchesters wore coordinated holiday sweaters.

It's a far cry from the *actual* past Winchester Christmas we were shown many episodes later, where adolescent Dean and Sam spent the holiday alone in another temporary efficiency apartment or hotel room. One of the sweetest—yet most painful to watch—flashbacks in the show was Dean doing his damnedest to give his kid brother Christmas because their father was out on a hunt and couldn't be bothered to make an appearance ("A Very Supernatural Christmas"). The first flashback in the episode featured a young Sam complaining that their father would probably forget Christmas, with Dean in the wifely role of trying to placate the whining child while at the same time defending the father. A following flashback had Dean declaring that John returned briefly in the middle of the night and left presents and decorations—a lie not even young Sam could believe after he opened gifts that were all intended for a girl. Dean admitted to stealing the wrapped presents from a nice house.

In the djinn dream world, Dean not only had a steady job that required no bloodshed, he had a steady girlfriend who was a nurse, which he proclaimed to be "so respectable." The character who once said he'd blow his brains out if he lived somewhere with a manicured lawn became nearly giddy at the chance to mow the Winchester's yard . . . which was surrounded by an honest-to-goodness white picket fence. Even after Dean realized that the djinn world was an illusion and that the "real" Dean was being slowly killed somewhere, he was reluctant to give up the dream.

The djinn-perpetuated characters in Dean's fantasy argued convincingly for him to succumb rather than fight, even after he asserted that none of them were real:

> FAKE MARY: It doesn't matter. It's still better than anything you had. . . . It's everything you want. We're a family again. Let's go home.

Dean Winchester's hopes and dreams in a nutshell: love, comfort, and safety. The fake Sam pointed out that Dean wouldn't have to worry about him anymore; the make-believe girlfriend held out the possibility of a future, Dean building his own family. After Dean escaped from the alternate reality, with some help from Sam on the outside, he admitted to his brother that, even knowing it wasn't real, "I wanted to stay. I wanted to stay so bad" ("What Is and What Should Never Be").

Of course, letting himself give up was never truly a possibility, not when Dean is drawn so strongly to the real world and his obligation to "raise" Sam.

It was Dean who, years ago, had the Talk with his younger brother—even if it was about the existence of demons and not sex . . . although they probably had that chat along the way, too ("A Very Supernatural Christmas"). It was Dean who made sure his brother ate, admonishing Sam to "eat your vegetables," even if the veggies in question were Funyons ("A Very Supernatural Christmas"), and who gave up his own dinner of the last of the Lucky Charms when Sam balked at the SpaghettiOs he'd requested earlier ("Something Wicked"). It was Dean who tried to mediate family differences by making sure Sam knew John was *not* disappointed in his youngest son and even used to sneak by Stanford to check up on Sam, an assurance Dean followed up with the reprimand, "It's a two-way street, dude. You could have picked up the phone" ("Bugs"). It was Dean who sought to protect his fully grown and not-so-little brother in "Heart" (2-17), by offering to kill Madison so that Sam wouldn't have to do it.

Ultimately, it was Dean who raised Sam from the dead by exchanging his own soul ("All Hell Breaks Loose [Part 2]"). When Sam later tried to discuss this sacrifice and possible ways to free Dean from the deal, Dean shut him down in the most maternal way possible:

DEAN: Sam, enough! I am not gonna have this conversation.
SAM: Why? Because you said so?
DEAN: Yes, because I said so! ("Bedtime Stories," 3-5)

Many mothers believe they'd be willing to die for their children, but few of us—thank God—are tested in as literal a way as Dean Winchester has been nearly all his life and in nearly every episode. He takes his responsibility solemnly and in repeated episodes has referred to protecting Sam as his "job." He's definitely felt the heartbreak parenting can bring, when you don't know what to do, when your kids push you away, when they reject your attempts to help, or when you witness them hurting. The upside, though, is that Sam turned out smart, strong, and under the circumstances, incredibly well-adjusted, which means Dean was almost as successful at mothering as he is at kicking demon butt every week.

Oh, and Dean? Just for the record, being a mom and being a bad-ass aren't mutually exclusive.

Award-winning author TANYA MICHAELS (who also writes as Tanya Michna) is in fact a minivan-driving soccer mom. Though she feels heroic whenever she makes someone laugh or meets a deadline, the closest Tanya gets to being a literal bad-ass is defeating Nintendo bad guys with her kids.

Sacrifice and heroism: can one exist without the other? Does sacrifice make the hero or does heroism demand sacrifice? Do the sacrifices each of the Winchesters has made inform the kind of hero he has become? Is Sam any less of a hero than Dean for having sacrificed his family? Is Dean more of a hero than Sam for having sacrificed his sense of self in order to support his father?

Amy Garvey examines the choices and the sacrifices made by the Winchesters and how those choices and sacrifices have affected the type of men—and the type of heroes—they have become.

AMY GARVEY

"We've Got Work to Do"

Sacrifice, Heroism, and Sam and Dean Winchester

Sacrifice isn't part of my everyday vocabulary. I'm not usually asked to give up much that really means something to me. In my life, offering one of the kids the last chocolate chip cookie or missing an episode of *Supernatural* because somebody's got a recital or a baseball game that ran long qualifies as a major hardship. (Stop looking at me like that.)

The Winchesters, on the other hand, have "sacrifice" stamped all over their well-fitting torn jeans. It's not surprising—the Winchesters, as envisioned by Eric Kripke, are heroes, a family of men who fight the nastier elements of the supernatural and save lives in the process. And being a hero generally goes hand in hand with a boatload of sacrifice.

Look at some of the biggies, at least by popular culture's standards: Superman, Batman, Buffy. Each of them heroes in their own particular way, and each of them missing a fair-sized chunk of what most folks want out of life.

The Winchesters aren't superheroes, though. They lack the super-strength, X-ray vision, or a whole bat cave full of techno-toys that have to go at least a little way toward easing the pain of missing out on a normal life. Dean and Sam Winchester are simple, sturdy Kansas stock, at least when we meet them, and no more super-powered than a couple of sawed-off shotguns, a working knowledge of Latin, and a fine example of American heavy metal can make them. And their choice of family business—"saving people, hunting things"—requires a whole lot of sacrifice for both of them, even if what they sacrifice and how they look at the choice is very different for each of them.

Who are these guys? On the surface, they don't look like much. One half of the pair is an enormous, lanky guy in too many layers, with shaggy dog hair and a displeased bitchface that could fell an even bigger man at thirty paces. His other half is a startlingly pretty bad boy with a fondness for leather, classic rock, and waitresses, and about as much tact as most demons have, which is to say, um, none.

That's Sam and Dean for you. A college-educated research geek who can throw an awesome left hook, and a cocky self-taught mechanic who doesn't go anywhere without a knife in his boot and a scammed credit card in his wallet. No capes, no Batmobile (although the Impala is a pretty sweet ride herself), and no supernaturally enhanced powers (at least at first). They may not be *super*heroes, but they're heroes nevertheless. They tangle with werewolves, vampires, ghosts, and demons for absolutely no pay and very little recognition, all to save the general population from facing the often deadly truth about the monster in the closet. And they do it—well, most of the time—simply because it's the right thing to do.

Dictionary.com calls a hero "a man of distinguished courage or ability, admired for his brave deeds and noble qualities." Sam and Dean certainly fit that bill, although Dean's nobler impulses are sometimes hard to find under the glare of his enthusiastic hedonism. This definition doesn't particularly point out anything about sacrifice. Neither does Joseph Campbell's description of the hero's journey, unless you read between the lines—giving up safety, home, and family to set out on a quest sounds like quite the sacrifice to me. In practice, there are no heroes who give up nothing—sacrifice is integral to the notion of a person who cares more for the fate of others, or the world, than him- or herself.

Even so, I think Sam and Dean are a special case when it comes to heroes. Unlike Campbell's mythic figure, they don't accept a "call to adventure," they're thrust into it as children.

There is no Sam and Dean Winchester, not as we know them, without John Winchester, father, soldier, and vigilante. Before the demon came for Mary, the boys were average kids, a preschooler and an infant, safe in a suburban home with loving parents and all the expected trappings of childhood. It's easy to say Mary's death was the event that changed that, but it didn't have to; plenty of widowed fathers raise their children just fine after a spouse's death. No, John changed the circumstances of the boys' lives when he took Sam and Dean on the road in his quest to find the creature that killed his wife.

Did John make a sacrifice? A sacrifice isn't a sacrifice if it's something you don't care about giving up. Imagine asking a teenager to give up algebra homework or to please stop cleaning his room. Not a problem, right? For all intents and purposes, given John's choices, the only thing that mattered to John was Mary, and she was *taken* from him, not offered up willingly. When he dedicated his life to uncovering the more vicious supernatural creatures that prey on the innocent, he wasn't giving up anything that he valued. Or at least not anything he valued enough to think twice about, including his sons' welfare.

Vengeance was John's *raison d'etre* from there on out, and it became, by default, his sons' mission, as well. The boys' childhood was offered up to it, everything from decent schools and the safety net of a caring community and a stable, familiar home to a child's right to fantasy and innocence. As Sam told Dean in the series pilot, "When I told Dad when I was scared of the thing in my closet, he gave me a .45." Not your typical reaction to a boy's fears, is it?

Sam and Dean's childhood was sacrificed *for* them. And yet despite growing up with the same father, in the same circumstances, each handled their nomadic existence very differently. Much of that might be put down to the age difference between them—Sam doesn't remember his mother, or his home, since he was a mere six months old when Mary was killed—but I think a lot of it shakes down to a difference in temperament. It's the old nature versus nurture argument, of course, and there's never any way to prove concretely that one outweighs the other, but it's clear from the outset that Dean is a completely different animal than Sam.

In the third season episode "Bad Day at Black Rock" (3-3), Dean and Sam found a storage container of their father's that housed a trove of demon-hunting paraphernalia, but also a few mementoes of the boys' childhood. Sam found his Division Championship soccer trophy; Dean found the first sawed-off shotgun he ever made. It's more than a glimpse into how John viewed his boys; it's a telling indication of who the boys were as kids. It's telling that Dean's subconscious seems to agree; in "What Is and What Should Never Be" (2-20), Dean's version of Sam was entirely removed from the blue-collar life Dean had adopted in this dream world. Sam was the successful product of a suburban childhood, educated and relentlessly civilized, while Dean was, well, not.

Sam was protected from the truth of their father's quest far longer than Dean ever was, as "A Very Supernatural Christmas" (3-8) proved. Sam excelled at academics, eventually earning himself a scholarship to Stanford, and even managed to play soccer and participate in a school play ("Shadow," 1-16). Those last two examples show that John was willing to settle at least occasionally for more than a month or two at a time, but even so it couldn't have been easy for Sam to be the new boy on a regular basis and to make such a success of his scattershot schooling.

Even as late as the end of the third season, the viewer still isn't sure that Dean ever graduated high school, and the only evidence of an extracurricular activity is that sawed-off shotgun John saved. But Dean's first job in their grieving family was defined from nearly the moment of Mary's death: to take care of Sammy, as the pilot's flashback illustrated when John handed four-year-old Dean a squirming infant and told him to "take your brother outside as fast as you can, and don't look back. Now, Dean, *go*."

And there's Dean's purpose in a nutshell: take care of Sam. We saw it in "Something Wicked" (1-18) especially, as well as in "A Very Supernatural Christmas," a boy far too young to be a surrogate parent, but acting as one anyway. Dean's not a saint, or a martyr, especially as a child, but he takes his responsibilities seriously. The guilt and terror on his face when the shtriga in "Something Wicked" nearly devoured Sam was heartbreaking. No nine-year-old child should feel obligated to provide for the safety of his own sibling, and Dean's guilt was likely twofold: not only was he not off getting Sam dinner when the monster attacked, he was playing video games, the way any bored nine-year-old would be tempted to do.

The next time we saw childhood Dean and Sam, they were three years older, and Dean had learned his lesson well. The boys were holed up in a motel room so crappy it barely looked legal, and it was Christmas Eve, with no sign of John's return. With Sam asleep (and newly clued in, and freaked out, to the truth of their father's crusade), Dean sneaked out and returned with "Christmas," in the form of a straggly Charlie Brown tree and two stolen presents—both for Sam. There was nothing for himself; Dean clearly wasn't surprised that John didn't make it back to the motel, and he apparently didn't even think to make his ruse a little more believable by stealing gifts for himself as well.

Dean gave Sam the most "normal" childhood one could hope for under the circumstances. Because of that, Dean taught Sam to want a life outside of motel rooms and highway rest stops and dangerous confrontations with things that go bump in the night—even though Dean doesn't seem to want those things for himself.

We have to assume that as Sam got older, and more self-reliant, Dean's focus shifted from being Sam's surrogate parent to being the warrior his father wanted him to be. Honestly, nothing makes that point better than the fact that when we first saw the boys, Dean was fresh off a solo hunt in New Orleans while Sam had left the family and the family business.

The pilot episode was explicit in pointing out the differences between the young adults the boys had become. We met Sam, a college student who had aced his LSATs and had a law school interviewed planned, and lived in an apartment with a loving girlfriend. Then there was Dean, who showed up in the middle of the night breaking into Sam's apartment, and was still entirely focused on the hunt. Despite their common upbringing, it seemed Sam hadn't sacrificed anything he'd wanted for his life, while Dean had sacrificed everything in the name of the crusade. Sam said to Dean later in the episode, when they were looking for John, "I'm not you. This is *not* going to be my life." Dean's response? "You have a responsibility."

Is it really as simple as that? It's a given that anyone with the power to save others from harm, if not Big Bad Evil, should use it (hence, the reason Superman is Superman, and not just a defensive end on some NFL team), and certainly the Winchester boys have knowledge and skills very few other people do. As an adult, Dean has made a choice to continue his vagabond life, hunting down the things that go bump in the night, but is he ever free to choose differently? Is he really a hero if he believes the only thing he's good for is aiming a shotgun full of rock salt and burning bones?

Sam clearly never believed hunting was his fate. He made sure of it, in fact, and if Jessica hadn't died, there's no doubt he would have let Dean go back to the road, aced his law school interview, and married Jess shortly after he passed the bar. But Jessica did die, at the hands of the same demon that killed the boys' mother, and even if joining Dean on the road was an active choice, it was motivated by the same prime mover that motivated his father: vengeance. In fact, Sam made it clear to Dean that once they found and destroyed the demon, he'd head back to college and the "normal" life he'd always wanted.

That changed as the series progressed. Sam never defined himself strictly by his abilities as a ghostbuster, to borrow a term. At the end of the first season, and even the second, it wasn't a given that Sam would continue hunting forever, but the plot of the show always provided one more hurdle for him to clear before returning to the life he had begun to carve out for himself.

But the show's events have been more than simply additional hurdles. Sam has come full circle, from a boy who was willing to sacrifice the one thing his brother couldn't imagine giving up, his family, to a man who is now, in his words, becoming "more like Dean" ("Malleus Maleficarum," 3-9). To go to school at all, to turn his back on hunting, Sam gave up the only people who provided a constant in his life, the people who loved him and always protected him, Dean and John. It's still not clear that Sam will hunt forever, but it does seem clear that he's now willing to sacrifice everything else to stay with his brother.

Dean, on the other hand, seems never to have imagined any other life for himself. One throwaway remark in "Salvation" (1-21) about wanting to be a fireman when he grew up is as close as we get to a "what if" for

Dean, until "What Is and What Should Never Be."

It's a painful episode. Dean found himself living an alternate version of his life, thanks to a djinn who seemed to grant wishes, but with a twist: the djinn's victims experienced their deep-seated subconscious wishes as the djinn slowly killed them. The most disturbing element of the episode was that his "wish" catered to every member of his family but himself. He was back in his hometown of Lawrence, Kansas. His mother was alive and healthy, his father had died a natural death after a long and fulfilling life (complete with several seasons of recreational softball), and Sam was a virtual star, engaged to Jessica, excelling in law school, and happily living far, far away from his shifty, disappointing brother.

And Dean? Dean was a mechanic, although this was apparently so unremarkable that he never actually went to work while he was in the "wishverse." He lived with a young, pretty nurse named Carmen, but his interest in her was nothing compared to his pride in Sam and his relief about his mother. Every wish in Dean's subconscious was focused on his *family's* happiness, not his own. Dean was still himself, but maybe more so; when they were younger, Sam said, Dean had "snaked my ATM card . . . bailed on my graduation . . . [and] hooked up with Rachel Nave," Sam's prom date. Even sadder, everyone assumed Dean's odd behavior in this reality was because he'd been drinking too much.

Is this the way Dean really sees himself? Working a blue-collar job he doesn't much care about, drinking too much, tolerated by his family, especially Sam, who accuses him of stealing from their mother? Carmen wasn't even a girl Dean once knew, but a model from a beer ad. Way to value yourself, Dean.

Most telling was the fact that even here, Dean couldn't quit hunting. Sitting at his dad's grave, he asked, "Why is it my job to save these people? Why do I have to be some kind of hero? What about us? Mom's not supposed to live? Sammy's not supposed to get married? Why do we have to sacrifice everything, Dad?" And yet, Dean's idea of his own sacrifice was leaving the wishverse, shrugging off the comfortable fantasy of his family's happiness. He longed to stay there, the gray sheep if not exactly the black one, to set the world right for the rest of the Winchesters. Even his choice of words was telling; he didn't say, "Why can't I have my mom back?" He said, "Mom's not supposed to live?" That impulse is selfless, based entirely on Mary, not on himself.

Dean's entire identity is wrapped up in the mission his father gave him as a child: saving people, hunting things. Maybe that explains why Sam was able to have a relationship with Jess while Dean failed with Cassie. Sam was more than his history and experience as a hunter, and so he could close off that part of himself to offer Jess just the student, the normal college guy.

Dean, on the other hand, came clean with Cassie when he realized he was in love, and he was punished for it. That's Cassie's fault, not his, sure, but the fact remains that without his identity as a hunter, Dean has no identity. Dean is, in most ways, exactly what he looks like: a guy with a sly smirk and a hot car, no job, no home, and no education that means anything to the folks he calls "civvies" ("Long-Distance Call," 3-14).

The only thing Dean has that matters to him is his love and loyalty to his family. And that's the basis for Dean's biggest sacrifice of all. When Sam was killed in the first part of "All Hell Breaks Loose" (2-21, 2-22), Dean gave up the only thing he had to get him back: his life.

John made the same sacrifice to save Dean in "In My Time of Dying" (2-1), of course, but I think the circumstances were a little different. John wasn't quite at the end of his life, but he'd spent a lot of years fighting one battle. The cynic in me is also convinced that the act was more reparation than selfless generosity; he knew how much he took from his sons when they were growing up, and trading his life for Dean's was pretty clearly motivated by guilt, at least in part.

Sam was willing to sacrifice himself, too, during "Croatoan" (2-9). Faced with the unsettling fact that he had been somehow marked by the demon who killed Mary, Sam was ready to die rather than turn into the kind of creature they hunt. In the end, that sacrifice wasn't necessary, and it's notable that when Sam did die in "All Hell Breaks Loose," he was *angry* at Dean for bringing him back. Did he feel guilty, too, for what Dean had done? I'm not sure he did. Sam is a lot more objective about freedom of choice than his brother is.

Nothing's easy for the Winchesters. Dean brought Sam back from the dead, sure, but it turned out that Sam may be Hell's answer to a Boy King. Dean gave up his natural life for a single year on earth, but was that sacrifice or selfishness? He got to live every remaining day with the one person he loves, yes, but it meant Sam was facing the possibility of a lifetime without his brother.

John knew that he was making a choice, when he took his very young sons on the road, even if he didn't feel good about all of them. Sam, too, is pretty clear about who he is and what he chooses to do, not only in leaving for Stanford, but in giving up Stanford after Jess's death, and even in fighting against an army of demons calling him their Great Evil Hope in season three. We know John made a conscious choice to take up the hunt after Mary's death, even acknowledging it as vengeance. John and Sam, as often as they tangled, are far more alike than either of them liked to admit, and it's this ownership and knowledge of their choices that connects them.

Dean, though, is another matter. And that brings us back to that pesky nature versus nurture debate. Sam lived the same life Dean did until he was eighteen and left for college, but Sam's identity isn't tied entirely to hunting, or to his family's traditions or expectations. Dean, on the other hand, is nothing but hunter, and not, it seems, a completely original one, at least in the darkest, nastiest corners of his head.

In "Dream a Little Dream of Me" (3-10), Dean was confronted with his dream self, and boy, was he a lot more vicious than "our" Dean ever is. Calling Dean as "mindless and obedient as an attack dog" and "Daddy's blunt little instrument," Dream Dean made sure to point out that the few things that identify Dean outside of hunting aren't even his own. "You car? Dad's. Your favorite leather jacket? Dad's? Your music? Dad's."

In the end, what Dean has sacrificed, consciously or not, is himself. As the third season wound down, Dean was finally realizing what he'd given up. For all his enthusiastic pleasure-grabbing at the beginning of the season, with no thought for cholesterol levels or the possibility of STDs, by the time we reached "Long-Distance Call," Dean was afraid. Dean was going to Hell, where he would become what he hated most, and he knew, as he told his dream self, that he didn't deserve it. And yet he didn't back down—he didn't allow Sam to turn him into some twisted zombie version of himself, and he didn't run when the Hell Hounds finally came slobbering and growling to tear him to shreds.

Does this make Dean more of a hero than his brother, or his father, or even other hunters like Bobby, who certainly have made their own sacrifices that keep them awake at night? No. Even someone operating from a solid home base, with money to fall back on, is making a huge sacrifice in risking their lives.

But what's most interesting to me is Dean's lack of self-awareness. When Sammy was lying dead in Cold Oak during the second part of "All Hell Breaks Loose," Dean blamed himself. He told Sam that he screwed up: "I guess that's what I do, let down the people I love." And yet Dean is the one who never gave up, who never abandoned his father, who saved Sam a dozen times over, who moments after this speech sacrificed the only thing he had left to give his brother back his life.

All of the Winchesters are heroes. Dean is simply the only one who doesn't know it.

AMY GARVEY is a former editor who now works on the other side of the desk as a writer, and watches a lot of TV. She's currently working on her next romance novel, saving up for her own vintage Impala, and stocking up on rock salt, as Sam and Dean have taught her to—just in case. Check out her Web site at www.amygarvey.com.

In the modern world, not all heroes wear capes, or even carry guns. Aid workers, paramedics, doctors, parents, teachers, social workers—unlike soldiers or police officers or firefighters, whose heroism lies in acts of overt courage, these modern heroes demonstrate their heroism through acts of kindness, compassion, and selflessness.

So is fighting evil, slaying monsters, and generally holding back the things that go bump in the night enough to qualify the Winchesters as "heroes"? Or does their real strength lie somewhere else?

Sheryl A. Rakowski examines how the word "hero" is defined in the world of the Winchesters.

SHERYL A. RAKOWSKI

A POWERFUL NEED

Heroism, Winchester-Style

> *"They don't need you. Not like you need them."*
>
> —YELLOW-EYED DEMON, "Devil's Trap" (1-22)

The day little Sammy Winchester learned there was no such thing as Santa Claus, his big brother tried to soften the blow with another revelation: "We have the coolest dad in the world. He's a superhero" ("A Very Supernatural Christmas," 3-8). Dean was just a boy himself when he issued that naïve affirmation, but it wasn't a sentiment he'd be quick to outgrow. That unshakable faith in his father became so central to Dean's personal worldview, so essential to his sense of well-being, that it constituted a lifeline for him, keeping the powerful currents and crashing waves that enervate mortal existence from pulling him away and dragging him under. But when John made his deal with the devil in an effort to save his eldest son, he severed that lifeline. Dean was left feeling abandoned and disconcertedly betrayed. It seems likely he would have felt the same no matter what John's bargain had been, even if John had forgone the additional cruel blow of the "Sam bombshell". . . . If the devotedly vigilant big brother could not save the youngest Winchester, Dean would have to kill him. Kill Sammy. On the surface of it, you had to wonder what was going through crazy John's head when he extracted that heartbreaking promise.

Perhaps, though, there was a method to his madness.

That's not how it appeared at first, of course. In the initial weeks after their father's death, Sam spent a lot of time worrying about his older brother, and with good reason. Dean was "erratic" and "scary." He was "tail-spinning" ("Children Shouldn't Play With Dead Things," 2-4). Little brother tried to extend himself as another lifeline but that tether seemed flimsy somehow, as if it were frayed and unraveling before our eyes. Little did we know, John's final words had damaged the fraternal bond that was Dean's last remaining connection to family, and with it his last, best survival instinct in a world too filled with "random, unpredictable evil" ("Houses of the Holy," 2-13). As a result, when season two approached its climax and Sam's self-appointed guardian watched in horror as Sam was stabbed in the back, history was poised to repeat itself. It was almost hard to imagine the concept of free will being applicable to Dean as he followed in his father's desolately sacrificial footsteps. "I couldn't live with you dead," he eventually confessed to his younger brother, "couldn't do it" ("The Magnificent Seven," 3-1). Given the who, the what, and the when of the situation, Dean might just as well have said that winter cannot help but follow autumn—daylight is always an antecedent to the dark of night. He'd get no arguments from me.

It may seem like I'm on a path to an analysis of destiny versus free will. I'm not, although I think it would be another fascinating framework for a *Supernatural* discussion. Instead, the point that I'm reaching for is this: Whether or not Dean's offering up life and soul to resurrect Sammy was a matter of choice, it certainly was not a surprise.

> *"Now, if it's the last thing I do, I'm gonna save you."*
> —DEAN WINCHESTER, "Born Under a Bad Sign" (2-14)

Perhaps it was because Sam was entrenched in his own personal crisis that he was able to find the reassurance he needed in those words, spoken, it seems now, a lifetime ago. But if tail-spinning Dean had said the same thing weeks earlier, before he revealed the specter of fratricide John had invoked, Sam would likely have demonstrated the same deep concern felt by many of us who were on the outside looking in. You didn't need to be a Psychic Kid to have a sense of foreboding, nor did you have to be a literature major to read the writing on the wall. But seemingly, the one thing you couldn't be and still have a grasp of the legacy of John Winchester's final hours was John himself. How could he not know that in authoring his deal with the Yellow-Eyed Demon to "save" Dean, he was creating the recipe for his son's self-destruction?

For those of us drawn to the Winchester family saga, it may be a bit of a challenge to decide whether John earned that ticket to Hell by pulling Dean back into the land of the living the way he did. What's less debatable, however, is that he painted a big red bull's-eye on himself as a target for criticism with respect to the "save Sam or kill him" admonition. No doubt many a fan has linked the words "straw," "camel," and "back" to that particular plot twist. I know I did. But perhaps Papa John was on the receiving end of a bit more criticism than he was due. As Sam observed in "Dream a Little Dream of Me" (3-10), no one can save Dean if he doesn't want to be saved. Would it be a huge surprise if John understood that too? When Dad yanked his eldest back from the brink, a question was left unanswered. Would our heroic and world-weary young soldier have given himself over to the rest he yearned for and deserved, or would his sense of duty, born out of love and fear for his family, have held him back? The doctors made it clear how hard Dean was fighting to hang on. Sam told his father he could feel his comatose brother's spiritual presence.

Did John sense what was transpiring between Dean and the reaper that had come to collect his soul? If so, he may have realized death was not the greatest threat Dean was facing, and saving his son's life may not have been his mission after all. Suppose John knew in his heart the choice Dean was about to make, or thought he did, and that it would leave his son trapped in a nightmarish solitary confinement of his own making. The immediate threat to Dean was his inclination to accept a disembodied existence in a soul-eroding netherworld and, being ill-equipped to push his son toward Heaven, John's only option was to pull him back to Earth. His deal was a stop-gap measure. It rescued his son from becoming hopelessly and irretrievably lost, but it only forestalled the danger Dean posed to himself as a result of his desperate need to hold on to his family, no matter the cost.

Simply put, a desperate need is a "powerful weakness." But the latter turn of phrase has an almost paradoxical ring to it, which can stimulate a curious mind. Moreover, since these are Winchester men we're talking about, any characterization that is "simply put" is also inherently suspect. Perhaps additional insight can be gleaned from turning the spotlight away from weakness and refocusing the discussion on what has, by implication, presumably been lost, stolen, or given away: strength.

> *"You're stronger than Dean. You're better than him."*
>
> —CROSSROADS DEMON, "Bedtime Stories" (3-5)

John's strength of will combined with that special brand of firepower he brought to the table (namely, the Colt) were all the resources he needed to buy Dean's life back. But if his "twisted and broken" son ("The Magnificent Seven") were to throw that gift away at the first opportunity, what good would that do anyone? Clearly, it wasn't enough to merely give Dean his life; John also had to buy his son some time—time enough to want to be saved. More than that, Dean had to find the personal strength to value his own salvation more than he valued his connection to his family. And herein may lie the rationale for Dad's vexing "final words," because the kind of time his son needed doesn't come easy or cheap. Apparently, however, it can come with a certain amount of irony attached. If Sam could hold his brother together for those first rocky months after their father's death, Dean's devotion to his family could do the rest, at least for a time. John had damaged the fraternal connection between his boys, but the significance of that fraying lifeline is, to a certain extent, a matter of perspective. Dean could be compelled to hold on tight, not because he was concerned about being set adrift himself but because his kid brother, securing the other end, might be lost if he let go.

"If it's the last thing I do, I'm gonna save you," Dean promised ("Born Under a Bad Sign"), and on reexamination maybe that wasn't the reflexive death sentence it appeared to be at first. As long as doubt exists that his little brother has been well and truly saved, Dean isn't free to go anywhere. His word is his bond. That bond is driven by his need. And his need is his weakness, but it is also his strength. Dean would be lost without that which he needs most, his family, and yet in so many ways, he is a better man, a bona fide hero, because of them.

In the shifting priorities set by the ebb and flow of the Winchester brothers' trials and tribulations, Dean's need for his family has been a constant, rarely out of sight and never on a holiday. Evidence of it goes all the way back to the pilot episode, which highlighted Dean's dependence on family against a backdrop of Sam's apparent independence. The elder brother could only handle three weeks being completely cut off from loved ones before he sought out the only family member he could find. In contrast, his younger sibling had apparently been incommunicado for two years, and the corresponding familial rift might be there still if an outside force, going by the name of Yellow Eyes, hadn't conspired against it.

Thus, when we were first introduced to the Winchester brothers, Sam gave no evidence of needing his family. He was a normal, albeit overachieving, pre-law student taking a self-actualized path to what would no doubt be a productive, well-adjusted, and chaos-limited life. There's no way anyone would have attached the label "needy" to this kid. On the contrary, direct and indirect references to how smart and strong Sam is, and to the power he possesses, have been made by multiple characters. Of course, while many a lawyer could be said to fall into the category of everyday heroes, they aren't in the same league as a Winchester when he's saving people and hunting things. Normal life is not without challenges for normal people, but is it a daunting, life-or-death test of heroism and strength of character? Not so much.

> *"If I'm gonna fight this war after you're gone, then I gotta change."*
>
> —Sam Winchester, "Malleus Maleficarum" (3-9)

As a consequence of his girlfriend Jessica's death, Sam made a partial, temporary commitment to hunting. It wasn't until he lost Dad too that he gave himself over to it completely. In death as in life, it seems the only way the boys know how to connect with their father is through the family business. Even before Sammy fully embraced "the life," however, signs that he wouldn't be able to breeze through it on autopilot abounded. Bouts of insomnia led to the recognition that the job isn't something Sam can leave at the door the way his big brother can. No one in their right mind chooses to become a hunter, hunting chooses them, and that choice is predicated on devastating personal loss. What separates the heroes of the hunting community from the "serial killers" Bela Talbot was more familiar with ("Red Sky at Morning," 3-6) is how they respond to having their hearts laid bare, cut into, torn asunder.

The first member of the Winchester clan we observed in a proactive state of denial over an impending family tragedy wasn't Dean or even John; it was Sammy, in "Faith" (1-12). When Dean's heart was literally damaged beyond repair, Dean mused aloud that little brother was not about to let him die in peace. Sam, whose heart was also breaking, albeit metaphorically, responded with a resolute, "I'm not gonna let you die, period." He wasn't kidding. The desperate young man managed to pull a rabbit out of his hat on that first occasion in which Dean found himself living on borrowed time. Regrettably, however, the miracle Sam conjured amounted to nothing more than trading one life for another and, although Sam claimed ignorance, you couldn't help but wonder: Would he have done the same even if he had known the price beforehand? Later, "Bobby" enticed a coldly obsession-driven Sam to return to the "Mystery Spot" by dangling the prospect of him getting his dead brother back, and we got a disturbing glimpse of what the answer to that question might be.

The Winchester family history essentially rebooted itself during Dean's contract negotiation and started to retrace a familiar path. Apparently, erratic and scary tail-spinning is every bit as much a part of the family business as saving people and hunting things. Of course, after John sacrificed himself to save his eldest son, Dean was the one being asked if he was all right, whereas the second time around it was Dean who was doing the asking. Big brother thought Sam should be "go[ing] on about the sanctity of life," ("Malleus Maleficarum") but Sam was just too busy trying to kill "as many evil sons of bitches" as he possibly could

("Wendigo," 1-2). In fact, by the time the brothers found themselves struggling to escape *Supernatural*'s life and death version of Groundhog Day, their old nemesis, the Trickster, had some insight to impart to Sam and to the rest of us: "Whoever said Dean was the dysfunctional one has never seen you with a sharp object in your hands" ("Mystery Spot").

Looking at Sam in the aftermath of his brother's "Wednesday death," we see that there's more to heroism than the deeds you do. The sole survivor of the Winchester clan still had all the right moves. He was still hunting things after his brother was gone and presumably still saving people, if only by default. But he was clearly just going through the motions. His heart was no longer in it, or perhaps it was just frozen into a heavy, protective numbness. When the pain and the fear get to be too much, the Winchester men hide in plain sight, but each brother goes about it in a different way. Dean puts his game face on—any changes only go skin deep. Sam, on the other hand, tries to adapt from the inside out.

> *"You've got one advantage that Max didn't have. [...] Me."*
>
> —DEAN WINCHESTER, "Nightmare" (1-14)

The youngest Winchester's malleability in response to his environment is, at times, a valuable asset but it can also be a dangerous liability. In "Dead Man's Blood," Sam experienced a rare moment of quality time with his father and observed how alike they were. Mary Winchester's death fed into the obsessive side of her husband's nature so that all he could see was the evil around him. If John managed to avoid transforming into an emotionally dead exterminator á la Sam in "Mystery Spot," if he managed to stop short of becoming Gordon Walker, it was the family he had left that saved him from that. He needed his boys to be a light in the darkness, perhaps his eldest son in particular. In his final moments, John recalled with loving gratitude how when he'd come home, wrecked from a hunt, Dean would lay a hand on his father's shoulder and tell him everything was okay.

John needed Dean to keep the home fires burning, or the campfire, really, that kept the wolves at bay. And Sam is his father's son—he needs Dean every bit as much. Well, that's not entirely true. Sam can be a regular guy living a normal life without his brother, a feat Dean himself may be less able to accomplish. But what the youngest Winchester cannot do on his own is be a hero. Oh, he can try, and the Trickster has shown us what will happen if he does. Of course, if there was a villain in "Mystery Spot," we have no one but the demigod to cast in that role, so perhaps we shouldn't trust the vision he presented to us. I can't say that I doubt it though. What I saw rang true to me.

Certainly, when Sam is listening to his better angels he can spot the innocent human inhabited by the werewolf, argue that not all vampires are evil, offer the mercy of imprisonment to a misguided hunter who had unmercifully marked him for death. . . And yet this same young man who tried so hard to save fellow Psychic Kid Max Miller also jumped all too easily to the conclusion that innocent Andy was using his psychic abilities to kill people. Yes, when his fearful and dark obsessions get the better of him, Sam's lesser angels have been known to shout down his better ones. Immediately after burying the woman he loved and leaving his hoped-for normal life in smoldering ruins, Sam had his worried brother characterizing his behavior as "all . . . shoot first, ask questions later" ("Wendigo"). Several months down the road, Dean had to physically restrain Sam from acting on a self-destructive impulse to rush into a burning building in the hope of exacting revenge on the thing that killed Jess . . . and Mom.

When discussions of *Supernatural* venture into moral compass territory, I always peg Dean as magnetic north, a constant to be relied upon. I've yet to participate in a similar conversation about celestial navigation, but I think such a metaphor may be even more apropos. Dean is Polaris for the hunting Winchesters, a bright light in the expansive darkness that is essential for finding and keeping your bearings. North may not always be the way to go, but if you're "in tune" with your environment and the North Star is in sight, you'll be able to find your way.

> *". . . for the same reasons you do what you do. . . . Loyalty. . . . Love."*
>
> —MEG, "Shadow" (1-16)

Forget about Roy Le Grange. If anyone qualifies as a faith healer in the

*Supernatural*verse, it's Dean Winchester, who also happens to be a guy who looks in the mirror and hates what he sees. "Desperate, sloppy, *needy* Dean" ("Bedtime Stories") offers comfort and security to John and Sam who, in turn, provide Dean with his purpose and sense of self-worth. And as it turns out, the Winchester family's need for one another is the stuff heroes are made of, which means I'm simply not prepared to call it a bad thing. Dean himself did "a one-eighty" on the function (or dysfunction) of family in the space of a handful of episodes in season one. In "Shadow" he told his brother, "Dad's vulnerable when he's with us. He's stronger when we're not around." But in "Dead Man's Blood" Dean changed his tune: "We're stronger as a family, Dad. We just are." This may have seemed a maddening inconsistency to some but it was merely a reevaluation of the power of familial need in the face of changing circumstances and dissimilar threats. After the near success of Meg's trap, Dean realized that he and his brother could be used by Evil to manipulate John into suppressing his survival instinct for the sake of his children. But later, when John planned to go after the Yellow-Eyed Demon on his own, Dean recognized that the boys could also serve an equal and opposite purpose: to protect their father from his own obsession-driven recklessness.

From the moment in the pilot when Dean let it slip that he could not go looking for Dad alone, need and weakness have been recurring, overt themes in *Supernatural*. While it is rarely if ever Sam who directly puts these matters front and center, a dark preoccupation informs the series' presentation of these themes, which is suggestive of Sam's point of view. This perspective is a slave to the environment which, in season three, was dominated by a slow, dispiriting dying of the light—Dean Winchester's light. "Dean's your weakness. The bad guys know it too," the Trickster warned ("Mystery Spot"). In this context, if Sam needs his brother, if Dean can be used to cause Sam harm; he's a liability, a weakness. While such thinking isn't really wrong, it *is* nearsighted (if understandably so). Fixating on the connection between need and weakness promotes a kind of tunnel vision that can obscure another equally important truth about what it means to need. Winchester need is a powerful need, but power in and of itself is a value-free commodity. It's how power gets used that determines whether it is a force of Evil or a force of Good, whether it is destructive or generative, whether it is a weakness or a strength.

If heroism is to be valued, that which makes a person capable of leading a heroic life should be looked upon as a strength, should it not? For the Winchesters, needing family and having the ability to acknowledge and sustain that need is the wellspring for their mission of "saving people, hunting things" ("Wendigo"). It is both the weakness and the strength implicit in the clan's loving interdependence that lies at the heart of their heroism. And it is why, for the Winchester men, hunting is and must always remain . . . a family business.

SHERYL A. RAKOWSKI is something of a born-again *Supernatural*phile. Initially, she practically went out of her way to avoid this supposedly youth-targeted "horror" series. In fact, Sheryl didn't become a true believer until the summer of 2007 when she came home from the video store with season one, disk one of *Supernatural*. By the start of season three that fall, she had made a pilgrimage through all forty-four of the preceding episodes. Sheryl has a master's in genetics, a passion for amateur motorsports, an appreciation for television that transcends mindless entertainment . . . and a yen for written expression.

Doomed mothers and girlfriends, demons, witches, and damsels in distress—are these the only roles available to women in Supernatural? *Is the show merely a male reaction to a perceived emasculation of the horror genre perpetrated by* Buffy the Vampire Slayer, *an attempt to reclaim TV horror/fantasy for the guys?*

Mary Borsellino examines the role of women, and specifically Jo Harvelle, in Supernatural, *and whether the show perpetuates misogyny as an integral part of the Winchesters' journey.*

MARY BORSELLINO

BUFFY THE VAMPIRE SLAYER, JO THE MONSTER KILLER

Supernatural's Excluded Heroines

Whether it wants to or not, *Supernatural* exists in a world and genre which is unarguably post-*Buffy*. You can't be a popular, fashionable show beginning life on the WB Network and featuring attractive young people killing monsters without summoning the ghost of Slayers past in the process. But this legacy has always sat uneasily on *Supernatural*'s shoulders, and the tension has rarely been as obvious as it was when it came to Jo Harvelle, the supporting character who first appeared in episode 2-2, "Everyone Loves A Clown."

To understand why the saga of Jo shook down as it did, we first have to look at *Supernatural*'s relationship with gender and genre, and especially at its views on another small, blonde, female demon hunter.

THE GUY WITH A CAR, THE GIRL IN A GRAVE

Eric Kripke, creator of *Supernatural*, is a self-confessed acolyte of the

"Hero With a Thousand Faces" school of character arcs. One of the pivotal moments in this story-form is the "return from the dead"; sometimes this journey is metaphoric, sometimes literal.

In the opening episode of season six of *Buffy the Vampire Slayer*, the heroine of that show is brought back to life and, struggling to live, thrusts her hand up through the earth of her grave. This image is repeated in the second episode of *Supernatural*, but here the possibility of a young woman's return has become monstrous, the stuff of nightmares—Sam awakes from the dream of his girlfriend Jessica's resurrection in horror.

There is a female character in the first season of *Supernatural* whose character arc can be mapped onto the Hero's Journey, mirroring as it does the Sam's progression from the ordinary world into the realm of a supernatural quest. Meg, the woman in question, is shown moving through a "death" and then returning. Like Buffy, she is a young, fair-haired woman with demonically imbued strength.

Meg is one of the central adversaries of *Supernatural*'s first season, and a serial murderer. She is also one of only three prominent female characters in the season; the other two are "good" women, and are both killed off incredibly violently after only a couple of scenes apiece (just enough time for the show to establish that they are "nice" girls). They return in later episodes to swan around the afterlife in floaty nightgowns. Meg, the only one with agency or initiative, is thrown out a window, shot in the chest, and put through an extended and apparently torturous exorcism before dying with what sounds like every bone in her body broken.

I'm not suggesting here that Meg is a hero done wrong by the text. She's a villain. But there are no female heroes in the first season of *Supernatural*. There are strong female characters in a number of the episodes (though the ratio of them to the generic, simpering damsels leaves a lot to be desired), but they are never the ones to solve the mystery, kill the monster, or help the helpless.

This can be explained by the fact that it is, after all, the hero's prerogative to save the day, and Sam and Dean—the heroes of *Supernatural*—are both male. But the masculinity the characters attempt to embody is one which reinterprets tropes introduced into the postmodern horror genre by *Buffy*, and the ways in which *Supernatural* seeks to recontextualize these images is distressingly easy to read as an attempted regression away from the new frontiers *Buffy* opened up.

Jared Padalecki, the actor who portrays Sam on *Supernatural*, was asked in the August 2006 edition of *AXM* magazine what he thought of his show in comparison to *Buffy*. He responded with "That was a great show and obviously went for several seasons and had a huge fan base, but I like to think that our show is different. I think it is less campy. . . . Our show is more of a blue collar, in-your-face scary horror."

Padalecki's remarks are particularly interesting in light of the fact that Sam's own Hero's Journey is centered around his wish to leave behind his "family business" (hunting monsters) in order to attend college and become a lawyer. Kripke's frequent invocation of Star Wars as a classic example of a pop *bildungsroman* underscores the role that discontent with the family legacy plays in a story such as Sam's: Luke Skywalker doesn't want to be a farm boy; Sam rejects the "blue collar" class-coding which Padalecki marks the show as embodying.

If *Supernatural* is "in your face," then the implication is that *Buffy* is something else: tricksy, complicated, smug, compared to *Supernatural*'s honest straightforwardness? A more concrete contrast between the two programs can be found in two of *Supernatural*'s season two characters, Gordon and Madison.

Gordon shares many similarities with the *Buffy*-universe character Charles Gunn. Gordon and Gunn are both Black men who kill vampires, and each of them is forced to kill his sister after she is turned into one

In Gunn's case, this killing was framed as an act of mercy, a final display of love. In Gordon's case, this same act was depicted as a blood betrayal—something more unnatural and monstrous than any creature could be. To kill someone you love, even if they have become something evil, is a heinous act. This theme was the driving force behind season two, in which Dean faced the prospect that he might have to kill Sam.

When writer Sera Gamble stated in a *Sequential Tart* interview that Madison, who became Sam's lover in the then-unaired episode "Heart," would not become a "brunette Buffy" or the third inhabitant of the brothers' Chevy, the same backlash against the seminal horror-genre heroine reared its head once again.[1] Fans had no reason to worry at such an out-

[1] http://www.sequentialtart.com/article.php?id=439

come, though: *Supernatural* put this female werewolf down like a dog, and left the firing of the shot to Sam.

To kill those you love is terrible, says *Supernatural* . . . except when the alternative to death is for her to become (horror of horrors) a Buffy-type character.

Another, more detailed example: *Buffy*'s male offsider, Xander Harris, is a screwball sidekick often played for laughs. Of the three core characters, and the wider ensemble as well, he is the one without easily definable skills: he's not a Slayer, like Buffy, nor a witch like Willow. In a season three episode, "The Zeppo," Xander's seemingly tenuous place within the group became the central narrative element.

In "The Zeppo," Xander attempted to prove his usefulness by becoming "Car Guy. Guy with the car." The car in question was a classic Chevy, which Brett Rogers and Walter Scheidel point out "brilliantly evokes American car culture and cinema in the late 1950's [sic] and early 1960's, an era when cult heroes like James Dean were making movies about tough teenage rebels and dangerous chicken fights of masculine bravado."[2] The Chevrolet is a symbol of a particular kind of mythic branding in American pop culture. In *Buffy*, it was played for irony, for hypereality—"imagery of the 1950's [sic] appears repeatedly in 'the Zeppo,' reinforcing the connection between the Chevy and a specific brand of rebellious American machismo"[3]—while in *Supernatural* it was straight-faced.

In another car-related plotline in *Buffy*, Xander spent the last months of his time at high school reading Jack Kerouac's *On the Road* and planning a road trip across America. Buffy mocked him for this dream and, by extension, could be seen as mocking the particular brand of mid-twentieth-century, male-centric romanticism which such narratives invoke. Xander's travel plans were thwarted when the engine fell out of his car in Oxnard, California.

Sam and Dean of *Supernatural* are named for the two central characters of *On the Road*, and their endless road trip is a direct counterpoint to—and, I would argue, a refutation/backlash against—Xander's inabili-

[2] *The Online International Journal of Buffy Studies*. Vol. 13/14. October 2004. <http://slayageonline.com/essays/slayage13_14/Rogers_Scheidel.htm>

[3] Ibid.

ty to tap into a traditional form of American masculinity.

Xander and Dean are very similar characters in many ways—they both pepper their conversations with references to popular entertainment, their libidos are extremely active, and they both tend to avoid emotional vulnerability with quipping and wisecracking. Neither is as formally educated as those he fights alongside. Dean is, it can be argued, what you get if you strip the irony away from Xander's make-up. But where *Buffy* thwarts opportunities for Xander to be a hero through traditional masculinity, it is exactly that traditional masculinity that Dean typically uses to save the day.

The real irony of this is that Xander's eventual ease with himself, and confidence in his abilities, affords the character a far less generic and more honest concept of himself as a man than he would have found by simply adhering to the motifs later taken up by *Supernatural*.

Another way in which *Supernatural* directly addresses ground previously covered by *Buffy* is in each show's relationship to firearms. While Buffy will use them when she needs to (season two sees her wield a rocket launcher), she doesn't put any faith in them at all: "These things? Never helpful" ("Flooded," 6-4). In contrast, guns are Sam and Dean's primary weapons, and make up the bulk of their arsenal. Firearms, like the Xander/Dean figure, are given back their traditional signification and narrative place by *Supernatural*, a role from which *Buffy* had removed them.

Finally, and perhaps most obviously, a parallel between the worlds of *Buffy* and *Supernatural* can be found in season six and the episode "Hell House" (1-17) respectively.

Season six of *Buffy* featured a trio of villains—a group of young men who fit the stereotype of the sci-fi nerd. They collected action figures, hung out in a basement, attempted to dabble in the occult, spoke with exaggerated self-importance and earnestness, and dreamed of the day when they might have sex with a girl. The characters were intended to be, for the majority of their appearances, read as comic figures, but were eventually revealed to be extremely dangerous.

Supernatural's season one episode "Hell House" featured a pair of characters who adhered to almost exactly the same template as *Buffy*'s three. They collected action figures, hung out in a trailer, attempted to dabble in the occult, spoke with exaggerated self-importance and earnestness, and dreamed of the day when they might have sex with a girl.

In one scene, as the pair attempted to gather their thoughts, one reminded the other of their mantra: "What Would Buffy Do?"

This, then, strongly suggests what *Supernatural* really sees *Buffy*'s legacy as: bumbling, inept, absurd male characters out of their depth in the world—no matter what role these characters were put into within *Buffy* or what other nuances and strengths various depictions of male characters on the earlier show may have had.

Buffy gave the world a story in which the traditional roles of masculine hero figures were questioned, and *Supernatural* responded not only by attempting to restore those pre-*Buffy* tropes, but also by putting the girl back in her grave and leaving her there.

Jo Harvelle

Just as "Winchester" conjures images of guns and mysterious houses, and did so even before it was associated with *Supernatural*, so too is "Harvelle" a name laden with meaning: it's Old English for "warrior woman." Jo Harvelle was a young barmaid at a roadhouse diner frequented by demon hunters, and her life intersected with those of Sam and Dean shortly after their father's death at the beginning of season two.

The original name for the character in the first script drafts was Alex, and both "Jo" and "Alex" share the common trait of being androgynous names. Carol Clover, who studied gender in the horror genre in her book *Men, Women and Chainsaws*, observed that the "final girl"—that is, the only one to survive the slaughter in a fright-fest—usually has a name of this sort, listing off Stevie, Marti, Terry, Laurie, Sam, Stretch, Will, Joey, and Max as examples from the movies of the seventies and eighties. This pattern has continued into the era of self-aware, referential horror to which *Supernatural* belongs: *Scream* gave us Sidney, *Final Destination* has Clear. Armed with a surname ready to fight, and a first name—be it Alex or Jo—ready to survive, this character appeared primed to take on whatever the writers threw at her.

After the name shift to Jo, no two creators could seem to agree on what "Jo" was short for—her blog, accessed through the season one DVDs, listed her name as Josephine, as did the comic-book series *Supernatural: Origins*, while the sixth episode of season two, "Hunted," had her mother refer to her as "Joanna Beth." Her age, likewise, was never really pinned down: *Origins* had Ellen remark that Dean and Jo were the same age, giving her a birth date sometime in 1979, while her blog put her birth date as April 7, 1985.

Such are the pitfalls of multiple-author texts. Rather than undermining the integrity of a character like Jo, however, such discrepancies create a different kind of "truth": a legend. *Supernatural* deals primarily with a world shaped by folklore, hearsay, and contradiction—the information that all hunters rely on and live by is information they heard secondhand, which may or may not be true. As part of that world, it's appropriate for Jo's past to be a little shady, a little mysterious.

In the first drafts of "Everyone Loves a Clown," Ellen referred to Jo as "Annie Oakley." Annie Oakley is one of the key female figures in the rich American frontier history on which *Supernatural* draws on so strongly, a markswoman who was nicknamed "Little Sure Shot" for her incredible aim. To invoke such a figure in Jo allowed *Supernatural* to make room for a strong woman within its own mythology. After the sexism of the first season, it seemed like the show was finally going to start getting it right.

The Annie Oakley line never made it into the aired episode.

Jo's blog showed this same pattern, of a brave beginning giving way to a cop-out. The first blog, which lasted only a few days before it was replaced by a very different version, was the diary of a young woman at ease with herself and her place in the world. The entry for March 18, 2005, read in part,

> *I'm not sure why I decided to add my own journal [to the blog site]. I mean, I guess one thing that struck me as I read was the fact that there are almost no other women out there hunting, or at least writing about it on the site. . . . Maybe these entries will help someone along their path, or at least comfort them a little.*

Other entries, copied into the blog from Jo's childhood diaries, tell of her friendships with John Winchester and Caleb, a hunter from season one, and season two's Gordon.

The writings of previously voiceless and disenfranchised groups are often vitally important historical documents, as they provide researchers the opportunities to put absent pieces back into the puzzle of the past. The first blog of Jo Harvelle was, for the mythology of *Supernatural*, just such a document. Actively and deliberately so, in fact: Jo set out to become a visible hunter in the community, a public voice with her own connections—heretofore unmentioned by the men involved—in the world . . . and she set out to do it because she couldn't find other women who'd done it already. If nobody else was going to stick themselves in the story and say, "Hey, women are fighting demons too! We're not all stuck down in graves or being tied up and killed!", then she'd do it herself.

The March 18 entry of the blog, along with the references to Jo's friendships with John and Caleb, were deleted within days, and in the four scant episodes in which Jo appeared she ended up both trapped in a coffin underground and tied up at knife-point, and each time she was rescued from certain death by the Winchesters. Begun with the best of intentions, the character had rapidly become everything she'd originally stood against.

The second version of Jo's blog contains some of the same backstory—though greatly reduced and edited—but a wholly different story of Jo's first love.

The first blog had contained the tentative, ultimately tragic story of Jo's hunting partnership with a young man named Rick:

> *I'd gone out on a hunt with him once before, just a quick day job one city over. But then, over the holidays . . . the hunt was supposed to be me, Rick, and Jake Reilly, but two days into it Jake was called away—a spirit he thought he'd taken care of was back and he had to go deal with it. So Rick and I had to handle the case. . . . I can't say much about it, but it was complicated, it involved a demon and an exorcism. I'm sure Rick has seen much worse, he said as much . . . but, he also said he needed me there, because it was definitely a two-man job. And I've never felt as in sync with another hunter as I did with him. . . . [W]hen we fin-*

ished off the spirit, and saw that the victim was gonna be okay, it was such an amazing high. And Rick felt it too. One thing led to another, and, well. . . .

Like I said, just the facts. And the fact is, Rick and I are dating now. We told my Mom about it and everything. I think she's pretty happy about it. . . . Rick is a damn good hunter and, like I said, the guy you'd want watching your back, and Mom always likes to know that someone's got my back. I think we're gonna be going on out on a lot of trips together.

Nine months after they began, however, Rick went out on a solo hunt and never returned. Jo version 1, while sad, seemed to cope with the loss relatively well—it's a fact of the hunting life that people die.

Jo version 2.0, however, had a different experience with Rick in the re-written blog:

He's been coming in the bar for a while, and we always got along fine. Over the holidays . . . well, he started coming into the bar more often and I caught his eye looking at me. It was the kind of look you don't forget and I don't know why the possibility that Rick could be after anything besides a hunt had never occurred to me. It was awkward at first, but I sort of liked the attention. I started paying attention to what I said around him, what he was looking at when he was stopping by, and finally, well, one thing led to another, and. . . .

Like I said, just the facts. And the fact is, Rick and I are dating now. We didn't want anyone else in the roadhouse to know, especially my Mom, she'd flip if she knew I was dating a hunter. But she's got eyes and ears and one time called us out on it . . . but we both lied. I know she doesn't believe me and it's getting hard to hide so many things from her. The last thing she wants is me falling for a hunter, but who knows what's best for me anyway? Me or my mom?

There would be nothing wrong, of course, with introducing this revisional, less mature Jo into the show, rather than the original version . . .

if the show had then taken the time and effort to allow her character to grow.

Fan reaction was volatile on the subject of Jo from day one, with most of the nicknames for the character being unprintable here. Rather than stick with the plan for season two as it was originally envisioned, the creative team bowed and scraped to placate fans as fast as they could, with executive producer Eric Kripke telling *TV Guide,* "While we're on the subject of the roadhouse characters . . . we read the boards, we pay attention, and we take your concerns seriously. . . . [W]e're not going to pursue anything on the show that's not working."[4]

Seven months later, again talking to *TV Guide*, Kripke said of Jo that "we feel we've learned from that mistake. . . . [W]e conceived the character wrong."[5] One can't help but wonder which particular conception of the character Kripke considered a mistake.

Another of the show's executive producers, Peter Johnson, went so far as to promise that future printings of the old issues of *Supernatural: Origins* would include no mention of Jo whatsoever, effectively excising her from the mythology completely—writing her back out of the history she'd tried to reclaim her place in. Johnson went on to say of Jo and her unceremonious expulsion from the show that "that issue remains dead and buried."

You can take the girl out of the grave, but in the end *Supernatural* always puts her right back in her place, six feet under.

Jo's mother, Ellen, is a strong and fascinating female character in her own right, a tough yet maternal single mother with a mixed opinion of the world of hunting. Fans responded more positively to her than to Jo, leading Eric Kripke to joke that perhaps Dean should "score some hot MILF action!" MILF is, of course, slang for "Mom I'd Like to Fuck." While it's a positive step to see an older female character perceived as remaining sexy and attractive to younger potential lovers, Kripke did not choose the most respectful term he might have to describe that. In a world where women seem to be either minxes or mothers, Ellen is

---

[4] http://www.tvguide.com/News-Views/Interviews-Features/Article/default.aspx?posting={376215DE-10D7-4281-AF13-9EBF86F8AB5E}

[5] http://community.tvguide.com/blog-entry/TVGuide-Editors-Blog/Ausiello-Report/Supernatural-Exec-Wont/800019020&start=15

described as both minx and mom and nothing more.

The season two finale saw Ellen's character arc pulled up sharply, with the bar she owned burned to the ground and her role reduced to nothing but a hostage: in the climactic showdown between good and evil, telekinetic villain Jake Talley forces Ellen to turn her gun on herself, assuring Sam and Dean that if they make a move, "You'll be mopping up skull before you get a shot off," and referring to Ellen as "sweetheart."

Rather than a character in her own right, Ellen is ultimately a pawn and passive catalyst within the stories of the male characters. This categorization for women on the show would become even more evident in season three, but was rarely more blatantly evident than in this shift from dame to damsel for one of the few stereotype-breaking females the show had managed to leave alive beyond their first appearances.

In the end it's Meg, the female demon punished for her agency through multiple gory deaths in season one, who teaches Jo that she'll never have a place of power in the Winchesters' story. Back from Hell and possessing Sam, Meg pays a visit to the bar Jo now uses as a home base for hunting (still unable to get the message that women's stories have no public place on *Supernatural*, Jo's hunting journal was then taking the form of postcards she sends home to the roadhouse). Meg ties Jo up and threatens her with a knife, telling her that she's nothing but "a schoolgirl" and "bait." To be tied up was the final act of violence a man inflicted on Meg before killing her last time, when the Winchesters bound and beat her before her fatal exorcism, she simply sneered at Dean that it was "kind of a turn-on, you hitting a girl."

Now, having crawled back from Hell, Meg's taken over a male body as her human form; she's not gonna make the same mistake again. Girls don't stand a chance, not in *Supernatural*'s world.

Dean saves Jo, Meg shoots Dean, Jo saves Dean. As Dean prepares to go after Meg, Jo has her final moments on the show.

"I'll call you," Dean promises.

"No, you won't," she answers, not sounding all that dismayed about it. And that's the end of that.

MARY BORSELLINO is a writer living in Australia. She likes comic books and loud music and other things which grown-ups are supposed to be too clever for, such as obnoxiously lurid hair dyes and staying up past bedtime. You can find interviews she's done with the cast and crew of *Supernatural* at http://monkeywench.net/supernatural, and her e-mail is mizmary@gmail.com.

On the surface Supernatural *appears to be completely male-dominated: two good-looking guys in a muscle car drive around Smalltown, USA, shooting, stabbing, and blowing things up as they search for their missing father and vengeance against the demon that ruined their lives.*

Why, then, does Supernatural *have such a huge female fan base? Are the aforementioned two good-looking guys in the muscle car the only reason women viewers could possibly have for tuning in?*

Jacob Clifton examines gender in Supernatural, *and how an ostensibly male-oriented show can ultimately be grounded in the feminine.*

JACOB CLIFTON

SPREADING DISASTER

Gender in the *Supernatural* Universe

I: KANSAS

(Three men watch as their house burns, huddling together on the hood of their car. The youngest is six months old.)

Every dramatic universe, just like ours, has its laws. They define the tone and intent of the story as much as they are affected by it, because they describe what is possible. The rules of a given show are its narrative physics; they also describe what it is that keeps viewers coming back. A show that falls off the beam, so to speak, has let its viewers down by not obeying its own rules. Either by making sense with the stuff that happened before, or by retroactively redefining the laws themselves, each new episode of a show has the duty of integrity. (The revelation, in the show's final seasons, that the power of the Slayer comes from a not-so-divine source, for example, puts *Buffy the Vampire Slayer*'s ethics on shout in a way that could hardly have been presumed from the start, but definitely fit with the show's overall ethos.) Everything prior in the story must agree with new events, or else they must be explained in the stories to come. Otherwise, you'll have your viewers jumping ship.

Coming-of-age dramas, like other basic forms of storytelling—fairy tales and classic mythologies, for example—bear a further responsibility to their own integrity. Every Young Adult novel or teen show is also a mystery story, because its entertainment derives from the fact that the characters are learning about the particular societal rules of their universes: they are stories about negotiating the physics of the narrative, and we're along for the ride. While every Hero's Journey is, in part, about finding one's place in the world, that journey is most explicit in teen and coming-of-age stories, because that searching and negotiating are just as central to the teen experience *outside* the narrative realm. No matter how old we are, every one of us can name books, stories, or television series that helped us to understand the world and our place in it. They take their position in our personal mythology and help to guide us through the mysteries of the real world: life, love, labor, and happiness.

Supernatural teen drama, by extension, is able to take those queasy subconscious forces and contradictions and represent them explicitly, as outside forces, in the life of the show itself. Myth and classic tropes, which linger in the margins of all fiction, are brought to the fore. Two clear examples, which have perhaps defined supernatural teen drama for modern television, are *Smallville* and *Buffy the Vampire Slayer*. In both cases, the central characters exist in opposition to an often confusing, antagonistic universe: the characters learn how best to adapt to and, more importantly, understand the rules of these worlds. Teen drama characters conquer inner demons, and learn to negotiate between their inner desires and potential (often signified by actual supernatural power), and outward social acceptance. But in the supernatural genre, those demons aren't always internal, and those potential powers are a bit more dramatic.

In these sorts of shows, natural psychological responses are mirrored by unnatural occurrences in the world itself. To explore the psychic and mythic content in these shows—and their instructive value—we must begin by looking at the overall qualities, positive, negative, and neutral, of these worlds, and the ways in which they differ from our own. Every story contains multiple points of entry for the viewer or reader: Are you

Buffy? Willow? Xander? Giles? Or none of these? The challenge can also become finding a place to stand in a story that seems to resist you as an individual. Does the nature of a given story, for a most basic example, privilege a masculine or feminine viewpoint? What gendered qualities does it most value in its heroes? Who is it that defines the characteristics of this world? Who is it that defines what a "hero" in a given story must do or say, or avoid? And how can we align these criteria with real masculine or feminine experience?

Another way to ask these questions can be found within the narrative of the shows themselves: Which of the characters within them are representative of and identified with the ego—the personhood of the show and viewer—and which represent the shadow, the twisted mirrors of the main cast, the Other? In cultural criticism, this defining point of view is often referred to as "gaze." It's a way of describing the central unifying perspective of the show (or book, or writer) in and of itself; in the terms we're describing now you could call it the gender of the show itself.

Smallville is a male-gaze[1] show: its threats mostly take the form of science, weaponry, science-fiction violence—all classic male tropes. Its development and history descend directly from the most classic possible masculine wish-fulfillment story since Hercules, a story that has been told month in, month out, through every medium, for the last sixty years—Superman's. *Smallville*'s strong female characters are gifted with independence and strength within this world, and recommend it highly, but the cast is unified by their connections to and disconnections from Clark's "secret," Superman being the story's endpoint and reason for existing to begin with. The show's characters and props represent elements of a *masculine* world and narrative: an environment which is itself bent on investigation, invasion, domination. By regularly focusing on—and then protecting or transcending—the "secret," and the vulnerability that goes with it, the show reinforces and protects Clark's own sovereign male nature against invading masculine intent.

Buffy, on the other extreme, is a story about magical and intuitive threats, written from a feminized viewpoint. Its world is dreamlike, as

[1] I will use "masculine" and "feminine" from here forward interchangeably with "male" or "female," without intention of drawing a distinction between these archetypal qualities and physical gender.

subconscious elements—dream-figures, classical nightmare tropes, and monsters representing figurations of the characters' own secrets and fears—arise to be conquered, vanquished, or assimilated. The world of *Buffy* itself is a female landscape; to say this is pejorative only to the degree that we as a culture undervalue women's experience. Changeable, unlawful, and illogical, as only dreams can be, Sunnydale is a Land Without Fathers, without strict categories or unbendable rules. The feminine gaze orders itself around self-defined concepts of rule and systems of control and justice, rather than taking external cues. In a masculine environment, these concepts are handed down from the father and other authority figures; in Buffy's world, the rules are a lot bendier—the world itself seems to withhold absolute answers, and often it's up to Buffy herself to define basic morality. There is little rigid division between the emotional lives of *Buffy*'s characters and the world that they inhabit, because that world, too, is bendy. Situational ethics triumph over traditional rules, patriarchal systems of control are regularly deconstructed and overcome, and the inner world is privileged over orthodox social construction: friends become enemies become lovers and so on.

To put it another way: While it's *possible* that Jack Bauer (from the less magical, but no more realistic *24*) will—like Buffy in her final battle against season four's Adam—dream himself into an avatar of prehistoric feminine power, and then use that magic to turn bullets into doves, it's unlikely at best. He lives in a male world and plays by male rules.

So then, why am I talking about *Smallville* and *Buffy* when we should be talking about cute boys? Because in both those cases, the gender basics of the shows in question are not compromised. A dreamland visit in *Smallville* will always find itself bound to scientific mental manipulation or male control, while Buffy's first experience with a scientific and martial threat (Adam again) leads back to the show's most dreamlike and evocative occult investigations yet, which in turn leads directly to an episode that takes place within the subconscious minds of the characters themselves.

Smallville's season four storyline involving reincarnated witches, and *Buffy*'s season six story about alienated male "geek" villains, are both gradually and completely subsumed into the show's respective mythologies. In the former case, Lana's supernatural abilities eventually lead the story back to Clark's Kryptonian heritage. In the latter, the trio of geeks eventually leave the ranks of the hard science-fiction stereotypes that once defined them. One is murdered by another in a magical ritual and thus connected bodily with the forces we're talking about, the second is skinned alive by a vengeful witch (see the *Season Eight* comics for the continuing story there) and becomes an embodiment of the First Evil, and the last eventually becomes a (mostly) trusted member of Buffy's own organization. Like any given psychological system, be it the personal psyche or a religion, the rules remain the same: While any story necessitates the introduction of antithetical characters or worlds, eventually you find you can't escape the specific qualities of the unique narrative universe forever. If you could, no show would be definable or contiguous with itself, and the serial nature of television being what it is, viewers would simply desert camp. Every world must obey its own rules, or explain very carefully that the rules have been retroactively changed.

Supernatural, having finished three seasons at this writing, puts both concepts—the masculine coming-of-age, the feminine emotional landscape—in a blender, by placing two classic male Hero archetypes in a classically intuitive realm. Like *Smallville*, the viewpoint characters are undeniably male both in representation and in their response to the genre elements the show throws at them: overpowering, self-insinuating, destructive. But like *Buffy*, the narrative universe of *Supernatural* is one where the landscape itself can rear up and swallow you if you're not careful, and where blood and birthright and spiritual states are quantifiable and often dangerous. Like Buffy, the boys are hunters of the supernatural, and like her, their resistance to its influence often presents obstacles to their own self-understanding and empowerment.

Masculine characters traversing a female landscape, addressing it through archetypally male modes of heroism: that's a gender double-twist. What this *should* mean is that anyone can find a place to stand in order to experience the show, involving as it does both male and female aspects of the supernatural adventure. But the show still draws upon a classically male gaze, leveling desire and objectification at bodies, and rejoicing in its images of violence and physical terror and destruction.

Where *is* the place for the female or queer viewer in such a strongly defined masculine story? Whence the show's overwhelmingly female fan base? This is a show created by men, about men, but watched in great numbers by women. Yet the show is self-consciously meticulous about defining the gender of its perspective: Whenever the less typically male lead (Sam) goes too far into alien (feminine) territory, the more strongly delineated male lead (Dean) is there to mock him back into place; queer characters, when they are introduced at all, are mocked or killed in shockingly blasé ways. (When Ghostfacer Corbett is duped into sacrificing himself by squicked-out straight man Ed, his death is shrugged off with a snarky, "You were teaching us about heart, about dedication, and about how gay love can pierce through the veil of death and save the day" ["Ghostfacers," 3-13].) And yet fan response is often predicated on queer issues seen to be lingering around the edges of the show, imputing homosexual desire even to the normally off-limits fraternal relationship. Is it simply the fact that the male characters themselves are just as objectified by the camera's eye, or is there something more going on? And in an age where fan participation, ancillary and derivative works like licensed novels and recaps, and fan creative output are just as important to the demographic as the canonical work itself, is describing any given television show as having one centralized "gaze" even still a workable concept?

II: The Chalice of Blood

(A demon girl speaks to her father, face reflected in the blood of an innocent.)

The story of *Supernatural* is, as all good fairy tales should be, a story of deferred contact with the parent. Sam Winchester begins the story having distanced himself from his father and brother, choosing college and the real world over their demons and monsters. Sam's attempt to ignore his world's magical content is invalidated by his girlfriend's supernatural death, and older brother Dean returns to tempt Sam into that most classic of Hero's Journeys: to locate and reconnect with their father. The journey will mean contact with the supernatural, and the transformation this implies.

The first present-day supernatural event in the show, Jessica's death at the hands of Azazel, carries with it a connection to Mary, the boys' mother. The search for the father will also, clearly, necessitate contact with the mother: both parents dwell in and are marked by the night world of the supernatural through their layered and mysterious relationships with Azazel, and John through his chosen vocation. Both searches will involve personal experience with demons and ghosts for the boys. The further they press into the shadow, both their own and that of their narrative world, the closer they will come to reconciliation with both parents.

The feminine nature of the shadow, as is typical with a male hero and show, is terribly evident, especially in the first season. A woman in white, a water wraith, a murderous ghost, a girl possessed by an evil preacher, a demon with a chalice of blood, and a vampiress (who is sacrificed for the magically phallic Colt) are among the overwhelmingly feminine iterations of darkness. And, as in any hero trope, the victims are female as well: the story is predicated on saving women from themselves, or in Jungian terms, redeeming the innocent feminine from its own darker appetites.

The rules become more complex in season two, as is usual as a show (or person) becomes more sophisticated. The boys defend a group of nonviolent vampires against a rogue hunter, upending their season one loyalties, almost at the start. And while there are female zombies and a rampaging female ghost, there is often a sense that the most apparently pure threats are less generic shadow content and more sympathetic, human aberrations: sad in effect but not horrific in and of themselves. Vampires begin to question their own lifestyles; poltergeists are revealed as victims in their own right. One episode balances the dark and light sides of the mother archetype by pitting the boys against a classic "black widow" nurse ghost, while allying them with a brave female public defender. We meet the Crossroads Demon, who becomes intimately tied to the boys' own troubled relationships with the shadow as, until Sam kills her mid-season three, she mediates their deals and administrates their communications with Hell itself. In a fascinating pair of episodes, the female "client" turns out to be the monster of the week—a ghost, and the next week a werewolf—and in both cases the client is even more sympathetic and pitiable for her association with dark forces.

This latter episode is a major turning point for Sam: he learns the truth only after sleeping with the client, and finally—after a speech on her part that echoes his own two episodes earlier, begging Dean to kill him to stop his demon-possessed destruction—agrees to kill her himself, even after Dean offers to do the deed on his behalf. It's an important and brutal step toward Sam's acknowledgment of his own connection to the underworld, accepting this responsibility for violence in order to protect the greater world. Perhaps only a werewolf could properly symbolize the uncontrolled violence that unmediated contact with the subconscious, which is to say unfiltered experience of his own supernatural potential, might inspire in Sam. The werewolf is a universal symbol of that moonlit madness: a narrative gloss on psychosis, or worse.

The feminine supernatural is tweaked further in the third season, as two female foils are brought in for the boys. While Ellen and Jo provided a season two mirror for Dean's relationship with John, Dean's double in season three is Bela: whereas Dean has always kept his distance from the supernatural by commodifying it, retaining his identity as an impersonal hunter, rather than a killer, Bela approaches hunting from an amoral, capitalist viewpoint. There is no honor in her dealings with the underworld. She represents the dangerous aspects of Dean's ongoing estrangement from the subconscious by illustrating its endpoint: dangerous and mercenary vigilantism. And in the end, Bela's fate—though it arises from what you might call a more selfish place—lands her in the exact same place as Dean: ripped from the world by the hounds of Hell. Although we do learn more about her reasoning and justifications, it's worth noting that in both cases, what drives these two hunters' destiny is denial: of accountability, of debts come due, and of the encroaching darkness that eventually claims them both.

While the show's first seasons focused on Dean's search for their father, and collaterally Sam's own rekindled bond with John, John's final release into death opens the way in season three for a radical shift: not Dean's search for the father, but Sam's search for the mother. Ruby, as emissary and guide through the grayer areas of the darkness, takes on a nearly maternal role, spurring Sam to discover Mary's story while entering into a secret alliance with Dean to prepare Sam for the coming war. Where season two began with a whispered secret from John to Dean, we now find Sam holding back information about Mary.

If season two radicalized the boys' relationship with darkness and the feminine, in season three the lines are almost completely redrawn. Hints throughout point to the season's Big Bad, Lilith. A newly freed demon queen, she views Sam as a rival, implying equality and possibly shared characteristics; her overarching plans involve everything from Dean's Crossroads deal and coming death to Ruby's presence. She the third season's dark mother, as implicit and unmentioned as Mary is in the earlier seasons. We are told explicitly in the final acts of the season that she holds all the cards: she holds Dean's contract and Bela's, she employed the now-dead Crossroads Demon, and she deliberately constructed the season's final battlefield in order to trap the boys and send Dean to Hell.

An early episode brings all three levels of the motherhood question—parental, mythic, and narrative—into alignment: The boys fight a "mother changeling" who steals human children, just as it's suggested that Mary was more involved in Azazel's demoneering than originally believed. Dean learns he may have a son of his own, and must contend with the threat of adulthood, new responsibility, and fears that he might reenact his father's effect on his own childhood. Most importantly, Ruby begins to influence Sam's investigations into Mary's life and death. In another episode, we encounter a town being slowly corrupted—in parallel to Lilith's manipulations—by a female demon, Casey, who is powerful enough that she is able to give the boys new information about both Azazel and Lucifer.

For the first two seasons the show never personifies its darkness as anything larger than something the boys can kill, with one exception—Azazel, whose position as a dark and paternal influence on Sam extends back (it is implied) to before Sam's birth. While Azazel was eventually destroyed, of course, this came at the cost of John's own life, another parallel between the show's real parents and their demonic counterparts. Several of the demons that appear in the first season (in particular Meg) and the Special Children like Sam in the second are both referred to as Azazel's children. He is a dark father. In season three, after both John and Azazel have been shot by the Colt, and killed, the tables turn: the darkness itself has a feminine presence and name, and it's closing in from every corner. Each mystery seems linked, week by week, to the central storyline of Lilith's involvement in the boys' lives. Even female monsters of the week are newly drawn, ever more complex and sympathetic—

most memorably the unwitting vampire in an early episode, whom the boys protect, unthinkably, from a fellow hunter.

An episode featuring a seemingly textbook coven of suburban witches (who affect Dean viscerally and eventually with life-threatening physical responses, while Sam is virtually unaffected) resolves with the revelation that its least impressive member, the passive and seemingly powerless Tammi, is actually a demon, impervious to the Colt and connected with Lilith herself. We learn that Bobby (another surrogate father) had to kill his wife, who was possessed by demons; Sam learns that Mary was involved with Azazel in an unspecified manner and that all her friends have died mysteriously. Even Dean's complex relationship with John, a lynchpin of the show and its masculine tropes, takes a beating in Lilith's presence: a mysterious phone call from "John"—even though the episode itself revolves around similar phone calls causing suicides left and right—leads him to track down Lilith even after numerous warnings.

The truth and beauty of the familial, fraternal, and filial love between the three men has been the show's one constant; if Lilith can pervert even these connections, how much power does she really wield over the narrative itself? The answer is implicit in the season's final act: the black dogs of the Crossroads are not defeated, Lilith easily overcomes Ruby's usually reliable strength, the Knife is no help, and even Sam's newfound ability to deal with demons and willingness to kill has no effect. Dean is carried off, physically, to his damnation. A tense balance, played all season long, ends in perhaps the most shocking way imaginable when Dean's fate is finally sealed. The story's strongest bastion against the dark, whose person seems entirely dedicated to defending his brother from any growth or transformation, finds himself in the bowels of Hell, being ripped apart. And if Ruby and his own visions are correct, his own transformation has begun.

III: The Double

(Two identical men stand in a dusty cellar: one with black eyes, the other holding a candle against the darkness.)

As befits a story with dual protagonists, the Winchester brothers have a marked predisposition, like twins, for dividing and intensifying the characteristics of the singular Hero, a metaphysical Everyman. Their competition within the story, the way the story switches story priority and vulnerability between the two, creates a dynamic, alternating current of transformation and personal change. If Dean is the Body and Sam is the Soul of this hypothetical ego, only by developing and broadening both characters in tandem can the show accomplish its remit as a true Hero's Quest.

Dean is the strong, well-versed, street-smart brother: grounded, connected to the earth. His fear of flying serves the dual purpose of demonstrating this essential quality while enhancing his connection to the Impala: he "prefers to drive." As a male symbol, and the more sexually virile of the two characters, Dean represents a viewpoint that seeks to conquer and destroy subconscious content. He moves from hunter, focused only on tracking the next monster, to a rogue blamed for the opening of the Devil's Gate, to a man marked himself by the supernatural.

Dean's deal with the Crossroads Demon at the end of season two, to save Sam's life, puts the next year of his life into a personal and occupational tailspin. Touched by the underworld and the uncanny, Dean becomes reckless and hapless, to a degree that terrifies his brother. A real-world analogy with terminal illness (which Dean has faced before) is not out of place, given Dean's personality and identity. An adrenaline junkie, as befits such an earthy, body-centered character, must never know when his death is coming. Dean does, and this—combined with his sudden new connection to the spiritual realm, sealed with a demon's kiss—is a trap to which he responds like a wounded, cornered animal.

At the show's beginning, Dean's connection to the supernatural is greater than Sam's, given his association with the hunting world. In fact, an important trope for season one is the idea that the boys are following clues left in their father's journal—a paternal grimoire of mysteries. But Dean's feelings about his role fighting the shadow realm are no simpler than his feelings about his father, and the twisted hunter boot camp John made of both his sons' lives. As a shapeshifter says, while in Dean's form, "Maybe this thing was born human but was different. Hideous and hated. Until he learned to become someone else." And later, speaking as

Dean himself, "Deep down, I'm just jealous. You got friends. You could have a life. Me? I know I'm a freak. And sooner or later, everybody's gonna leave me" ("Skin," 1-6). We learn that Dean's first love dumped him when she learned about hunting, and when they meet again, she still rejects his lifestyle and association with the supernatural.

Dean spends the first episode of season two suspended between life and death (of note is Sam's ability to sense his brother's spirit). And while in the end his relationship with John is strengthened both by his father's self-sacrifice and their shared knowledge of Sam's destiny, while comatose Dean expresses his resentment for the ways his father's lifestyle has changed him: "I've done everything you've ever asked me. Everything. I have given everything I've ever had. . . . What the hell kind of father are you?" ("In My Time of Dying," 2-1). Because Dean glories in the violence of hunting, it's easy to overlook his conviction that his childhood, and continued hunting, have effectively evicted him from the natural world, or the chance to succeed in it. He lives in the shadows, and each time he tries to leave this life—or bridge it—he is rejected. His resentment of the shadow realm thus takes him further into it, even as it marks him as its own.

After John's death, Dean reconnects with a secondary family of hunters, spending time at Harvelle's Roadhouse and bonding with Jo over their fathers' shared exploits and fates. He is strong enough to turn down the Crossroads Demon at their first meeting (she offers Dean ten years and the return of John's life in exchange for Dean's eventual damnation) even when she reveals that John is suffering in Hell. Midseason two, Dean has advanced to the point that he can reveal John's secret: that Sam may have to be killed, should he come into his birthright as one of Azazel's "Special Children." This move represents a new willingness on Dean's part both to share John's memory with Sam, and to soften his authoritative and protective stance toward his younger brother. The ongoing softening of Dean's approach—even as Sam is becoming harder—is mirrored in Dean's estrangement from and sometimes antagonistic interactions with the other hunters. As much of the season involves Sam's growing acknowledgment of his own ties to the subconscious content of the narrative—in fact, as Dean helps him deal with it encroaching on seemingly all sides—it makes sense that Dean's parallel development would itself come out of concern for Sam. Throughout the story, when one brother grows we can see a compensatory change in the other.

This contrast and conflict, between Dean's brave rejection of and assaults on the unknown and the shadow and his intensifying connection to it, are played out in a pivotal episode of season three, "Dream a Little Dream" (3-10). In what would have been, prior to the 2007 WGA strike, halfway through the season and is now two-thirds through, Dean is able to physically confront his fears through interaction with a dream-world demon double: Having learned from Ruby and Tammi that at least some demons were once human, twisted by their time in Hell, Dean realizes that he's agreed not just to his death, but his eventual damnation. When Dean says that no one can save him, Sam responds, "No one can save you because you don't want to be saved."

A nightmarish version of Dean, with a demon's black eyes, speaks to him directly about his fears, his sense of worthlessness, his self-hatred. It points out to him that all he has in the world is his brother, whom he is failing by dying; his father's feelings for him amounted to the respect due a good soldier, or cannon fodder; and John loved Sam more than Dean. If all of these are worries and neuroses typical of the classic masculine hero, what does it say about Dean that they are eventually transcended? Dean finally calls his father an obsessed bastard who couldn't protect his family, who let Mary die, and who wasn't there for Sam when he needed it most. He acknowledges that he didn't deserve the burdens John raised him to carry, that he mourns the life he never had, and maintains that he doesn't deserve to go to Hell. Although this dream experience drastically changes Dean's waking relationship to his own salvation, the episode ends with a terrifying image: the nightmare double, snapping his fingers as though to suggest Dean's dream of escaping his deal is just that—a dream, a fantasy. And while Dean can be forgiven for assuming the worst, there were few viewers prepared for this last vision to be proven true.

IV: The Car, the Colt, & the Knife

(Two men sit behind the wheel of an immaculate black '67 Chevrolet Impala, arguing over the radio.)

Being uncomfortable with overt emotion or affection, as is the wont of the Western Hero, much of the show's most important emotional content is expressed through objects: the Car, the Gun, the Knife. Just as the objects in a Tarot deck express more than their simple use, or proper names, these objects spend as much important time onscreen as the boys themselves—almost characters in their own right, certainly more than mere props or MacGuffins.

In Dean's case, the Impala is a symbol of masculinity, both as a virile signifier in its own right and as a sign of the family's legacy of protection and violence. The story begins with the car, as John holds his sons tightly in front of it while their mother and home burn. The car provides continuity, comfort, and movement from place to place; these are also the things Dean provides, as a brother and father figure, for Sam himself. Provided by John, it also signifies Dean's alpha status: in the absence of their father, Dean is the authority figure. He's the driver.

Dean's acceptance of his fate—and of Sam's right to independent manhood—is made explicit when he ends a season three episode by teaching Sam to repair and care for the Impala, showing the transmutation of his protective role into a more guiding paternal approach. If Sam must carry the family name on his own, once John and Dean are both dead, then he will be the true heir, both of the Impala and of the Winchester Hunt. It's both touching and generous, one of the most emotional scenes for both men's stories, and a serious redefinition of the roles of both characters, and of the rules of the show itself.

(A boy trains a pistol against the darkness; behind him stands the spirit of his father.)

Even as the Impala represents Dean's role in the family and his connection to John, the Colt has come to be associated with Sam's own approach to the hunt: objective, hands-off, investigative. It's an intriguing reversal: A car is not necessarily lethal, and in fact provides comfort and transportation, and sports cars are fetishized sexual objects, phallic and feminized at once. In contrast, guns are made to do one thing only. They are the prime phallic object, in fact—as we'll see, even knives are made to do more than kill, and have ritual and mythological ties to the feminine that balance their obvious phallic qualities—and yet while Dean is responsible for the Impala, it's Sam who is the owner, for all intents and purposes, of the Colt. (Consider that the inventor of the Colt handgun was another Samuel!) In both cases, of course, they are passed down from John, but the reversal is informative, as the objects are externalized parts of their respective owners' less-developed masculine qualities.

Dean's story is that of a lone wolf, damaged by childhood, rootless, who through caring for his brother and humanizing his own mission grows to be more nurturing and accepting of intimacy and love. Sam's story represents an earlier part of the classic Hero story: that of a young man coming into his own sexual and masculine power. John has given his sons just the tools they need to become the men they need to be: Dean a roving home for his family, and Sam the destructive capability he's only now developing, to complement his own sensitive and intuitive powers.

But as we know, both John and Mary are familiar with Azazel, which the boys and the show's explicit narrative seem to actively ignore. Psychologically, it's a master stroke, illustrating the subconscious power of the parents, both as mother and father archetypes and as our strongest developmental influences. If it's an especially male story that identifies the feminine with magic and the subconscious, it's every story that does the same for parents. For Sam, season two is an exercise in striking out beyond those familiar connections, investigating his new "special" family and spiritual lineage, and thus he is unable to make a claim on either object, gun or car, throughout. When the Colt reappears in the end of season two, it's Dean who uses the last bullet to kill Azazel, rendering it useless.

It's only Ruby's reappearance, working with fellow surrogate parent Bobby to restore it, that gives Sam the chance to claim its power for himself. Ruby, representing feminine and supernatural balance, is able to repair the gun just as she facilitates a new relationship between Sam and the darkness itself. As he moves into a more protective and functional role, working to keep Dean tethered to this world, Sam is finally able to claim the gun. Bela, associated with Dean's ongoing rejection of the supernatural, then makes off with the gun—after Sam is unable to kill Lilith's servant demon Tammi with it, notably—and the boys spend the latter half of the season tracking her, and it. However, it's not the gun that the boys bring to their final showdown with Lilith and her demons, but something much older, and darker, and carrying a much stronger feminine power.

(A black-eyed angel holds out a wicked blade, point-first; behind her stand two boys, wreathed in darkness.)

Ruby's knife is not the first one we've seen. We see a curved blade in Sam's overnight bag in the pilot, which he packs when he's leaving his home in Palo Alto to join Dean's quest. It is also seen in one of the first promotional images marketing the series. In the picture, Dean holds a sawed-off shotgun and faces the camera, while Sam stands behind him, looking almost over his shoulder behind us. The Impala shines its brights in the background, a large bag of salt propped against her front fender, symbolizing not only her role in the illumination of the darkness but also the safety she promises, and has provided since the Winchester house burned.

Compositionally, the flashing bright headlight leads down across Sam's backside, to the knife; the line then leads to Dean's hand, holding the gun, and ends on his groin. The elements of the image are emblematic of the boys' roles and characteristics: active Dean, confronting and attacking the darkness head on, while passive Sam's relationship to the enemy, and his own power, are more questionable. Dean's shotgun tells us that he is DIY, a soldier on the front; Sam's knife speaks of an older, archaic or mythic connection to ritual. Together, they represent a lineage of hunters, from knife to gun, from spirit to body. It's a powerful image, and one which rings true three years later.

Before Ruby appears, Sam's Colt is the only known weapon capable of killing demons. Its creator built the devil's trap in Wyoming that keeps Hell at bay, and wrote much of the literature on which the Winchesters depend. Ruby brings with her not only a revitalization for the Colt—and Sam's journey toward manhood, which it signifies—but another, less male weapon. When Tammi stops Sam's bullet in midair, Ruby tries to kill her with the knife, and Dean—perhaps implying his own proximity to and growing connection with the supernatural and the feminine—

takes up the knife and succeeds. Now that Lilith has escaped from Hell and established herself as a major player in the American West, the Colt is no longer as powerful as the men once thought it was. It is natural to assume that the stakes are higher: the Colt took out Azazel, the main antagonist for the show's first two seasons, and yet does nothing against Lilith's handmaiden. The Knife provides a third alternative, and takes center stage as the third season winds toward its conclusion.

As we learn, it's Lilith who controls Dean's contract, and thus his life—and the narrative itself—throughout the third season. A totally male, totally human, hunter weapon like the Colt cannot be expected to hold its own when the universe of the story, and the souls of the boys themselves, are growing so comfortable with the feminine, demonic darkness. By claiming Ruby's demon knife for the final fight, the boys are adding a third object to their arsenal of props—and without even considering whether there will be consequences for claiming and using a demonic weapon.

They've crossed the line into acceptance of their own darkness and complicity with the feminine, come close to accepting Ruby as a member of their coalition, and know that they must combine all the assets at their disposal in order to save Dean's life, and go on fighting. A compromise with darkness, after all, is better than being taken by it utterly. But the irony in any deal with darkness, as we see time and again, is the way in which it carries with it its own derangement. The back-and-forth with Ruby resolves in a terrible betrayal as even she is overtaken by the Lilith demon, and the hounds of Hell carry Dean off to his reward.

V: THE RUNAWAY & THE CROSSROADS

(A boy turns his back on the darkness; he does not see the snake at his feet.)

But if Dean displays all the conventional markers of heroic masculinity—his connection to the father; the Odyssean gift of gab; the ability to make stern and unemotional decisions—where do we find the masculinity in Sam Winchester? He's not a damsel to be rescued, although he is often in need of rescue. He's not identified with the supernatural in the same way as the episode's throwaway female characters. He's definitely male. How best to illustrate, in the mid-2000s, the concept of the spiritual male, as opposed to Dean's physical approach?

Sam's relationship to the supernatural is all-or-nothing, and creeps from the inside. While Dean rejects the monsters on a case-by-case basis, killing them one by one, Sam's first adult decision was to absent himself from the world of darkness altogether. Only threats to his family tempt him to cross the lines again. And once there, almost immediately, he is confronted from within. Sam reveals early in the first season his gift for premonitions, and admits that they began six months prior to the events of the first episode. He shares a kiss with Lori, the repressed girl whose own subconscious content summons the Hook Man—a very important theme for Sam, suggesting that connections to the shadow must be faced and assimilated, lest they control us, or hurt the people around us.

Midway through season one—after once again leaving Dean behind—Sam meets Meg, whose connection to Azazel and Sam will determine the next season and a half. Next, Sam's obsession with saving Dean leads them into a complex ethical situation wherein a faith healer is commanding a bound Grim Reaper. The boys begin to amass knowledge of other children chosen by Azazel, a story to which nearly every plot twist can be traced. Mary and Jessica's deaths and the psychological implications of these for all three Winchester men, Dean's quasi-death and John's sacrifice, Sam's death and rebirth, and Dean's deal with the Crossroads Demon: all arise from Azazel's selection of Sam.

Sam's mental or spiritual powers increase to include telekinesis in this episode, although it only arises from a need to protect Dean. Telekinesis is one of the few classic psionic powers that crosses the boundary from the entirely mental to the entirely physical: in terms of the mind/body dichotomy the boys illustrate, Sam is using his Sam powers to effect a Dean change in the world, linking his passive mental abilities to the kind of physical movement, or violence, in which his brother excels. No wonder it's painful.

Leading up to the first season finale, Sam meets and mourns the lost innocence of a boy in "Something Wicked" (1-18) who—after being used as bait to tempt a demonic witch—will never be able to live ignorantly in a world free of monsters again. The feelings of resentment this provokes lead directly into the next episode, in which the boys finally rejoin their father. John retrieves the Colt, a magical gun and the only weapon known to kill demons, and saves Sam's life, opening the door to their relationship's rehabilitation. They bond over the identical deaths of Mary and Jessica, and the trio finally hit the road together. It's a short ride: by the season finale, Dean has killed Azazel's demon son with the Colt and Sam has shot his possessed father with it, and all three Winchesters end up in critical condition.

John's secret knowledge of Sam's fate—that Azazel's plan for him might necessitate that Dean kill his brother—is revealed halfway through season two, driving a wedge between the brothers just long enough for Sam to meet the next of the Special Children, Ava. Just as Dean was led to reconnect with his hunter family at the Roadhouse in the wake of John's death, this final break and posthumous betrayal by his father leads Sam narratively to his magical family, the putative children of Azazel.

Although Sam seems, in the aftermath of the Devil's Gate, to have lost his powers, his association with the darkness has only increased. Azazel hints to Dean that his brother may not have come back "one hundred percent pure" ("All Hell Breaks Loose (Part 2)," 2-22), and early in the third season a demon refers to Sam as the "Boy King" of the demon armies. He also, most importantly, enters into a relationship with Ruby, a demon—self-described in "Sin City" (3-4) as "the little fallen angel on [his] shoulder." It's a new kind of interaction, in which there are promises made and loyalties presumed, that never could have existed in prior seasons.

Early in season three, we encounter another a client whose uncontrolled subconscious, as with the girl from "Hook Man," threatens to overwhelm everyone around her: a little girl playing out the grimmest of fairy tales. This is an important thematic element for Sam, whose representation as the spiritual half of Everyman brings with it the responsibility not only to confront the darkness, but to master or assimilate it. Unlike Dean, who spends the series fighting demons, Sam is set upon a harder path: to find a way to coexist with darkness itself. The show's curious and sometimes virulent homophobia rears its head momentarily and memorably in this context, as Dean taunts Sam for his knowledge of these tales. Any cultural or folklore expert can tell you that being conversant with fairy tales is not a sign of the mental illness the show makes of homosexuality, but it is a substantial advantage in hunting. The connections Dean seems to draw between femininity, weakness, and homosexuality are essential in his ongoing project to train Sam in masculinity, whether or not those connections are even rational. The manhood game is as much about exclusion of non-masculine qualities as it is about absorbing or performing masculine qualities and acts.

This struggle—Dean versus Sam's alignment with darkness and the feminine—plays out as Dean threatens again and again to kill Ruby, against Sam's protests, and through Sam's near-obsessive need not only to save Dean from his fate but to ease his pain on their travels. Sam's nurturing qualities are both helpful for the boys' survival, and a hindrance in Dean's intention of making sure Sam is strong enough to survive without him. Watching Dean combat his own association with the demonic world for the first time, Sam is pushed into accepting his own implication in the world and systems of the supernatural. As Dean is dreaming of his double, and retrieving his own will to live and escape the demonic deal, Sam dreams only of rescuing Dean. But this struggle is not without consequence: on several season three occasions, even Dean is surprised by Sam's newfound willingness to kill when necessary, even when the perpetrators are all too human. There's a beauty in the irony: Dean is just as offended when Sam becomes "harder"—more masculine, in Dean's construction—as when Sam shows signs of femininity or passivity.

There is also a motif throughout in which Sam requires Dean's grounded presence to keep from being carried off by darkness altogether. Whenever the boys split up, Sam loses his anchor to the real world: he meets Meg, or becomes entangled in the machinations of Azazel. There are also positive benefits to these frequent abductions: it's Sam's kidnapping by the leader of a nonviolent vampire collective that readjusts the boys' attitudes toward the human qualities of some monsters and demons, and also radically affects their view of the fanatical nature of some hunters, including their own father.

Rogue hunter Gordon, a recurring and frightening character, is the villain in the latter episode, and becomes a serious threat in season three, not only tracking the innocent vampire Lucy but working with the mercenary Bela to find Sam, whom he believes is the Antichrist. While the possibility that Gordon is technically right is unquestioned, the experience makes clear the degree to which the boys' approach, methods, and philosophy have diverged from that of the average hunter. While in season one this move might have been unthinkable, the hunters become a neutral element in the story: the boys have been exposed to the human darkness, and the revenge element, implicit in their father's loose army of vigilantes, and eventually find it as questionable and mixed in value as any darkness they've come across. It may be, in fact, that the loss of the hunter as a possible ideal is a contributing factor to the breakdown of Dean's own identity in season three.

(A man and woman, moon overhead, locked in a kiss, each with fingers crossed.)

Which brings us back to the problem of the viewer. As the story of the Winchester boys' compromises with and accommodations of darkness continues, the only element that seems to have taken fans by surprise is the introduction of Bela and Ruby to a cast that has, over the years, contained many female allies and villains. The outcry started before the third season had even begun, with worries that the show was trying to expand its demographic or, worse, introduce permanent love interests for the boys. Bela's initial prowess as a hunter, matching or overwhelming Dean's own, seemed like betrayal. Sam's acceptance of Ruby's ability to come and go as she pleases, and her production of a tool more powerful than the Colt, seemed likewise to dilute his character.

I maintain that this is as a natural outgrowth of the central tension provoked by the series itself, from the first episode: the story takes place in a universe of Otherized and fetishized femininity that surrounds the narrative's all-male viewpoint. If Dean is teaching Sam to be a man, who's teaching Dean? By watching these boys learn and test their own limits, and explain to themselves and each other their own masculinity and traditions, we see a modern portrait of manhood that's been recapitulated a thousand times. Behind Dean's swagger and sexual bravado there lies the implicit accusation that his own learned masculinity comes less from real life experience than from television and movies—and perhaps that's the only answer the modern man could give. But introduce female doubles (who swagger twice as much!) and you've unlocked something that's been brewing in the show since Sam's first premonition: the interpenetration of the male world of the protagonists and the female world in which they live.

As a compromise of the characters themselves and their code of honor, the darker developments of the latter parts of the series are troubling enough—perhaps only acceptable because when one brother is threatened, the other is there to save and comfort him. But once the brothers start taking on and accepting their own magical implications and become more willing to compromise, as a united front, the show itself takes a dramatic turn toward complexity.

The story ceases to be an explication of the boy's journey toward manhood, and starts being a reflection of the human journey toward wholeness. Part of this latter journey expresses itself through the breakdown of male control and power: giving up reliance on absolutes and rigid rules, and on establishing control of the world around us. To stop hunting demons, and start talking to them. In season three, the boys' journey stops being a spectator sport, and the boys themselves stop being so easily objectified. It's hard to stand separate from the story when the story seems so intent on implicating the viewer in its ethical conundrums, and a lot harder to sexualize or fetishize the boys when their hurt/comfort tropes become more thematic than based in a given episode's particulars. The story element that best expresses this relaxed view of the world as black and white is the introduction of characters—not faceless demons or goddesses or dead parents, but identifiable people, in the same age bracket and of the same idealized physical attributes—who know more than the protagonists, or are more powerful than they are. By giving Bela and Ruby existence, and backstory, independent from the Winchester-eye view of the world, the viewer is put into the position of seeing them as more than just symptoms of the landscape: they become true doubles.

And if these new doubles for the Winchesters were male—stronger, better, faster, more ethically variable men or demons—the show would be over. The rules of the Hero's Quest dictate that this is an impossibility. In a show so relentlessly dominated by the feminine yet negotiated entirely by the masculine, the idealized and contradictory mirrors represented by Ruby and Bela must be played by women. And because it's television, they have to be at least as hot, as appealing and intriguing and multifaceted and funny, as the leads themselves. Our hypothetical female or queer fan, already feeling pushed out by the conflicted masculinity and morality of the show's deepening complexity, finds herself pushed even further out by these new arrivals; as companions on the journey, our place has been taken up by these new, powerful characters. Accusations of the "Mary Sue" were flying thick and heavy at both characters before they even debuted on the show proper: a sure sign that the characters were meant to be simultaneously real characters unto themselves, and meant to work as plot elements as well. Identification with the boys, and simultaneous identification with the new girls, results in a viewer paradox: as rivals to the central characters, the girls are to be hated, while as characters in their own right, they are to be respected. What's a viewer to do?

Which is as it should be. Trained as we are, by the nature of the show, to the portrayal of the feminine through the show's monsters—or occasional allies, and often dead ones—we are invited through the girls' relationships with Sam and Dean to confront those aspects of the feminine, the unconscious, and the questionable within ourselves. Queer or straight, male or female, we've spent years learning to read the show, but in order to follow the boys on their season three journey, we are asked to lay down the rigid categories and assumptions that we spent the first two seasons building, in contract with the show itself.

The introduction of these new characters puts the viewer, perhaps for the first time, in the exact same position as the protagonists: mystified by or jealous of the new characters' abilities and knowledge, suspicious of their motives and shifting allegiances, worried by their unseen connections to the larger picture, and tempted by hints at their own rich histories and futures within the universe of the show.

Questioning Ruby and Bela, then, might be the best thing a participating fan could do at this stage of the game: it finally takes us out of the realm of passively watching the Winchesters' journey, and sets us on the road right beside them. Confused, perhaps; definitely looking forward and wondering what happens next; lost in a world where black has begun to bleed into white, and where the knight errant, Dean, is in need of a little rescue himself. And so I think for the first time, maybe, the problematic viewer is able to stand alongside the Winchesters, and see exactly what they see.

JACOB CLIFTON is an Austin novelist and staff writer for the Web site Television Without Pity (www.televisionwithoutpity.com).

Mary Winchester's fiery demise in the opening teaser of Supernatural's *pilot episode is surely one of the most shocking and most memorable images not only of the series, but of recent television in general. This one event informs the entire show, as well as the actions of the main protagonists—Sam and Dean would not be the men they are without Mary's death and John's obsession to "find the thing that killed her."*

So in a show based ostensibly on myth and folklore, does the image of "Mom on fire on the ceiling" demonstrate Supernatural's *attempt to create its own unique American mythology out of the old and the familiar? Carol Poole investigates.*

CAROL POOLE

Who Threw Momma on the Ceiling?

Analyzing *Supernatural*'s Primal Scene of Trauma

Here is how the series *Supernatural* begins, with its own origin myth. It's a dark night, late autumn. A big, comfortable-looking house doesn't seem to know it's being stroked by spooky shadows of bare tree limbs. Inside the house we see a young family just brimming with its own goodness and naïveté. Mom, Dad, and four-year-old Dean are saying good night to baby Sam in his crib.

Already the show has begun to use one of its favorite tricks: studding each scene with pop-culture references. Sam's bedroom is a stock set of the genre, the scary nursery where the mobile spins for no apparent reason while the music slides off key. *Supernatural*'s opening scenes are so saturated with familiar tropes that one doesn't expect to see anything exactly new here. But maybe we don't care. Such scenes draw audiences again and again, if only because, as Sigmund Freud discovered, people have a way of needing to repeat certain experiences endlessly. *Supernatural* winks at the viewer with knowing references that say *we have all been here before*, while at the same time asking us to care as much as ever.

When the foreshadowed bad thing happens it's as scary as you'd expect, but there *is* something new about it. In the dark nursery room, just above Sam's crib, Mom is splayed across the ceiling. Victim of a gravity-defying demon, she grimaces in terror while blood drips from a gash in her abdomen. A few moments later she bursts into flame. The fire burns into the viewer's retinas this horrific view of her—hair swirling, one leg bent to the side in a grotesque parody of a cheerleader's kick—then consumes the house, leaving the Winchester males homeless and emotionally scarred.

As far as I know, this is a new image in American pop culture: a wounded mother burning to death on her baby's nursery ceiling. Eric Kripke, the show's thirty-four-year-old creator, has said that "Mom on fire on the ceiling" was "the start of it all,"[1] the first image he had in mind when he began to develop the series.

But what might it mean? This is the question I want to explore here, using depth psychology to try to understand more than one layer of meaning. I want to look at how "Mom on fire on the ceiling" resonates as an image of soul trauma. Within the plot, their mother's death is the catalyzing event that sets Sam and Dean off on their scary yet meaningful quest for redemption. But it can also be seen as a key to the show's artistic ambition, which I think is to make myths that are uniquely American and newly imagined.

Of course, one could argue that "Mom on fire on the ceiling" is just the obligatory gross-out scene every horror show needs. Like Regan's 360-degree head spin in *The Exorcist*, the scene aims to shock.

But gore is just one side of *Supernatural*, which has three-dimensional characters we're meant to care about and features big moral themes like death and redemption. Emotionally, the show has as wide a range as any serious drama, from rage to humor to love, loss, and forgiveness. It also has a meta-narrative, with its continual pop culture references and in-jokes.

What sets *Supernatural* apart from a lot of genre fiction on TV is the

[1] DVD commentary, "Pilot" (1-1).

way it plays with different layers of story and source material. Its sources are an eclectic mix of pop culture, history, folklore, and urban legends—the flotsam you might find in any teenager's mind, or your own. In a way that seems at once ironic and heartfelt, *Supernatural* creates a specifically American mythology out of this stuff littering our mental attic. Kripke names such influences as Neil Gaiman's *American Gods* and Joseph Campbell's *The Hero's Journey*[2]—serious mythologists, both, suggesting that Kripke has ambitions as a myth maker himself.

If so, "Mom on Fire on the Ceiling" appears to be the core, origin scene in the myth Kripke set out to create in *Supernatural*. It's a powerful, disturbing image worth taking a closer look at.

A NOTE ABOUT MYTH AND PSYCHOLOGY

The study of myth has been important to psychology ever since Freud pondered Oedipus's unhappy family life. More recently, Jungian analyst James Hillman is one of the better-known proponents of using myth to illuminate psychology. He defines myth as traditional stories which help us understand our lives, making meaning out of our experiences in a poetic, dreamlike way that feeds the soul:

> *Myths talk to psyche in its own language; they speak emotionally, dramatically, sensuously, fantastically. . . . One beauty of mythic metaphors is that they elude literalism. We know at the outset that they are impossible truths. Like metaphor itself, the power of which cannot satisfactorily be explained, a myth also speaks with two tongues at one time, amusing and terrifying, serious and ironic.*[3]

Maybe this is why, while the dramas on television can be irritatingly superficial and sensationalistic, some of the most searching truth-and-beauty meditations on TV can be found in ironic genre shows like *Buffy*,

---

[2] Boris, Cynthia. "Eric Kripke: Satan's Head Writer." *TV of the Absurd*. 25 July 2008. <tvoftheabsurd.com>

[3] Hillman, James. *Re-Visioning Psychology*. New York: HarperPerennial, 1975. pp. 154–155.

Battlestar Galactica, and *Supernatural*. Outlandish, impossible images talk to us in the language of dreams, while literal shows about "reality" such as *ER* or the endless crime-fighting dramas often seem psychologically implausible.

In this spirit, I don't aim to explain in rational terms why "Mom on fire on the ceiling" has such impact, but do hope to explore at least some of its resonance, both in terms of its impact as a formative event in Sam and Dean's story, and as a defining image of *Supernatural*'s world—and, maybe, the viewers' world as well.

"Mom on Fire on the Ceiling"—A View from the Crib

If like me you're a woman and apt to identify with women you see onscreen, your first thought about Mary Winchester's death might be simply, "Ow." Your second might be, "Why should I watch this kind of sadistic, misogynistic crap?" Within the campy yet scary world of a show that speaks with two tongues, it's hard to know how to feel when the family's only female member makes such a horrifying final exit in Scene One. But for the sake of understanding the attraction of this intense imagery, let's just stipulate that Mom is clearly not a subject of her own experience in this story; her role here is to be the object of other people's feelings. Mary is Mom, the most important person in a baby's world, and when she dies her baby's world comes crashing down in flames.

The view from Sam's crib is a scene of overwhelming horror. From the ceiling, Mom can no longer hold him or offer him any kind of safety or comfort. In the scenes leading up to her death, Mary appeared as a likeable, down-to-earth woman who would be more at home in *Dawson's Creek* than in *Rosemary's Baby*. But on the ceiling, she's no longer down-to-earth; the laws of gravity no longer hold her, and her face is a mask of panic. She seems out of her mind. The wound in her belly suggests that her very ability to carry and nurture life is what the demon is out to destroy.

This imagery is all the more potent in light of developmental psychology, which tells us that at Sam's age his mother plays a key role in his psychological development. In recent decades, psychological research has confirmed that there is something very powerful and awe-inspiring about the relationships between babies and the people who mother them. Human minds and nervous systems develop through closely attuned, comforting yet stimulating relationships.[4,5] In order to develop normal emotional and psychological capacities, in fact in order to survive at all, babies need to be held, played with, soothed, and talked to as much as they need to be fed.[6] Psychoanalyst Thomas Ogden has described this life-giving early relationship with mother as "the matrix"—mother—"of the mind."[7]

It seems that something very important is being attacked in this nursery. By destroying his mother and his home, the demon takes away from Sam the sustaining matrix of emotional safety he needs in order to develop a mind and a sane, ordinary sense of self. Of course, Sam has a father, too, but in the Winchester family Mom is obviously the one who provides primary emotional safety. While Dad snoozes in front of the TV, Mom is alert to Sam's cry in the night. As the story goes on it soon becomes clear that John Winchester is a difficult dad, at least after Mary's death. He's deeply attached to his sons, but his obsession with demons makes him more scary than nurturing. Sam's mother and his home both seem to represent the life-giving qualities of safety and nurturance. Without them, he grows up in a world of demons and ghosts.

One of *Supernatural*'s ongoing themes hints at a dark connection between the demon and Sam. The Yellow-Eyed Demon, we eventually learn, kills Sam's mother in an effort to redirect Sam's development, to make him special and superhumanly powerful, and also to warp his morality, to turn him toward the demonic side.

The imagery in this scene provides some hints toward the demon's motivation. The fire that consumes her suggests fiery feelings. The demon seems offended, enraged even, by the thought that Sam might be

---

[4] Stern, Daniel. *The Interpersonal World of the Infant: A View from Psychoanalysis & Developmental Psychology*. New York: Basic Books, 1985/2000.

[5] Schore, Alan. *Affect Regulation and the Repair of the Self*. New York: W.W. Norton and Co., 2003.

[6] Mitchell, Stephen A. and Black, Margaret J. *Freud and Beyond: A History of Modern Psychoanalytic Thought*. New York: Basic Books, 1995. p. 38.

[7] Ogden, Thomas. *The Matrix of the Mind: Object Relations and the Psychoanalytic Dialogue*. Northvale, NJ/London: Jason Aronson, Inc., 1986.

an ordinary baby who will grow up to be an ordinary person. Ordinary babies need mothering, and will die without it. Some psychoanalytic thinkers believe that we are all apt to feel rage about this dependence, so that our love for our mothers naturally has to contend with unconscious feelings of rage and hate about our human limitations and needs. According to this line of thought, there's a part of each of us that wishes to be a superhero instead of an ordinary, vulnerable person who can suffer and cause suffering to those we need and love.

Whether or not this is true about people in general, I think it is true of the Winchesters, who can never seem to need a woman without setting off terrible consequences. A world where Mom burns on the ceiling is a world where we can expect to find mother issues.

Brave Little Soldiers: Sam and Dean as Motherless Heroes

Sam and Dean's story resumes twenty-two years after the fire. We learn that their mother was never replaced, nor was their home. Instead John raised the boys on the run as demon hunters, seeking revenge on the demon that killed their mother. Sam has rebelled by opting for a conventional life—he has a girlfriend, he's applied to law school. But nothing about the fire has been resolved, and Sam soon learns that he can't escape its ramifications.

Like Luke Skywalker—another hero inspired by Joseph Campell's understanding of hero myths—Sam and Dean are propelled into heroism by losing their mother and home in a traumatic way. Maybe part of what makes them heroes is that they survive losses which ordinary humans can't endure. And as Americans, they're heirs to a tradition of John Wayne–style heroes for whom "masculine" is just another word for "independent." After all, this nation began in war with its mother country, and in Sam and Dean's world, *someone* is making war on Mom.

In the pilot episode, it soon becomes uncomfortably clear that Mom on fire on the ceiling is not only felt to be a trauma, it also represents freedom from the tyranny of needing Mom. Sam's not a baby anymore, he's a young man, but questions about needing Mom can bubble up out of nowhere when a boy is in mid-transition to manhood. Does Mom make a young man strong, or weak? Does he need her, or is he supposed to be the strong one who protects her? Is she an angel offering solace and love, or a demon threatening to weaken and emasculate him by making him endlessly dependent on her instead of allowing him to become strong in his own right? What place does femininity have in a man's psyche, anyway?

It's all very confusing, and so is the scariest, darkest question of all: can he survive without her? The pilot episode of *Supernatural* poses this question sharply when Sam asks his girlfriend, Jessica—who strongly resembles Mary Winchester—"What would I do without you?" She smiles and says, "Crash and burn."

But Sam's big brother Dean shows up in his black '67 Chevy Impala, like a ghost from Sam's demon-ridden past, and soon they're riding off to find their father, who has gone missing. An AC/DC song blasts on the car's antiquated stereo system:

> *Let loose*
> *From the noose*

Before the pilot is over, it is Jessica who has crashed and burned, on the ceiling—killed in exactly the same way as Mary. But this time it's not a baby's mother who is killed, it's a young man's future wife, a woman who represents stability and responsibility and belonging in a world of law and order, a world where things make sense.

Jessica's death throws Sam back into the arms of the person who really became his mother after the fire: big brother Dean. Like their father, Dean is a misfit in the mainstream world, a "hunter" who fights dangers most people don't know exist. He likes beer, girls, and his Impala, and the vintage cheese rock he plays on the car stereo like the soundtrack to his soul—equal parts tough-guy stoicism and soppy sincerity, with a saving edge of humor. Dean is the kind of guy who can bully and charm you into admitting that you secretly love Journey, too.

Honestly, it's Dean who charmed me into liking *Supernatural*. I didn't want to; feminism is close to my heart, and there is no way to construe this as a feminist show (though you could argue that some of its female characters have a post-feminist flair). It's a story where the heroes belong to one demographic—pale, young, and male—and the rest of us have to be content with identifying with characters who generally die or turn evil.

But then there's Dean, a wisecracking, soulful dude who just wants to save the American soul from all the demons and ghosts that populate its nightmares and haunt its folklore. He's *funny*, and genuinely touching. Who wouldn't rather ride off with him than go to law school?

In fact, while Sam and Dean are on the run from their losses, and don't seem ready for relationships with women, they do make a family with each other. Traveling the country in Dean's Impala, working together to protect people from demons, the brothers develop a relationship that survives every test. They save each other's lives again and again. They even survive their constant bickering and the strain of their endless road trip's logistics, the shared motel rooms and hours in the car.

What's great about these two is the way they're searching to heal themselves and each other by developing what every girl or woman watching this show knows they need: to reintegrate the sanity represented by Mom and home back into their damaged lives, without losing their independence in the process. I might go out on a limb and say they need to resurrect the nurturing feminine wisdom in their own souls. They live in a world of monsters, haunted by old traumas, but in their relationship with each other they keep trying to learn how to live with their own demons with tolerance, and even humor. I would say "love," but I think it's important for Sam and Dean to have their own way of saying that dangerously comforting word:

> SAM: Jerk.
> DEAN: Bitch. ("Pilot")

HUNTING: *SUPERNATURAL*'S QUEST FOR A NEW AMERICAN MYTHOLOGY

"Mom on fire on the ceiling" is the disaster that propels the Winchester brothers out of a conventional life. This event sets their story in a post-traumatic world, haunted by stories that need resolution. But their world is also a postmodern one, because their story is set in an America of immigrants and survivors, people whose Old Country traditions have been lost or fragmented by displacement to the New World where the old hierarchies and value systems have been thrown drastically into question. Instead of a unified religious or folkloric tradition, the Winchesters' America is a place where feelings and meanings, deep and shallow, wander around all lost and overlooked, waiting for someone to notice them and put them either to rest or together. Here, Sam and Dean's trauma seems like everyone's. A nation that began in war with its mother country is haunted by the same intensities of rage and need, and the same ambivalence about need versus independence.

In this postmodern landscape, Sam and Dean fit right in. As characters, each of them is a collage of pop-culture references. Eric Kripke has said that *Supernatural* was conceived as *Star Wars* meets *Route 66*, and has also cited the 1950s TV Western series *Have Gun, Will Travel* as an influence.[8] I've described it myself as "Kind of like *X-Files* meets *The Hardy Boys*, except darker." It's impossible to watch a single episode of this show without being reminded of all of the above, plus *Ghostbusters* and *Men in Black*. It's quite a canon.

Then there are the show's historical references. The name "Winchester" is a blatant nod to the Wild West era.[9] If Sam and Dean are postmodern knights on a quest for justice and redemption—or at least a so-called life—their Excalibur is a magical Colt revolver. They have a special relationship with guns and gun symbolism which sometimes seems glossed-over and troubling. Let's not forget that the "demons" killed by actual Colts and Winchesters in the nineteenth century included Native Americans demonized by the settlers who shot them. The show hasn't yet addressed this kind of historical complication in its gun imagery, but it does have a way of lurching unevenly sometimes between light camp and heavy heart-of-darkness violence. (How were viewers supposed to feel when, in "Heart"(2-17), Sam shot his new girlfriend to death?)

The heaviest episodes show Sam and Dean longing to know that they're good, but wrestling with their power to do harm. Even in the

[8] DVD commentary, "Pilot."

[9] A true story, worthy of being made into a *Supernatural* episode: an heiress of the Winchester rifle fortune was a believer in the occult who was terrified she'd be haunted by the ghosts of everyone killed by a Winchester rifle. The Winchester Mystery House in San Jose, California, is a monument to her superstition.

tongue-in-cheek mode of *Supernatural*, it's painfully confusing to try to be good men in a world of violence, in a country that was "won" at the end of a rifle. As demon hunters, Sam and Dean struggle to figure out where the line is between being warriors—protectors—and thugs, an anxiety highlighted when Bela accused Dean in "Red Sky at Morning" (3-6), "You're a stone's throw from being a serial killer." The difference is not always clear. As Dean put it in "Wendigo" (1-2),

> I mean, our family's so screwed to hell, maybe we can help some others. Makes things a little bit more bearable. (long pause) And I tell you what else helps. Killing as many evil sons-of-bitches as I possibly can.

I think this question—"Are we good guys or bad guys?"—is at the heart of the show. *Supernatural* is a story about two American men in search of redemption from pain and destruction, trying to learn how to be strong, how to survive, but also how to use their power for good. But what is good? Is it just the opposite of evil? *Supernatural* explodes that simple notion through the character of Gordon, the demon-hunter whose worldview is dangerously two-dimensional. Gordon's self-righteous loathing of demons makes him the moral equivalent of a demon himself—sadistic and murderous, unwilling to think about what he's doing. He lacks empathy.

Supernatural seems to understand the appeal of this kind of thinking. It's not so different from the fantasy that a magical revolver can kill any enemy. In this fantasy, men don't need the feminine trait of receptivity; they can just point a projectile and make the Other disappear. But this isn't the only fantasy being acted out in *Supernatural*. There are also fantasies about containing demons in magic circles, and putting ghosts to rest by learning about them. The way Sam and Dean put ghosts to rest is to bring new understanding to the traumas of the past, find out where the bones are buried, and cleanse them with salt and fire. There's also a kind of cleansing that happens when the brothers restore meaning to a ghost's disrupted story. Unlike Gordon, the Winchester brothers are on a quest to repair and resurrect life, love, and meaning—which seems to parallel the show's quest to resurrect and restore meaning to cherished but neglected bits of America's mythology. When *Supernatural* resurrects historical figures such as H. H. Holmes, the serial killer who plagued the Chicago World's Fair in 1893 ("No Exit," 2-6), or puts a sinister twist on Scandinavian tree folklore ("Scarecrow," 1-10), it piques the viewer's desire to know more about our history and the beliefs that have shaped it. In other words, the show appeals not only to our desire to kill what we fear; it also invites us to try to understand.

CONCLUSION: YES, CHICK-FLICK MOMENTS

Why don't I just come out and say it: Beneath Sam and Dean's macho exteriors are two young men trying to heal from the traumatic loss of their mother, which also seems to mirror America's traumatic loss of the coherent, stable mythologies of our mother countries. Dean in particular seems to take on some of the functions of mothering even while he struggles to find himself as a man. If Sam is in some ways the eternal baby of the pair—endangered, but also endowed with scary potential and unknown powers—Dean is how the baby gets by without a mother, the baby's ersatz protector. Eric Kripke has called Dean the Han Solo to Sam's Luke Skywalker.[10] He's the one who provides the closest thing the brothers have to a home—his car—and an ambience—his music. The box of cassettes in his car is garage-sale junk from the '70s and '80s—AC/DC, BTO, Creedence Clearwater Revival—but Dean loves the stuff, without irony or apology.

Which is basically what *Supernatural* does with neglected scraps of American folklore: "Bloody Mary" in the mirror, the "Woman in White" legend, the mysterious disappearance of the Roanoke colony. *Supernatural* isn't interested in historical authenticity; anyone who wants to know what "Croatoan" means to historians had better look elsewhere. Instead, it weaves new stories out of bits of old, semi-forgotten ones, raising a puzzling question: Is *Supernatural*'s postmodern pop sensibility a demonic force dismembering traditional stories into mixed-up fragments? Sometimes, yes. In "Wendigo" (1-2), for example, we are asked to accept what is obviously Pacific Northwest coastal rainforest as

[10] DVD commentary, "Pilot."

a scene in the Rocky Mountains, a demonic abuse of America's regional integrity. If our history is worth learning, so is our geography. Still, for the most part *Supernatural*'s way of mixing and matching recycled cultural references seems creative, a way of bringing new life and meaning to older traditions.

Stories can do for a culture what a mother can do for a baby: They hold us, and help us develop our minds and souls. They help us link our own experiences with larger meanings, and work through personal and collective traumas. So I enjoy *Supernatural*'s attempts to find storylines in the back roads of American myth and legend and pop culture. It's as though the show were speaking to the viewer in Dean's voice, saying, "Okay, we Americans are kind of shell shocked and lost, we have no sense of history, and we don't understand where anything or anyone comes from or belongs. All we know is that some things out there can hurt us—and have hurt us—and we can hurt them, and what does that make us? But what the hell. We can try to put something together; we have to start somewhere."

CAROL POOLE, MA, is a psychotherapist practicing in Seattle. She is a graduate of Pacifica Graduate Institute in Carpinteria, California, with a strong interest in the conjunction of psychology, mythology, and pop culture. She is a member of the Northwest Alliance for Psychoanalytic Study and a frequent contributor to its literary publication, *The Forum*.

As Supernatural *blurs the lines between fantasy and reality, creating a realistic world inhabited by fantastic creatures, its characters themselves must by necessity also live outside of the "normal." Sam and Dean Winchester are anti-heroes who get by on hustling pool and credit card fraud, who are wanted by the police, and who don't "live regular." In response to this transgression of society's norms,* Supernatural's *fans have embraced the concept of transgression, and the freedoms offered by the show's lack of boundaries, as well—specifically, in fanworks. Emily Turner examines the phenomena of Wincest, crackfic, and genderswap fanfiction, and how these stories themselves transgress the boundaries of the* Supernatural *universe, and our own.*

EMILY TURNER

Scary Just Got Sexy

Transgression in *Supernatural* and Its Fanfiction

Supernatural is a text packed full of themes of transgression. That is to say, to "transgress" is to go beyond a boundary or limit, those boundaries and limits often pre-set or prescribed. In the case of *Supernatural*, two core examples of transgression occur both within the plots and premise of the show—the boundaries of reality as we (the viewer) know it are transgressed by the existence and behavior of supernatural elements (ghosts, cryptids, demons)—and at a meta-textual level—both the creators and characters refer to outside films, shows, comics, and other texts, transgressing the boundaries of *Supernatural* as a discrete text itself. The themes of transgression trickle down into countless aspects of the show, both trivial and key to narrative. Sam and Dean transgress the boundaries of their own society to live as nomads and work the system with their fake IDs and lack of permanent address. They transgress the boundaries of life and death by repeatedly dying and bringing each other back to life, even as demons and spirits transgress boundaries of human bodies to possess victims.

Each week Sam and Dean drive in their big black muscle car from text to text, transgressing boundaries of state lines and city limits to enter into existing worlds drawn from everything from folktales to popular culture: *The Ring* ("Bloody Mary," 1-5), an *X-Files* episode ("Tall Tales," 2-15), *The Blair Witch Project* ("Ghostfacers," 3-13). In solving the mysteries and vanquishing the villains, often in ways different than in the text that is being appropriated or referenced, Sam and Dean reread and rewrite existing stories and characters. At the same time, Eric Kripke and the rest of the production team are doing the same as they write these scripts and set up these shots. This blatant celebration and transformation of the countless other horror texts being appropriated is not that different from fans' transgression of *Supernatural*'s boundaries as a TV show—a legitimate cultural text (aired on network television, made by professional and paid staff)—as they appropriate the *Supernatural* world and rewrite and recreate its existing stories and characters.

This is particularly true of the group of fans who engage with the show by producing fanworks such as fanfiction, fanart, and songvids. Just as not only the construction but the content of *Supernatural* reflect themes of transgression, so too do these fanworks explore transgression not only in their creation but in their plots and premises, as the themes and practices of the show sift down into the fan communities. But unlike the show itself, which exists within the restrictive ideological requirements that come along with being produced by an industry for the commercialized mainstream, *Supernatural* fans are free to explore and express creative responses to *Supernatural* any way they wish, able to publish them freely with no editorial requirement beyond access to the Internet and skill to use it. Writers of fanfiction may construct any scenario they wish for the characters to exist within, the only guidelines the community standards of characterization and effective suspension of disbelief—guidelines that are not enforced, and remain up to each individual reader.

With *Supernatural*, the suspension of disbelief guideline leaves lots of room for fans to move. In a 'verse where supernatural occurrences are a given, fanfiction that explores narratives beyond the boundaries of our reality doesn't seem too far-fetched. In *Supernatural*, the boundaries between "life" and "death" are transgressed by both ghosts and Lazarus-like revival (and let's not forget the zombies); psychic characters can "see" through the boundaries of time into the future, or transgress another character's mental boundaries to read or control their thoughts; and as mentioned above, even physical boundaries are transgressed—the boundaries of human bodies crossed or broken by the demons possessing them—and societal boundaries also in the Winchesters' frequent subversions of the law. What we think of as "reality," fantasy, and fiction are thrown together rather than delineated as separate.

In *Supernatural* fanfiction, fan writers also construct narratives of transgression both societal and metaphysical. A considerable amount of *Supernatural* fanfiction is classified as "Wincest"—the vernacular term for slash between members of the Winchester family (Sam, Dean, and John). "Slash" is fanfiction (or other fanworks) that posits two characters of the same gender in a romantic or sexual relationship (the name "slash" is derived from the virgule that joins the names in the pairing). In the case of the *Supernatural* fandom, this is predominantly Sam/Dean fanfiction, and of a huge volume; according to the research conducted by one fan recording and analyzing the stories posted through the daily newsletter, the fanfiction in editions 1 through 600 was almost 40 percent Wincest; 37 percent was "gen" (general, non-sexual or romantic stories), approximately 15 percent was "het" (stories with male/female romantic or sexual relationships), and the rest of the pie went to miscellaneous other categories.[1]

Obviously, the theme of transgression in Wincest is more explicitly related to the transgression of the boundaries of societal prohibition and taboo—namely, incest. Although the scenario of incest would never occur in the show itself due to its context as a mainstream media text (the same context that restricts it from making the two lead characters queer, related or not), *Supernatural* itself does not necessarily negate the possibility of a homoerotic interpretation. Homoerotic subtext between characters in mainstream texts has long been identified as an inspiration for writing slash about characters. Pairs—often professional partners—

[1] See the Supernatural Fic Link Archive page on the SupernaturalWiki for more information on this research: http://supernaturalwiki.com/index.php?title=Supernatural_Fic_Link_Archive.

in buddy movies have always provided especially rich fodder (these days, some movies are even playing up this homoeroticism, sharing with the audience their awareness of it, such as in 2007 British action comedy *Hot Fuzz*), and Sam and Dean's partnership in *Supernatural* is frequently reminiscent of such "buddy pairs." In these traditional partnership models, slashers reread moments of intense emotional connection into somewhat fleeting instances of eye contact, loaded dialogue, or physical connection between male characters who are restricted by social mores from expressing their affection more openly.

In *Supernatural*, however, the two male protagonists—Sam and Dean—are already coded within the text as being in a loving (if fraternal) relationship. The fact that they are brothers allows a freedom to engage in and display both emotional and physical intimacy with each other that is prohibited in non-related pairs. Their mutual devotion is constantly reiterated via both their dialogue and their emotional behavior (embracing in times of stress as in "Mystery Spot," fighting and reconciling with strong emotional language, discussing their emotional need for each other—albeit in often stunted ways, as in "Shadow" [1-16]). It's hardly a stretch to read the characters of Sam and Dean in *Supernatural* as lovers *instead of* brothers—something that occurs even within the text (they are mistaken for a gay couple in both "Playthings" [2-11] and "Something Wicked" [1-18]) suggesting that their fraternal connection displaces the homoeroticism of Sam and Dean's relationship onto a more platonic level where the "romance" is merely symbolic, excusing any infringement on the boundaries of hetero-centric mainstream media heroes.

In Sam/Dean slash fanfiction, however, it's rare that the author will subvert the transgression of incest by creating an alternate universe for their story wherein Sam and Dean are not related. On the contrary: Wincest seems to revel in the transgression of that particular taboo. Often, the problematizing of Sam and Dean's relationship through incest is re-appropriated by slashers as a site of pleasure. The illicitness of an incestuous relationship between Sam and Dean may be lingered on by the style of the story, where the language lovingly emphasizes the familial bond in moments of romantic intimacy, indicating the pleasure taken in it for the author and/or reader, or indeed may be elaborated on within the story by the characters themselves. Wincest stories often take their transgressive cues from the text itself; often when Sam and Dean are seducing each other in Wincest stories, the more reluctant of the two is convinced to engage in the relationship when the other reiterates that they are already outsiders in society, already isolated from the "normality" of their world—why should the prohibition of incest stand in their way when they have already broken so many other laws?

Whereas the incest element of Wincest is by default challenging societal boundaries, a different form—often more symbolic—of exploring transgression can be found in fanfiction narratives belonging to a genre called "crackfic." Crackfic is classified by its premise, which generally breaks from the accepted reality of the original text, often in an absurd or supernatural[2] sense. (The word "crack" here has dual meaning: you'd have to be high—on crack—to write it; and reading it is, like crack, addictive.) Some crackfic scenarios include characters transforming into animals, swapping bodies, swapping gender, swapping consciousnesses with inanimate objects, becoming inanimate objects, de-aging rapidly (from twenty-six to six in the space of seconds), and traveling through time (to name just a small handful). Crackfic often literalizes themes of transgression—bodies transforming, the metaphysical borders of "reality" being crossed—themes which, we know well, are not so ridiculous within the *Supernatural* 'verse. The reality of *Supernatural*'s world permits these crackfic scenarios to occur without diverging much from what could conceivably occur within the original. The result is a proliferation of fanworks that explore narratives of transgression as fans play with the permissibility of *Supernatural*'s supernatural world.

As with Wincest, the outcomes of these transgressive narratives—the stories themselves, the issues they raise and explore—are varied; just as the fan has freedom to transgress the boundaries of reality with the premise of the story, so too are they free to either transgress or adhere to the societal and often ideological boundaries placed on the original text. In terms of Wincest, fans are transgressing boundaries that relate to the portrayal (or lack thereof) of queerness in mainstream media, and soci-

[2] "Supernatural" in that it breaks from the accepted reality of the original text, a reality often similar to our own. In the case of *Supernatural* crackfic, these classifications are somewhat looser (as discussed below).

etal boundaries that posit incest as taboo. In the type of crackfic known as "genderswap," fans explore the boundaries of "gender"—what it means; what maleness, femaleness, masculinity, and femininity are, and just how rigid those classifications are when it comes to portrayal of gender in mainstream television. No doubt elsewhere in this book authors are unpacking the problematic representations of gender and other topics in *Supernatural* through close textual analysis. Through constructing transgressive narratives, fans often engage in close textual analyses of their own, taking advantage of the permissiveness of the transgressive themes of the show to further traverse and explore gender boundaries. Sometimes fans use these opportunities to challenge the problematic representations, sometimes there is no challenge at all, and sometimes the representations are problematized in an entirely different way.

Genderswap is a term that describes the premise of its genre—in genderswap stories, the gender (or, more accurately, physical sex) of a character is spontaneously "swapped." Writing in the *Supernatural* world means that generally, all manner of premise that would usually be considered "crackfic" in other fandoms is par for the course. Within the first season of *Supernatural* alone, the text explores scenarios wherein characters have psychic abilities ("Home" [1-9], "Nightmare" [1-14]), divine beings animate corporeal bodies ("Scarecrow" [1-11]), villains physically mimic characters' bodies á la *Invasion of the Body Snatchers* ("Skin" [1-6],), characters (and inanimate objects) are possessed and animated by malevolent spirits ("Home," "Asylum" [1-10], "Devil's Trap" [1-22]), and all manner of urban legend, folklore, and supernatural creature are (if not encountered) discussed as being assumed to exist. Any of these could provide a valid explanation for a character to appear female despite being male, or vice versa. Twice, in fact, they have. Sam was once temporarily possessed by the female demon Meg ("Born Under a Bad Sign" [2-14]), and shapeshifters have taken on the form of both men and women ("Skin," "Nightshifter" [2-12]). That said, *Supernatural* continues to conform to the societal prescribed by its context. In other words, whereas it's more likely that Dean could end up in a situation where his anatomy spontaneously turns female on our screens some Thursday night than the same could happen on, say *Grey's Anatomy*, the context of *Supernatural* as a show that airs on a mainstream network in mainstream culture means that this kind of challenge to gendered norms via the bodies of its heroes is unlikely.

But just because a text's premise is based on a transgression does not necessarily mean that its theme of transgression extends to all its aspects. Genderswap fantexts have the *potential* to address issues of gender in mainstream culture head on by portraying gender in a way that challenges mainstream representation, but this is not a given. Genderswap fantexts have the option of not stepping very far (or at all) outside of the "boundaries" that construct gender in mainstream media and therefore the original text around which the fandom is based (*Supernatural*, in this case). It is impossible to make blanket generalizations as to whether fanworks challenge or adhere to prescribed mainstream ideologies, just as we cannot make blanket generalizations about, for example, the portrayal of gender in the medium of television, but rather must analyze *Buffy the Vampire Slayer* and *Heroes* as separate texts. The exploration of the themes of transgression in fanworks lies in a close reading of each individual fantext.

Supernatural fandom's genderswap fanfiction includes a diverse range of gender representation. Though it could be argued that the premise of genderswap alone undermines norms of gender and masculinity established by mainstream culture by at a base level constructing it as changeable, often genderswap fanfiction doesn't explore the transgressiveness of the situation beyond a change of anatomy. In a story wherein Sam suddenly switches biological sex, for example, he may subsequently undergo a change in mannerisms, interests, and sexuality. His emotional state becomes more fragile, he suddenly wants to go shopping for makeup and frilly underwear, and he is abruptly attracted to men (whereas, in a male body, he was attracted to women). This scenario, while playing with the permissibility of transgress-able physical boundaries of reality, simply adheres to the mainstream ideal that sex and gender (and sexuality) are synonymous—that having a vagina and breasts is what makes you like the color pink, shopping, and boys. While this can make entertaining reading due to the comedy that results, the transgressive nature of the story does not stray into that of the social construct of sexuality and gender.

Other genderswap stories similarly transgress on biology, but not on mainstream physical representations of gender. For example, instead of a mere change of anatomy, sometimes when changing sex Sam and Dean also become shorter (as if there are not women in the world as tall as Jensen Ackles or even Jared Padalecki), their hair spontaneously lengthens, and their body mass becomes more "petite." Such representations don't stray very far from the very narrow representation of body types in mainstream culture when it comes to women—representations that bear very little resemblance to the diversity of bodies in reality, which include those that are tall, fat, butch, and so on. Again, however, although these examples are not uncommon in *Supernatural* genderswap fanfiction, each text must be examined individually. For example, some stories may portray the above scenarios guilelessly, whereas others may deliberately construct such a situation not necessarily to adhere to but rather to draw attention to these prescribed representations of gender, engaging with *Supernatural* in a more ironic (but no less affectionate) way.

More sober challenges to the representation of gender in mainstream media (and of course, *Supernatural* specifically) occur in genderswap stories where the sudden change of anatomy is one that throws the character's world into chaos. A change of sex leaves the character experiencing a crisis of self, suddenly faced with the anxiety of possessing a body physically alien to him, not to mention one with existing (problematic) societal ideals inscribed upon it. In stories such as this, the author is able to address the very real boundaries of gender experienced by real people: how female bodies (and those women inhabiting them) are treated by the society they exist within, and how the representation of gender in mainstream cultural texts—that we see on our televisions every day—differs from the way gender exists in reality. These kinds of fantexts don't necessarily engage with the humor of such an absurd situation (as is largely typical of the crackfic genre in other fandoms); rather, in the *Supernatural* fandom, crackfic takes advantage of the show's permissibility to undertake extreme plot devices in a way that challenges the problematic ideas perpetuated by show as a mainstream text.

Some genderswap fanfiction in *Supernatural* fandom addresses similar issues without taking such a dystopian slant on the society it is critiquing. For example, the anatomical change from male to female may occur, but without any accompanying changes in personality or appearance. Dean may now have female sex organs, but he is still about six foot tall, bow-legged, short-haired, and attracted to women. These kinds of scenarios, rather than drawing attention to the fundamentally problematic nature of gender representation (as with the scenarios above), instead serve as kind of a celebration of transgression, a demonstration of how transgressing boundaries of gender (and indeed sexuality) is not as taboo or impossible as mainstream media seems to make it out to be.

To return again to discussing *Supernatural*'s themes of transgression at a meta-textual level (through its intertextuality and appropriation of other mainstream media texts), arguably fans who write both genderswap and Wincest (and other fanfiction that doesn't fit in these categories) are transgressing boundaries at a meta-textual level also, beyond a simple re-appropriation of the original text of *Supernatural*. In participating in these fan communities that create and consume fanworks, fans transgress boundaries at the level of construction and consumption—they both write and read *Supernatural* fanworks, occupying the triple role of consumer of *Supernatural*, creator of *Supernatural* fanworks, and consumer of *Supernatural* fanworks. Often this complex relationship between fan and text extends even to fans being creators of fanworks *for Supernatural* fanworks. The fanworks themselves have traversable boundaries; in responding to these stories fans may choose to write more fanfiction set in its 'verse, proliferating the transgression of these textual boundaries. Gender, too, comes into play in the creation and consumption of fanworks; in writing *Supernatural* fanfiction, women (and some men) animate male bodies, transform male bodies (in the case of genderswap), and in the case of slash, explore sexuality through male bodies.

Although it is important to not fall into the trap of analyzing fans rather than the work they produce—just as it is appropriate to analyze *Supernatural* but not Eric Kripke through it—it is perhaps accurate to say that the characteristics that draw fans to *Supernatural* are the same as those that make the *Supernatural* fandom such a fertile space for the kind of fanfiction discussed here. Fans that are drawn to themes of transgression have been drawn to *Supernatural*, and inspired enough by it to further explore transgression through their own *Supernatural* fanworks. Furthermore, given the amateur nature of the production of fanworks (that is to say, they receive neither the financial reward or mainstream respect that professionally produced work does), it's reasonable to infer that the currency of fandom is one of enjoyment—and in the case of *Supernatural*, a clear pleasure taken in transgression. Just as Kripke's enjoyment of the horror genre and filmmaking is obvious in his reveling in intertextuality, so too is fans' enjoyment of *Supernatural* and their creative engagement with it demonstrated in the sheer volume and quality of work produced by the *Supernatural* fandom.

Having studied media theory and toyed with the idea of being an aca-fan for five years, EMILY TURNER now works out her fan activism urges with the Organization for Transformative Works. Her remaining spare time is spent watching TV, thinking about TV, running Web sites about TV and writing fiction about TV. Sometimes on the weekends you may find her in her leather jacket, cruising the country back roads outside Melbourne in her (sadly compact) car.

Hunting on a budget. This is pretty much the story of the Winchesters'—and Supernatural's*—life. How do the boys manage to fight the forces of Evil with no job, no home, and no money, and only a gas-guzzling classic car to their name?*

Jamie Chambers gives us the lowdown on hunting evil on the cheap, demonstrating how financial backing, legitimate authority, or inherited superpowers are no match for detailed knowledge of the supernatural world, creative thinking, and good old-fashioned Winchester ingenuity.

JAMIE CHAMBERS

BLUE COLLAR GHOST HUNTERS

Flip on the television, head off to the movies, or open up a comic book. You'll see ghosts aplenty, monsters hiding behind every bush, and more evil than you can shake a stick at. Those that battle such terrors are inevitably endowed with superpowers, expensive high-tech gadgets, or an arsenal worthy of the legions of Hell. The conflicts in each of these tales are challenging, but you don't exactly see Everyman hunting dark forces in most pop culture stories. There seems to be an unwritten assumption that Everyman would get his ass handed to him.

Who you gonna call? The Ghostbusters were a for-profit corporation founded by three guys who each sported PhDs and came from cushy, grant-funded research studies at a major university. Mulder and Scully had the authority and resources of the Federal Bureau of Investigations, with an expense account, sidearms, and cell phones. Buffy Summers inherited superpowers and the insight of an ancient feminine legacy—one that even came with a snooty British guy who had most of the answers. Hell, even poor ol' Carl Kolchak had a steady job and a press pass.

The Brothers Winchester are playing in a high-stakes game where the deck is stacked against them and the dealer wants to rip out their soft and squishy parts. Sam and Dean aren't sporting proton packs. They have no superpowers to speak of (save a few unreliable incidents for Sam, and he can't count on them to even pick up a bar tab). There's no legal authority to back them up. Now, the boys *do* sport guns, law enforcement IDs, and high-limit credit cards. Too bad it's all about as legal as driving home after the fifth beer.

Hunting ain't exactly a pro-ball career. You're way more likely to end up shoving daisies through the topsoil than rolling around on mattresses covered in Benjamins. Normal people don't have any business trying to take up the life, and just eating a bullet is far quicker and less painful than what might happen to you during a hunt. Each man or woman who walks away from their nine-to-fives and mortgage payments to stake zombies and burn bones—even the random roughnecks polishing their Remingtons in Harvelle's Roadhouse—has a powerful motivation driving them down that lonely road. A hunter is risking life, limb, and a ten to twenty-five stint in a 9 x 5 cell to walk into the darkness and make it just a tiny bit safer.

Somewhere in the world there might be a rich hunter, the *Supernatural* equivalent of Richard Dreyfuss's character in *Jaws*. It might be interesting to see what such an independently rich person might do to make his or her mark on a dark world filled with angry spirits and the unquiet dead . . . but I somehow suspect it would be less compelling than seeing the Winchester brothers get by using what little they have.

A Little History

The Winchesters were never swimming in loot. They didn't look desperately poor when we first saw them (at a point where Dean was a year shy of kindergarten and little Sammy was still sucking formula from a bottle) but they did look like they were scraping out the bottom end of middle class. It seemed likely they inherited the split-level home rather than mortgaged it on John's wages.

The senior Winchester was no moron, but it could be that he never earned so much as a G.E.D. The pictures and medals of his Vietnam days in the Marines showed him as a rifleman, and those with high school degrees were often sent to aviation or communications schools. After serving his country (and receiving a USMC Expert Rifle Badge, a Bronze Star, a Purple Heart, and Vietnam Service Medal in the process) he ended up working as a mechanic. Mary appeared to be a housewife and stay-at-home mom, taking good care of her sons but not letting them enjoy the kind of excess that the '80s were known for.

After the fire, John must have taken the insurance money and sold the property before hitting the road. He would have known it could only go so far, so stretched it out by living light. Roadside motels, greasy diners, and cheap beer were the order of the day for John.

But after a time his resources would have run out. Savings, loans, credit cards, personal possessions sold—it wouldn't have been enough to buy silver for the bullets, keep gas in the Impala, and pay for chicken wings at the local greasy spoon. But John Winchester was on a mission—to find and put down whatever it was that killed the love of his life and mother of his sons—and he wasn't about to stop long enough to find his fortune. Time to start taking other's people's fortunes. Stealing sounds ugly, but there are ways to buy ammo and supplies without having to knock over 7-Elevens.

Identity theft wasn't a buzzword back when John Winchester began the practice. Before the information age, you had to dumpster-dive for credit card carbons, steal cards, find the social security numbers of the invalid rich or the recently deceased, lie your ass off on a regular basis, and engage in some good ol' fashioned breaking and entering. John wasn't out to hurt any regular folk, he probably figured if those he robbed had a clue about the kinds of horrors he sent back to Hell they'd be scratching out thank-you notes.

These were important skills to pass on to the next generation, and so the boys learned how to steal badges from drunk off-duty cops, create fake IDs, design bogus business cards for nonexistent insurance companies, and do other things that would help them get where they needed to go in order to get the job done. One can't help but wonder how Sam felt much later as a pre-law student, learning just how many lifetimes in jail they could spend for every crime they'd committed over the years. It probably gave him pause, but not enough to stop him from going back to the life once he had strong enough reasons of his own.

How to survive without a job in a life of digging up graves and breaking into abandoned buildings wasn't the only thing John taught his sons. Their old man also instructed them on how to get the job done on a reasonable budget.

HUNTING ON THE CHEAP

Leave it to people named Winston and Egon to haul around expensive equipment and find scientific solutions to their problems. *Supernatural* is steeped in folklore—as in the "lore" of "folks," which doesn't exactly inspire images of lifestyles of the rich and fabulous. In the legends of old, people had to look to whatever herbs, roots, prayers, and traditions they had on-hand when bloodsuckers, pissed-off spirits, or other nasties set up shop. Add in some Yankee ingenuity, improvisation, and desperation, and it all leads to a supernatural formula.

It's from this fine tradition that the show gets its decidedly low-rent, old-school solutions to the problem that scare the hell out of us each week. Here are a few pages out of the Winchester playbook—all of the savings without having to clip a single coupon.

AVOID BIG PURCHASES

The easiest way to get your stolen (or falsely issued) credit cards noticed is to start buying big-ticket items. The red flags go up, the cops show up, you go to jail, and the spook/monster keeps on killing while you make nice with an over-friendly cellmate.

Dean loves his car, and would flip off anyone who suggested that he trade in his classic ride for something a little more fuel-efficient. But aside from the Impala's tendency to gas-guzzle, she's pretty cost-efficient; Dean wisely handles the upkeep and maintenance on his own (using the skills taught by his pro-mechanic dad). It's one thing to buy a new shotgun with a credit card bearing the name of Hector Aframian, another thing entirely to get yourself a new set of wheels with it.

Open the car's trunk, THEN pull up the hidden paneling, and you'll see a collection of guns, blades, and what may well be instruments of torture—enough to supply a whole S&M club with a full evening's enjoyment. Stolen, unregistered, or fraudulently acquired firearms let the Winchesters stay one step ahead of the law in an age of forensic criminalists and *CSI* reruns. Gunsmithing kits let the boys fix up their own weapons and cast their own silver bullets to take out werewolves and assorted shapeshifters. The machetes, bowie knives, and switch-blades are available for the critters that need more up-close-and-personal action. There's also a collection of knick-knacks, from crucifixes to hoodoo charms, to deal with demons and restless spirits.

Watch any ghost-tracking reality show and you'll see them haul around a utility van full of equipment. Cameras, video recorders, motion detectors, infrared imagers, and a host of other crap is set up all over a site for a period of hours to document the whole event. Each person carries a digital recorder for electronic voice phenomenon (EVP), along with a clunky gadget to record electromagnetic frequencies (an EMF detector; Dean has one of these, but he made his out of a busted-up old Walkman).

Not only is most of this junk spectacularly ineffective in tracking and dealing with ghosts, it draws attention and slows you down. The cops have a tendency to notice guys hauling a couple of mortgages' worth of electronic gear into an old house—and if you need to bail you might find yourself having to abandon your investment. Also, poltergeists aren't known to be friendly to delicate electronic gadgets, just so you know.

LEARN YOUR SYMBOLS

One of the cheapest, simplest things Dean ever did to hold off a creature was draw in the dirt. Okay, he traced Anasazi symbols in the earth to create a circle of protection against the Wendigo. But he did it with a stick.

Stick? Zero dollars. Dirt? Zero dollars and zero cents. Not becoming a freakish cannibal's winter snack? Priceless.

There are plenty of symbols that can be used for various purposes, from summoning to banishing to protecting and everything in between. Most of them don't require much more than a piece of chalk—though certain summoning circles and other pieces of business require some lit candles, maybe a little incense, or some burning herbs.

If you think you're going to be dealing with demons at any point, you might want to get familiar with a complicated doodle known as a devil's trap. Taken from the *Lesser Key of Solomon*, it's a pretty potent demon-catcher with plenty of bang for your buck. If you can lure a demon into the circle you've pretty much got it right where you want it. (Just hope it's not powerful enough to break the circle without touching it.) Once you've got a demon trapped you can perform an exorcism with impunity, and you might even be able to save the poor sucker it's possessed.

There's also a symbol used by Tibetan monks that can be used to manifest a creature from pure thought and belief, known as a Tulpa. This is not easily accomplished, and it's an incredibly dangerous thing to screw around with, so it's best to understand the symbol so you can wipe it out before it gets any real use.

If you're really educated, you might begin to recognize pictographs and symbols used in witchcraft or rituals from long-lost cultures. It's useful on a hunt, but that kind of education takes years and it ain't cheap.

Salt Is Your Friend

Salt has enjoyed a special place in human history, a fact that's largely lost on those who use it mostly to season French fries or de-ice sidewalks. But along with fire and the wheel, salt is one of the most important tools for human survival. It was one of the few ways to preserve meat back in the days before freezers and canning. It has been used as currency and as a symbol of both hospitality and fortune—which is why it's bad luck to spill salt and a good idea to toss it over your shoulder if you do (hey, you never know what might be sneaking up behind you).

The purity of salt repels unnatural things, including angry spirits and demons. Block the doors and windows with salt and you might earn yourself a good night's sleep or at the very least enough time to plan your next move. Surround yourself with a ring of salt if you're somewhere unsafe, and you might well live to see the next morning—just don't be stupid enough to break the circle or step outside of it.

Rock salt rounds aren't just for riot control anymore. Just as the ring of salt keeps the spirit out of your room, a blast of the pure substance might be just enough to disperse it or drive it back when it's trying to put its icy fingers around your heart. It would be naïve to think you're killing a ghost or even hurting it with the salt rounds, but you are pulling your bacon out of the fire long enough to plan your next move.

As satisfying as shooting a spook in the face might be, one of the surefire (pun intended) ways of dealing with the situation permanently is to salt and burn the bones. The purity of the salt combined with the destructive force of the fire is enough to break the spiritual anchor that lets the angry ghost hang around and cause trouble. Finding out just where some poor bastard was buried, digging up an old grave, and then torching some freshly salted bones is a giant pain in the ass—but it does the trick to be sure, and without breaking the bank. You have to wonder, though, how do Sam and Dean dig such perfectly rectangular graves with hand-shovels?

START FIRES

We touched on fire in relation to salt and burning bones, above, and the salt/fire combo is enough reason to keep any good hunter stocked with a gas can and some lighter fluid. But above and beyond that, fire can be its own solution.

Sarah Michelle Gellar's character had it all figured out in *The Grudge*. Ghost can't haunt a house if there's no house left to haunt—though that bitch of a ghost didn't let her finish the job. She should have salted and burned the bones instead of the house. Oh well. It worked well enough for Sam and Dean on the Hell House in Texas.

Some monsters are just asking to get lit up. Wendigos, for one, are ready to go up like dry kindling soaked in kerosene—assuming you can get a good shot at them. One well-placed flare gunshot to the chest and all you'll need is a pack of marshmallows. Curse-crazed bugs aren't too crazy about fire, either, nor are other animal-like critters. And fire will usually hurt even what it can't kill.

Lesson for hunters? Keep matches, lighters, sterno packs, and other sources of easy flame within easy reach. Fire is always a good, inexpensive plan B.

Crosses, Stakes, and Ol' Time Religion

Dis the classics all you want; they're in all the legends for a reason. Even if the stories don't always get it right, there are plenty of uses for crosses, holy water, stakes, and a few well-spoken Latin phrases.

Some of the exorcism rituals may take a little digging and some time in musty college libraries and used bookstores, but just about everything else can be found with ease. Keep a rosary and the correct ritual handy and you can turn a bathroom sink or even the steam pipes of an old factory into a makeshift font of holy water.

Holy water, by the way, is a must. You may want to keep a nearby flask of Jim Beam handy, but the smart hunter will fill it with holy water. A simple splash will tell you if the guy in front of you is possessed, and its judicious use is important in most of the Catholic-tradition exorcisms. If you don't know how to make your own, discreetly visit nearby churches to fill up before your next hunt.

A crucifix doesn't work the way you expect from television shows, but a well-brandished holy symbol can still hold many unclean things at bay—especially when you have the faith to back it up. Just don't expect it to work so well on vampires, because on Fangs it's just about as useless as . . .

Wooden stakes. Not so useful for vampires (who require decapitation to be sure), but often the first order of business when dealing with special entities from the Old World (Europe, for those who didn't benefit from higher education). Tricksters can be destroyed by wooden stakes dipped in the blood of at least one of their victims. Certain pagan gods can be taken out by an evergreen stake (or even the pointy end of a Christmas tree, if you're desperate). Zombies need to be nailed back into their own graves, which is even more of a pain in the ass than burning bones, and stakes will usually do the trick.

Desperation Is the Mother of Improvisation

The Christmas tree says it all. You'll never have everything you need right when you need it, but look around, you might be able to find something that will do. It may not work, but it's sure better than checking out without a fight.

Need a flamethrower? Grab a can of hairspray—or just about anything else with some kind of propellant—grab your gas-station lighter, and burn away. Need to blow up a cursed house? Turn on the gas and then make a homemade fuse with a pack of matches and a lit cigarette. You can make a lot of fire with just a couple of smart moves.

A hunter may not always have the right weapon when he needs it. Stuck in a bank with a psychotic shapeshifter? A silver letter opener may not be as comforting as a revolver loaded with silver rounds, but it'll get the job done—just as long as you have the stones to go toe-to-toe with an evil sunuvabitch.

Ghosts are often tied to their physical remains—which is where the whole burning the bones thing comes in—but sometimes the object that binds them to the world is something else. Could be anything: doll using the deceased's hair, a prosthetic that was never fully destroyed, a mirror that a victim stared in at the moment of death. Whatever it is, get rid of it and you'll send the damn thing back to Hell.

Sometimes you just have to break stuff (see mirror, above). You'll have to kick in your share of doors as a hunter, but this goes beyond that. Witches, cultists, and morons who picked up the wrong book may craft some talisman, altar, or satanic cross that lets them control a spirit or monster. These bozos think they're in control, but I'll bet you dollars to doughnuts that they're living on borrowed time. Spirits, monsters, and demons don't *like* to be controlled, and the moment you smash the mystical doodad to bits the one who's been calling the shots is the first target.

Technology can sometimes be your friend in unexpected ways. Some spirits that are invisible to the human eye can be picked up on certain kinds of cameras, like the ones found in a cell phone. Video cameras can pick up the strange flash of a shapeshifter's eyes. And phones, tape recorders, and the like can sometimes grab little supernatural bits of dialogue called EVP (electronic voice phenomenon). Look for whatever might come in handy and grab it. Just don't get caught if it's hot merchandise.

Hitting the Road

This doesn't even come close to being a comprehensive guide to hunting the supernatural without a trust fund to back you up, but it's a start.

Travel light and fast, be flexible, and don't get busted. Be ready to think on your feet and use whatever you have on-hand wherever you are.

Sam and Dean may not be the happiest guys in the world, but they've learned to enjoy draught beer, home fries, music from a tape deck, and themed motel rooms. They don't need the fancier things in life to get the job done while they hunt evil and raise a little hell. Neither should you.

JAMIE CHAMBERS grew up in north Georgia where he found a love for games and books, but apparently not mild winters and sweet tea—which is why he moved to southeast Wisconsin where he could get away from them and write stories and games for a living. When not writing long, run-on sentences, he is working on the *Supernatural Role Playing Game* and other projects. He lives in an old, creepy house with his wife and three kids. Follow his latest antics on the Web: http://www.jamiechambers.net.

Can the adventures of Sam and Dean Winchester be used as a template for day-to-day living? Is it possible to Fight the Good Fight following the examples they set? Should they be role models for disaffected male youth? Is Supernatural *really just some silly little show about the occult hidden away on a TV network aimed at teenagers? Or does the show have more to say—about family values, paternal and fraternal relationships, destiny, fate, determination, sacrifice, love, good versus evil?*

While it remains to be seen whether "love conquers all" for the Winchester boys, the love of Supernatural *certainly does conquer all in Heather Swain's fictional (we believe) account of two people discovering each other when fandom triumphs over the ignorance of the uninitiated.*

HEATHER SWAIN

A *Supernatural* Love Story

Dayton Daily Sun Sentinel Newspaper
"Ask Adam: Advice for Men" weekly column
October 5, 2006

Hey Adam,

First off, your column rocks, man. You really know how guys think. Here's a problem for you. The wife and I are having our first kid soon. She wants her mother to stay with us after Junior is born. I say no way. The lady is from Hell. What do I do?

Signed,

The Monster-in-Law Is Coming

Dear Monster-in-Law Hater,

This is a clear case of damned if you do and damned if you don't. If you let her come, she's going to drive you to drink, but if you keep her out, you'll be dealing with the wailing of the baby and your wife all on your own.

Demons come in all shapes and sizes, so you have to ask yourself, what's the worst that could happen? It's not like she's going to force your baby to drink her blood, or burst into flames and blow up your house, right? Look at it this way, maybe she'll help out. Take Junior for a stroll so you and the wife can get some rest.

Of course, if you think she truly is demonic, salt all the windowsills and doorways. That way she'll never be able to cross your threshold again.

Take it easy,

Adam

***

MEMO
To: Adam Shastenberger
From: Eileen O'Rourke-Dutton
Date: October 10, 2006
RE: "Ask Adam" Advice Column

Dear Mr. Shastenberger,

I regret to inform you that we have received several complaints about the advice you dispensed in your most recent "Ask Adam: Advice for Men" column.

I must admit, I was quite disconcerted by your tone and can understand why readers were upset. In the future, please try to keep your advice palatable for the general reading public.

Thank you for your attention to this matter.

Sincerely,

Eileen O'Rourke-Dutton
Managing Editor
Dayton Daily Sun Sentinel

***

10/12/06

Dear Ms. O'Rourke-Dutton,

Thank you for your letter regarding my column. I assure you that I never meant to be disconcerting or upsetting. However, I believe my advice column speaks for itself (metaphorically, that is). I must admit I'm unclear as to what in my column was objectionable. Could you please be more specific?

Sincerely,

Adam Shastenberger, MSW

***

MEMO
To: Adam Shastenberger
From: Eileen O'Rourke-Dutton
Date: October 15, 2006
RE: "Ask Adam" Advice Column

Dear Mr. Shastenberger,

Although I would think it's obvious, let me state clearly that in the future you must refrain from references (metaphoric or otherwise) to mother-in-laws (or other relatives) as demons, infants drinking blood, people bursting into flames, houses exploding, and/or salting windowsills to keep said demons at bay. No one is interested in such nonsense.

I hope this clarifies the situation.

Sincerely,

Eileen O'Rourke-Dutton
Managing Editor
Dayton Daily Sun Sentinel

***

10/17/06

Dear Ms. O'Rourke-Dutton,

As per your recent letter, I respectfully submit that demonic possession and its effects on family life interest more people than you might realize. For example, are you aware that over the past ten years television shows such as *Buffy the Vampire Slayer*, *Angel*, *Smallville*, and *Supernatural* have captured millions of viewers, many of whom are young men—the exact demographic of my readership, I might add? Isn't that evidence enough that my advice column is hitting exactly the right tone for the readership?

Sincerely,

Adam Shastenberger, MSW

MEMO
To: Adam Shastenberger
From: Eileen O'Rourke-Dutton
Date: October 19, 2006
RE: "Ask Adam" Advice Column

Dear Mr. Shastenberger,

I will kindly ask you to remember that we are a respectable newspaper and not some silly cable television network pandering to the whims of teenagers. Furthermore, you are dispensing advice for real people, not vampires, demon slayers, and superheroes. I insist that you keep your tone at the utmost professional level.

Sincerely,

Eileen O'Rourke-Dutton
Managing Editor
Dayton Daily Sun Sentinel

***

Dayton Daily Sun Sentinel Newspaper
"Ask Adam: Advice for Men" weekly column
May 1, 2007

Hey Adam,

I know guys usually write to you for advice, but my question concerns a guy, so I figured it would be okay. Here's the problem. My fiancé is a workaholic. I mean, big time. He's practically obsessed with his job. I know his work is important (he's a social worker so other people rely on him to help them out of their problems), but I keep telling him that work isn't everything. I love him so much, but part of me thinks that if he can't change, I'm not sure I want to spend my life with a guy who cares more about other people's problems than his own family.

Signed,

Lonely After Six O' Clock

***

Dear Lonely,

You know, sweetheart, some people have important jobs that have to be done. Take my friends Sam and Dean, for example. Their job keeps them on the road all the time. You think Dean doesn't want a good home-cooked meal every once in a while? Something that hasn't been microwaved at a minimart? You think he wouldn't love to take a vacation? See the Grand Canyon, maybe? You think Sam doesn't want to go back to college and have a normal life again? But they can't, sister. Because if they do evil will prevail, okay?

Not evil like "Oh boo-hoo, someone bilked an old lady out of her social security check." I'm talking evil feasting on the blood of innocent children and humans sacrificed to demonic scarecrows kind of stuff! So why don't you just back off and cut this guy some slack. Be supportive for once and realize that the world doesn't revolve around what kind of curtains you hang in your McMansion. Somebody has to be around to save us all from the clutches of dark forces, and maybe that guy isn't exactly your fiancé, but still, I'm just saying, Sam and Dean have no choice!

Take it easy,

Adam

MEMO
To: Adam Shastenberger
From: Eileen O'Rourke-Dutton
Date: May 5, 2007
RE: "Ask Adam" Advice Column

Dear Mr. Shastenberger,

I was under the impression that we had resolved the issue of inappropriate advice dispensed in your column last October. After further complaints about your propensity to refer to reapers, djinns, Wendigos, and other paranormal creatures, it has come to the attention of our legal department that your advice draws heavily from the CW television program *Supernatural*.

Our lawyers have asked me to familiarize myself with the program in question and review all your past columns. At first, your references to *Supernatural* seemed to be minor and perhaps even coincidental. (For example, is it really necessary to encourage men to purchase black 1967 Chevy Impalas rather than hunter green minivans, or to suggest "Burnin' for You" by Blue Oyster Cult as "the most kick-ass wedding song ever"?) However, over time these references have grown blatant and openly hostile toward those seeking your advice. Your most recent column was particularly troubling.

It was our understanding upon hiring you that you are a licensed therapist and couples counselor specializing in family dynamics. Our readers expect expert advice based on reality, not on some silly show about the occult.

Sincerely,

Eileen O'Rourke-Dutton
Managing Editor
Dayton Daily Sun Sentinel

5/8/07

Dear Ms. O'Rourke-Dutton,

Thank you for your recent memo regarding my weekly column for men. As far as your observation that I base some of my advice on the television show *Supernatural*, I believe Dean Winchester would say it best: "Thank you, Captain Obvious!"

Frankly, I find it troubling that you would so callously disregard the excellent lessons about brotherhood, father-son relationships, family loyalty, and fighting evil that I've explored in my columns.

You claim that I blatantly use plotlines from a "silly" television series about the occult. Nothing could be further from the truth. As you should realize by now, *Supernatural* is no mere television series, nor is it silly, and it certainly isn't about the occult, as you so indelicately put it. Each week, this piece of cinematic genius bravely and openly dissects the intricate personal lives of men and their relationships in the face of battling pure evil. What else do real men do, I ask you, if not this?

Sincerely,

Adam Shastenberger, MSW

***

MEMO
To: Adam Shastenberger
From: Eileen O'Rourke-Dutton
Date: May 11, 2007
RE: "Ask Adam" Advice Column

Dear Mr. Shastenberger,

While I agree that tackling relationship issues is of paramount importance, all I'm asking you to do is *keep it real*, as the young people say. In other words, please draw your examples from lives of actual people, not fictional characters such as Sam and Dean Winchester. No matter how imploring Jared Padalecki's beseeching hazel eyes may be or how enticing Jensen Ackles's crooked grin can seem, these young men are not real and neither are their problems.

Sincerely,

Eileen O'Rourke-Dutton
Managing Editor
Dayton Daily Sun Sentinel

P.S. Could you believe the way the writers left us hanging last night after "All Hell Breaks Loose (Part 1)"? Do you think Jake really killed Sam after Sam saved him from the Yellow-Eyed Demon? They wouldn't really kill Sam off, would they? How would Dean get by without his dad *and* his brother?

***

5/13/07

Dear Ms. O'Rourke-Dutton,

First of all, rest easy. I'm certain Dean will find a way to save his brother, as he sees this as his life's work. I only hope he can do it in a way that will not endanger himself. Dean, as I'm sure you've recognized, has a classic co-dependent relationship with his brother. Despite his seemingly callous attitude, he often puts Sam's needs before his own. Dean's rough, tough-guy exterior is merely a cover for the depth of emotion he carries. These emotions drive his actions and yet he is shamed by them and believes (erroneously) that they make him appear weak. Sam's possible death is the ultimate test for Dean, and I for one am anxiously awaiting his response.

Oh, but as you said, these aren't real people with real problems, so why should we discuss it?

Sincerely,

Adam Shastenberger, MSW

***

MEMO
To: Adam Shastenberger
From: Eileen O'Rourke-Dutton
Date: May 18, 2007
RE: "Ask Adam" Advice Column

Dear Adam,

I have purposefully waited a week to reply to you so we could be certain of Sam and Dean's destiny before continuing our correspondence. First off, I'll admit that I'm not entirely surprised by Dean's solution to sell his own soul in exchange for Sam's life . . . like father like son, wouldn't you say? I think Bobby summed it up best when he asked Dean, "How's your brother going to feel when he knows you're going to Hell?" How indeed? Given Sam's deeply humanist perspective, nothing could hurt him more than knowing his own well-being is tied to his brother's ultimate sacrifice and eternal damnation. One can't help but feel heartbroken for the brothers' fate and yet envious of their loyalty to one another.

However, despite my apparent emotional attachment to the Winchester boys, Chas McWilliams, lead counsel of our legal department, assures me that it is in the best interest of our newspaper that you refrain from using *Supernatural* as a template for advice.

Until next season, I remain yours sincerely,

Eileen O'Rourke-Dutton
Managing Editor
Dayton Daily Sun Sentinel

***

5/20/07

Dear Eileen,

The men who read my column are looking for role models that can lead them through the difficulties of being a man in today's world of uncertainty where evil can lurk around every corner. The Winchesters are fine examples of regular working class guys enduring such a task without special equipment or fancy degrees. I see no problem in referencing their experiences for my like-minded readers.

Perhaps we are not the ones with the problem. Perhaps Mr. Chas McWilliams needs a little holy water sprinkled in his bathtub. In short, as long as the Winchester brothers battle evil while working through the emotional grit of their family bonds, I shall continue to reference them as part of my columns.

Sincerely,

Adam Shastenberger, MSW

MEMO
To: Adam Shastenberger
From: Charles L. McWilliams, Esq.
CC: Eileen O'Rourke-Dutton
Date: 5/25/07
RE: "Ask Adam" Advice Column

Dear Mr. Shastenberger,

I do not take kindly to your thinly veiled threat to exorcise the Devil from my soul. No matter what you think of lawyers, I can assure you that I am not possessed. Should you continue to use such slanderous language, I shall be forced to sue you for defamation of character.

My role as lead counsel to the *Dayton Daily Sun Sentinel* is to keep our standards above reproach so as to avoid unnecessary lawsuits. I agree that the men who read your column need strong, positive role models, but the (fictional) Winchester brothers, who solve their problems with fists and weaponry, hardly qualify. While I understand that you feel differently, I believe two people should be able to disagree without resorting to name calling and lawsuits.

Sincerely,

Charles L. McWilliams, Esq.
Lead Counsel
Dayton Daily Sun Sentinel

***

5/27/07

Dear Mr. McWilliams,

First, please accept my apology for implying that you are "possessed." That was inappropriate and unwarranted. As you point out, reasonable people may disagree without resorting to drastic measures (such as exorcism or lawsuits—both the work of the devil, ha, ha, ha).

This leads me to my second point. I have never once in my column advocated violence as a solution to an interpersonal conflict. This is precisely the beauty of the Winchester paradigm for problem-solving. What you've disregarded as a show about weapons and violence is, upon closer inspection, an incisive look at the ways regular guys negotiate tricky emotional terrain.

As a licensed therapist and family counselor (as well as an ordained High Priest of the Green Grove Wicca Coven of Dayton), I take offense at your dismissive attitude toward the Winchester legacy. Who else in modern pop culture has explored the complications of joining the family business, finding job satisfaction, and communicating with macho emotional Neanderthals via an entertainment-driven plot?

Sincerely,

Adam Shastenberger, MSW

CC: Eileen O'Rourke-Dutton

***

MEMO
To: Adam Shastenberger
From: Charles L. McWilliams, Esq.
CC: Eileen O'Rourke-Dutton
Date: 6/1/07
RE: "Ask Adam" Advice Column

Dear Mr. Shastenberger,

Haven't you ever watched *The Sopranos*? Talk about a deep exploration of family dynamics! You should reference Tony, Uncle Junior, Pauly Walnuts, and Christopher in that low-rent column of yours. At least they deal with reality.

Sincerely,

Charles L. McWilliams, Esq.
Lead Counsel
Dayton Daily Sun Sentinel

***

6/5/07

Dear Mr. McWilliams,

I understand now why you would become a lawyer and I a therapist. *The Sopranos* is fundamentally a dark show that illustrates how vice and immorality can infiltrate and ruin family life. *Supernatural*, on the other hand, is about putting family first while kicking some evil sons of bitches' asses in the process! My readers love my column and if you try to stop me, your precious paper will suffer in the end.

Sincerely,

Adam Shastenberger, MSW

***

MEMO
To: Adam Shastenberger
From: Charles L. McWilliams, Esq.
CC: Eileen O'Rourke-Dutton
Date: 6/10/07
RE: "Ask Adam" Advice Column

Dear Mr. Shastenberger,

Despite the supposed success of your column, I insist that you end the practice of referring to *Supernatural* immediately or I will take legal action to permanently withdraw "Ask Adam" from the pages of our fine newspaper.

Furthermore, do not threaten me or this newspaper, unless you would like a restraining order (or perhaps a pair of cement shoes). I'd like to see your hocus pocus mumbo jumbo protect you then.

Sincerely,

Charles L. McWilliams, Esq.
Lead Counsel
Dayton Daily Sun Sentinel

***

MEMO
To: Adam Shastenberger
From: Eileen O'Rourke-Dutton
CC: Charles L. McWilliams, Esq.
Date: 6/10/07
RE: "Ask Adam" Advice Column

Dear Adam,

I'm so sorry it's come to this. Through your patient tutelage I have come to see the merit of *Supernatural* as a template for modern male interpersonal relationships. (Not to mention my newfound role as a number one J.A.F.—Jensen Ackles Fan, that is. He's a modern day James Dean and has rekindled my girlish crush on the rebel without a cause archetype.)

Unfortunately, as far as legal action against you, I'm afraid my hands are tied in this matter. Mr. McWilliams has me in a devil's trap of sorts. Please do what he says or I'm afraid you will be "exorcised" from our newspaper!

Most sincerely,

Eileen O'Rourke-Dutton
Managing Editor
Dayton Daily Sun Sentinel

***

Dayton Daily Sun Sentinel Newspaper
"Ask Adam: Advice for Men" weekly column
October 8, 2007

Hey Adam,

Here's a tough one. Due to a congenital birth defect, my brother needs a new kidney. Turns out I'm the closest match. The thing is, ever since he was a kid, everyone has bent over backwards for my brother because he almost died when he was a baby. I'm finally getting my life together. I met a girl I want to marry, got the job I've been after, and I'm ready to buy a house. My parents expect me to put my life on hold and get myself sliced open for my "special" little bro. Do I have to?

Signed,

What's Mine Is Mine

Dear Mine,

How far would you go for your brother? Give him the last taco off your plate? Let him crash on your couch if he was broke? Go to the Crossroads and sell your soul to bring him back to life? Vow to find a way to get your brother's soul back even if that means continuing to tempt your dark side? That's exactly what Dean and Sam Winchester do for one another, because they are true brothers. They've seen each other through thick and thin after they've lost everyone important (mother, father, girlfriend, fellow hunters). Sam and Dean are the kind of guys who realize that there is no stronger bond in this world than the bond of two brothers fighting evil.

But maybe you're not that kind of guy. Maybe you're the kind of guy who wants all his kidneys for himself. Well, fine. But you better watch your back when the soldiers from Hell come marching forth, because Sam and Dean won't be there, man. You and your two kidneys will be all alone.

Take it easy,

Adam

***

MEMO
To: Adam Shastenberger
From: Charles L. McWilliams, Esq.
CC: Eileen O'Rourke-Dutton
Date: 10/10/07
RE: "Ask Adam" Advice Column

Dear Mr. Shastenberger,

Well, it's the beginning of season three on the CW and, despite repeated good faith attempts to dissuade you from using *Supernatural* as your template for advice, you have once again done just that. Your last column was frankly the last straw.

The legal department of the *Dayton Daily Sun Sentinel* has taken immediate action to terminate your contract. Your services are no longer welcome at our fine newspaper establishment.

Sincerely,

Charles L. McWilliams, Esq.
Lead Counsel
Dayton Daily Sun Sentinel

***

10/12/07

Dear Mr. McWilliams,

Are you possessed? Has the Yellow-Eyed Demon taken hold of your soul? What else could explain this virulent attitude of yours? This cold-blooded disgust of what is sacred and holy? What is your problem exactly? Sure, you look normal, but do your eyes flash the dark of a moonless night when your inner demons rear their ugly heads at the mere mention of what is good and just in this world?

You sicken me and if we ever meet in a dank abandoned warehouse, be forewarned that I will rip you to shreds and send you back to the Hell you came from. Please consider our working relationship severed like the head of a black Hell Hound.

From now on my loyal readers can contact me via my Facebook page and of course find me posting under the name SuperShasty on the TV.com *Supernatural* chat forum.

Sincerely,

Adam Shastenberger

***

10/13/07

Dear Adam,

I'm terribly distraught! I'm so sorry the legal department at our newspaper can't recognize genius when they see it. Please know that I did everything in my power to keep you on board. I'm afraid there are no bones to salt in this case.

Most sincerely,

Eileen

***

10/15/07

Dearest Eileen,

Please don't worry yourself over this matter. I will prevail and *Supernatural* will be picked up for another season, I'm sure. What more could we ask for?

As for Chas McWilliams, I'm sure he'll get what he deserves. Evil always pays in the end.

Please know that you are always welcome at the Fan Club viewing party held every Thursday. We'd love to have your spirit with us as we root for Sam and Dean.

Yours truly,

Adam

***

Dayton Daily Sun Sentinel Newspaper
November 5, 2007
"Local Lawyer Missing"

According to Police Chief Steven Botch, Charles "Chas" McWilliams (local lawyer and lead counsel to the *Dayton Daily Sun Sentinel*) is feared missing. His wife, Liz McWilliams, reported that McWilliams left his residence at 4:25 p.m. October 31st for a business meeting but never returned.

Police Chief Botch offered no comment on the ongoing investigation of Mr. McWilliams's alleged involvement with an organized crime ring that has infiltrated area media and refrigeration businesses as well as narcotics trafficking. In September, Mr. McWilliams pleaded not guilty to charges of money laundering and extortion and is awaiting trial.

The police believe it is entirely coincidental that McWilliams disappeared on Halloween night, yet foul play has not been ruled out. "I don't think he was snatched off the street by some hobgoblin, if that's what you're implying," said Chief Botch. "Halloween is an ordinary day just like any other." There are no suspects at this time.

Dayton Daily Sun Sentinel Newspaper
November 5, 2007
Community Announcements Weekly Calendar

WEDNESDAY
The weekly midnight meeting of the Green Grove Wicca Coven will be held at the Miamsburg Earth Books behind Kinko's. Presiding High Priest Adam Shastenberger will discuss "The Occult and the Media: Friends or Foes" with former *Dayton Daily Sun Sentinel* managing editor Eileen O' Rourke-Dutton. All are welcome no matter what path they follow.

***

Dayton Daily Sun Sentinel Newspaper
January 10, 2008
Community Announcements Weekly Calendar

THURSDAY
The Dayton "*Supernatural* Fan Club" will host their weekly viewing party at the Delco Park Applebee' s in Kettering. New President-elect Eileen O' Rourke will preside. Drinks and appetizers start at 7:00. Free Tex-Mex Pizza Poppers for new attendees.

***

Dayton Daily Sun Sentinel Newspaper
May 15, 2008
Shastenberger/O'Rourke Wedding Announcement

Eileen O' Rourke and Adam Shastenberger were married in Hueston Woods State Park at sundown, on Saturday, May 12, 2008. High Priestess Katura Lloyd of the Green Grove Wicca Coven officiated the wedding. The couple, who are co-presidents of the Dayton area *Supernatural* fan club, are currently enjoying a cross-country honeymoon trip which begins in Lawrence, Kansas, and will end in Vancouver, B.C., Canada. "We're going to visit every town that Sam and Dean Winchester have been to," the groom explained. "Then we'll go to the set in Vancouver where I'll present Jensen Ackles with a needlepoint pillow I made bearing the likeness of his face," said the bride. It's a *Supernatural* love story.

Heather Swain is the author of two novels, *Eliot's Banana* and *Lucious Lemon*, and the editor of *Before: Short Stories About Pregnancy*. Her young adult novel *Me, My Elf and I* will be released by Puffin/Speak in summer 2009. Her fiction and nonfiction have appeared in literary journals, Web sites, and magazines. She lives in Brooklyn, New York, with her husband, two children, and dog.

When is a car not just a car? When she's Dean Winchester's 1967 Chevrolet Impala, of course. Home to the homeless, mother to the motherless, an essential member of the family: the Impala is all of this and more. She is one of the few constants in the Winchesters' lives and the only thing they can rely upon besides each other, even when she's been towed, impounded, or smashed to pieces by a demon-controlled truck.

Here, Jules Wilkinson looks at the various roles assumed by the Winchesters' heavy metal steed—protector, mother, home . . . and a constant reminder and symbol of their father, his place in their lives, and their own place in the "family business."

JULES WILKINSON

BACK IN BLACK

The Batmobile, the General Lee, Starsky and Hutch's Torino, Magnum's Ferrari, Knight Rider's KITT—cars have become icons in many TV shows. Mean, sleek, macho machines with an ability to burn rubber in the cause of a hot pursuit or getaway. Auto-erotic fixations for the heroes, valued for their grunt and stunts. However, one car is going full throttle beyond these conventions. In her break-out role on *Supernatural*, a '67 Impala Chevy is showing that a car can be more than just a bitchin' ride.

At first glance, the Impala appears to fulfill the usual TV-car stereotype. She fits the bill in the looks department: a classic, sexy and shiny, with a trunk full of weapons. Like all TV cars she never breaks down or gets covered in bird poop, and she always finds a place to park. Sure, the Impala might get dirty occasionally, but in the next episode she's certain to be gleaming again. (Unfortunately we have never seen Dean in a pair of cut-offs, sudsing her up. Of course, Dean "doesn't do shorts"

["Wendigo," 1-2], but viewers live in hope.)

Like her well-known brethren, the Impala, for all her distinctive looks, flies under the radar. Despite their eye-catching appearance, it's as if TV cars can cast a glamour over themselves to remain inconspicuous. The super villains of Gotham City never noticed the Batmobile parked on the corner and criminals never wised up to the fact that the arrival of a loud, red Torino meant Starsky and Hutch were on their tail. Similarly, on *Supernatural*, when the FBI takes an active interest in the Winchesters, the only disguise the Impala needs is a switch of her license plates: Kansas plates KAZ 2Y5 to CNK 80Q3 from Ohio. It's a bit like a fugitive from *America's Most Wanted* sticking on a fake mustache.

Along with their owners, who are usually breaking all the rules in their fight for justice, TV cars are mavericks. Like the Winchesters, the Impala is an outsider, marginalized from mainstream society. In today's world, she's transgressive—a gas-guzzler harking back to the days when gas was thirty-three cents a gallon and heavy with lead. The '67 Impala was built for cruising down the highway, not for zipping down to the mall. No airbags here, just a solid chassis of Detroit steel. This is no iMpala; she has a cassette deck that only plays mullet rock—no indie pop mp3 nonsense for her.

TV cars are known for their guts and their willingness to throw their metal bodies into danger without hesitation and the Impala is no exception. She's courageous, a hunter chasing down ghosts, demons, and vampires, along with the Winchesters for all the thrills and spills. The junk in her trunk is all high caliber and razor-sharp steel. She gets beat up, once smashed almost beyond repair, but like the rest of the Winchesters, death proves an impermanent condition. When Dean restores her after her late season one encounter with a demon-driven Mack truck, she makes her return to the screen in a long, sensuous scene, gleaming in the sun as she tears along the highway to AC/DC's "Back in Black."

But *Supernatural* is not just a show about battling evil; it's a show about family. The Impala is a character with as much depth and emotional resonance as Sam or Dean. She is the link to their past, to what they are fighting for, and present at all the significant moments in their life to lend support and comfort. She takes them on their journey and provides the only home they know. The Impala is not just a hot ride; she *is* a Winchester.

The Impala is established as an integral part of the family in the opening scenes of the pilot episode. When Mary Winchester dies on the ceiling of the nursery and their house goes up in flames, John Winchester, young Dean, and baby Sam are seen huddling on the hood of the Impala, supported by her, as life as they know it ends.

With the loss of mother and home, it is the Impala that takes on the role of nurturer and sanctuary, becomes the metaphoric womb for the Winchesters. This is the heart of her character.

The Impala carries with her the family history. She takes the Winchesters from suburban idyll to a nomadic life hunting the supernatural. When Peter Johnson, writer of the tie-in *Origins* comics, made the Impala a car that John acquired as part of becoming a hunter, fans were outraged. Johnson listened, and later altered this in the trade paperback edition, saying he now recognized what the car represented thematically "in the continuity of the family—before and after Mary's death."[1]

We know little of what happened to her during the intervening years, but twenty-two years after Mary's death it is the Impala that brings Dean to Stanford, to reunite him with Sam. (I'm pretty sure she had some work done in those intervening years because she looks pretty amazing for a girl approaching forty.)

The relationships in the Winchester family are intense. For twenty years, as they chased the creatures of myth and urban legend, cut off from normal society, this family had only each other: John, Dean, Sam—and the Impala, too, because as Bobby later reminds Dean, "Family don't end with blood" ("No Rest for the Wicked," 3-16).

The Impala signifies for both Sam and Dean the home they never had. In contrast to the never-ending series of quirkily decorated motel rooms, the odd house—preferably with a steam shower—to squat in, and the occasional weekend at Bobby's, the Impala is the only space that is truly theirs.

As a car, though, she can only provide so much in the way of a home. While the Winchesters travel in her, sleep in her, and eat in her, the

[1] http://blogs.mediavillage.com/sci_fi/archives/2007/06/supernatural_co.html

Impala really offers only the illusion of a private space. As anyone who has been caught singing out loud or picking their nose while in the car knows, the car is a private space open to the public sphere. Put simply—it has windows!

Having a car as the only recurring space on the show emphasizes the boys' isolation from normal social interactions. Most TV shows have three types of spaces: private space, such as a bedroom (or prison cell); a semi-public space, such as a living room in a sitcom or a workplace (think squad room or hospital doctors' lounge); and a contained public space, like the Bronze (*Buffy*), Central Perk (*Friends*), and those bars or dining areas that exist on every spaceship from *Enterprise* to *Galactica*.

The purpose of the recurring semi-public spaces is to allow social relationships to develop. It is where relationships may transition from friendship to romance. They are often an alternative space to both the private space of a home and the open public space of a crime scene or workplace, a place where characters of different status at work can interact more equally. They are a more public space than a home and allow antagonistic characters to interact with each other—think (early) Spike and Buffy.

The Winchesters have access to none of these. They did visit Harvelle's Roadhouse for a brief period before demons destroyed it, but they rarely interacted with any of the perpetually gun-cleaning hunters who frequented it. All Sam and Dean have is the Impala, primarily a private space, and rarely are other people allowed in. They do not have access to spaces in which to develop relationships with other people. That kind of interaction is limited because this show is all about Dean, Sam—and the Impala.

It is within the fragile private space of the Impala that the brothers have many intimate and often difficult conversations—the sort of exchanges either brother would prefer to walk away from, but which are inescapable when the Impala is powering along at 100 miles an hour. Whether it's Sam challenging Dean about his obedience to John or trying to tell him how much he means to him, or Dean insisting to Sam that he'll save him or later that he doesn't want to go to Hell, the Impala is the space that contains and holds them.

Many other significant events occur with the Impala present. At the end of the pilot episode, the brothers stand over the trunk of the Impala, guns in hand, side by side. Sam, having just lost the woman he loved to another incendiary ceiling, has to choose whether to leave his "normal" life and return to hunting and his family. The camera shows us the brothers from the Impala's point of view, waiting to support whatever decision is made. "We've got work to do," Sam says as he throws his weapon in, and the episode ends as he closes the trunk.

This scene is recreated forty-four episodes later, in "All Hell Breaks Loose (Part 2)" (2-22). *Supernatural* stands out in its use of a visual language more sophisticated than is usually found on TV. In particular, it uses the mirroring of scenes from previous episodes to provide a link to past events, and to indicate how characters have evolved since that earlier point, adding emotional resonance to the character arcs.

At the end of the season two finale, the Winchesters' mission is ostensibly complete—they have defeated the demon that killed their mom—and there is another pivotal choice to be made. As the brothers decide to carry on fighting the demons that have escaped from Hell, the scene from the first episode is replayed, again from the Impala's point of view. This time the brothers' positions are reversed, for in the second season it has been Dean who has repeatedly suggested that they leave hunting and so now it is Dean who tosses the Colt into the trunk, saying, "We've got work to do." There is no doubt, of course, that the Impala is along for the ride.

The Impala is also there when Sam and Dean first find out their father is alive, as they sit on her hood and listen to a voicemail message in "Phantom Traveler" (1-4). The Impala supports them as Dean shares his grief with Sam in "Children Shouldn't Play with Dead Things" (2-4), and as he collapses with the vision he receives from Andy in "All Hell Breaks Loose (Part 1)" (2-21). She looks on as Dean finally shares John's secret with Sam and later when he sells his soul to the Crossroads Demon, and again when Sam kills the Crossroads Demon. The Impala helps Dean carry Sam from Cold Oak after he is killed by Jake, and watches helplessly as Dean dies in "Mystery Spot" (3-11). She shares too in the most bittersweet moment of the season three finale, when the boys recapture for a moment the memory of happier times as they sing along to Bon Jovi's "Wanted Dead or Alive." In each instance, the Impala shares in the brothers' trials and their grief, and on rare occasions their hope.

Yet while the members of the Winchester family are more enmeshed with each other than most, the Impala undoubtedly has the closest relationship with Dean, and his affection for her is unabashed, as this exchange from "Bloodlust" (2-3) illustrates:

> DEAN: Whoa! Listen to her purr! Have you ever heard anything so sweet?
> SAM: You know, if you two want to get a room, just let me know, Dean.
> DEAN: Don't listen to him, baby. He doesn't understand us.

For all his teasing, Sam does understand; his Christmas presents to Dean in "A Very Supernatural Christmas" (3-8) are beef jerky and motor oil. As Dean says, "Fuel for me, and fuel for my baby." The final shot of the Christmas episode pulls back to frame Sam, Dean, and the Impala in the same shot, to show her sharing in this family occasion.

The Impala is Dean's only constant, as those closest to him, in one way or another, leave him. We see how strongly Dean is attached to the Impala by his reaction on the rare occasions when they are separated—and unlike Sam or John she never abandons Dean willingly. When the shapeshifter in "Skin" steals her, Dean complains, "The thought of him drivin' my car. . . . It's killin' me" (1-6). It takes Andy's "Obi-Wan" mind powers to part Dean from her in "Simon Said," (2-5), and in "Red Sky at Morning" (3-6), Dean has a full-blown panic attack when Bela has the Impala towed, a stronger reaction than he had when she shot Sam! Life without her is unthinkable, and even in the alternate reality created by the djinn in "What Is and What Should Never Be" (2-20), the Impala is present, no longer a hunter but a civilian like Dean, with just a copy of *Maxim* and some burger wrappers in her trunk rather than her usual cache of guns, knives, and rock salt. There is no stronger indication of Dean's love for the Impala than the fact that Dean's last words to Sam in "No Rest for the Wicked," as the clock strikes midnight and the Hell Hound sniffs at Dean's soul, are: "Keep on fighting, and take care of my wheels."

For Dean, being behind the wheel means being a man in charge:

"Driver picks the music, shotgun shuts his cakehole" ("Pilot"). But it's not just about choosing the tunes. When everything is going to hell in a handbasket around him (and in the world of *Supernatural*, sometimes this is happening quite literally) and Dean is overwhelmed with emotional turmoil, presenting Sam with the façade that he's coping becomes paramount. Significantly, as Dean struggles to keep it together in season two, burdened with grief and guilt over John's death and the fear of what Sam may become, Dean stays behind the wheel throughout and Sam is never seen driving the Impala.

Dean, he of the "no chick-flick moments" mentality, often relies on the Impala to help him express what he can't. In times of turmoil, Dean locks his emotions away more securely than the Impala's trunk with a devil's trap on it. When he is worried about how Sam is dealing with the trauma and grief of Jess's death in "Wendigo," he doesn't hug him, or have a deep and meaningful conversation about life and loss—he asks Sam if he'd like to drive. A significant gesture from him, made clear by Sam's response: "In your whole life you never once asked me that."

Later, in the aftermath of John's death, Dean can't articulate his grief. Like the Impala, he is broken, and he starts what seems to be the insurmountable task of fixing things, fixing himself. "We've got nothing, Sam. Nothing, okay? And the only thing I can do? Is I can work on the car" ("Everybody Loves a Clown," 2-2).

In season three, as Dean grapples with having less than a year to live, Sam again challenges him about having shut himself off. He pleads with Dean to be his "big brother" again. Dean allows Sam back into his emotional sphere by lifting the hood of the Impala to expose her broken inner workings, trusting that Sam can help fix things. There can be no clearer sign of unconditional trust and love from Dean than letting Sam near the Impala's carburetor with a wrench.

The Impala also gives Sam a chance to express his feelings, particularly about Dean. In season one, Sam rediscovers his role in the family, renewing his relationship with both Dean and the Impala. Dean wants Sam to stay, and is happy to let him in the driver's seat. In "Bugs" (1-8), Dean emerges from a seedy bar after a hard night of hustling pool to find all six-foot-four of Sam sprawled across the hood of the Impala. It's a sign that Sam is comfortably back in the family unit—and also that he's a typical bratty younger brother, subtly challenging Dean's position of older-brother–in-charge. Of course, in latter seasons Sam wouldn't lounge on the Impala. Not only has his relationship with Dean evolved, but he's bulked up quite a bit and these days he would crush her like a tin can!

On a more somber note, during "In My Time of Dying" (2-1), when Dean lies in a coma and the Impala lies smashed in a junk yard, Bobby suggests there is nothing of the car worth salvaging. Sam, however, counters, "Listen to me, Bobby. If there's only one working part, that's enough. We're not just going to give up on . . ." Bobby, God bless the sensitive heart under that gruff, pig hat-wearing exterior, knows immediately that it is Dean about whom Sam is talking.

Just like Sam and Dean, the Impala has Daddy issues. The Impala was John's car first; he was a mechanic, so we can assume he restored her. As his life changed, the Impala was the one reminder of the man he had been, before he became an obsessed demon hunter.

We know John gave Dean the Impala, and while we don't know exactly when, it must've been a significant occasion—an anointing, if you will, of his oldest son. To Dean, the car represents John and his mission. In accepting it, Dean stepped into his role in the "family business" and acknowledged that he wanted to be just like his father. We know that deep in his subconscious, which we visit in "Dream a Little Dream of Me" (3-10), Dean continues to see the car as John's and as a signifier of his father's influence on him even after his death.

After he gives the Impala to Dean, John retains his role as patriarch by replacing the Impala with a monster truck—bigger in every way than the Impala, with much larger, not at all phallicly significant, weapons. The separation of John from the Impala is a sign of him disconnecting from his family, his heart, and without her he becomes a loner, focused solely on his vengeful quest.

When John reunites with his sons in "Dead Man's Blood" (1-20), he makes a crack to Dean about the state of the car: "Dean, why don't you touch up your car, before you get rust? I wouldn't have given you the damn thing if I thought you were going to ruin it." John is reasserting his paternal authority—reminding Dean where the car came from and who the car represents. In other words: respect the car, respect me.

After John's death, with the Impala a wreck, Dean drives a loaner from Bobby in "Everybody Loves a Clown" (2-2): a family van with soft pop, rather than cock rock, playing on the radio. In Freudian terms, he experiences the loss of his father (the phallus-owner) as castration: "I feel like a freaking soccer mom." Beyond the purely Oedipal, this can more broadly be seen as Dean having lost the power to act. He has no clear enemy to fight, and he has no idea what to do with the enigmatic warning John has left him about Sam.

One of the arguably most powerful moments in the show—and in Dean and the Impala's relationship—comes when he turns against her at the end of this episode. Sam breaks down and reveals to Dean his deep grief over John's death and his regret that he never got a chance to reconcile with him. As he leaves, Dean turns to the Impala, which he has been repairing, and in a heartbreaking scene, pounds into her with a tire iron. Over and over. Seventeen times, as grief smashes into him, he smashes into the Impala. Demolishing what he loves, what he has been trying to restore. Expressing his rage at his father, for causing Sam this grief, for abandoning Dean, for leaving him with the guilt of knowing John died for him, and for charging Dean with the unthinkable: the task of killing Sam.

This symbolic destruction of the father, of that which John used to appoint his son as his successor, also suggests that Dean is going to follow a different path than his father. In the next episode, "Bloodlust," the Impala is back on the road with Dean at the wheel. At first, it appears as if Dean is following full-bore down John Winchester's road, as he takes on the hunt for vampires with a frightening intensity. However, by the end of the episode, Dean has started to question the values his father taught him—that everything supernatural is evil. This is developed throughout this season and the next, as Dean time and again tries to pull away from hunting, questioning the cost of what he and Sam do, and as he starts to see the world in more ethical shades of grey than John Winchester did.

To Sam too, the Impala represents his father and his mission. In "Scarecrow" (1-11), he is frustrated that John has made contact with them only to send them on another hunt while refusing Sam's plea to let him join in the search for the demon that killed Jess and Mary. Sam storms out of and then walks away from the Impala—symbolically rejecting his father's authority. Dean, however, accepts his father's directions, and stays with the Impala and the hunt. Later in "Dead Man's Blood," it is when Sam is driving the Impala that he ceases to follow John's directions, and uses it to stop John's truck in its tracks and challenge his father's authority.

Another example of how the Impala links Sam with John can be seen after Dean's death on Wednesday in "Mystery Spot." Sam transforms into a version of his father—fanatical and revenge-driven, although slightly neater. The Impala too changes back to John's car—complete with anal-retentively organized weapons in a pop-out compartment in the trunk.

And let us not forget that the Impala is integral to the story as a car. *Supernatural* is a quest story of the sort that has been around since Odysseus was a boy. All heroes need transport, be it Jason's *Argo*, Don Quixote's Rocinante, or the choppers in *Easy Rider*. Sam and Dean follow their heroes' path in a Chevy Impala. The physical journey is merely a reflection of the characters' internal journey, their own search for meaning and purpose and truth.

The Impala's meanderings back and forth across America with no clear destination or goal reflect the postmodern project of constructing self, where the old truths are broken down and nothing is assured. The boys are on the road to nowhere—and everywhere. The mission statement for the Winchesters—"saving people, hunting things"—is continually challenged and disrupted as the series progresses. Sometimes the people are evil, and the things need saving. Later it turns out the things (ghosts and demons) actually used to be people. Even saving each other is problematized for the brothers, when it turns out Sam might be the Antichrist and saving Dean from his deal may mean losing a war against Hell. And in the Winchesters' world, not even death—or at least staying dead—is certain.

The Impala fights alongside Dean and Sam, nurtures and supports them, and undoubtedly would charge into Hell to save them. Her role in *Supernatural* has gained her an enthusiastic following from fans, who have christened her "Metallicar" in reference to her favorite type of music, and her image can be found on merchandise from trading cards to collectible plates. The Impala isn't just another TV muscle car; she embodies the heart and soul of this show. The Impala *is* a Winchester.

JULES WILKINSON was raised by television in the wilds of suburbia in Melbourne, Australia. This explains a lot, particularly her ability to sing the alto harmony to every TV theme ever written. Her extensive work as a freelance writer includes news reporting, ghost writing a health advice column and reviewing everything from restaurants to gay porn videos. Jules' stand-up comedy has confused, and occasionally amused, audiences at festivals around Australia. She is also part of the team behind the Wiki site www.supernaturalwiki.com, which documents everything about *Supernatural* and its fandom.

One of the more unique aspects of Supernatural *is the fact that it has only two main characters: Sam and Dean Winchester, the show's central protagonists. Sure, other characters come and go—most of them die horribly—but apart from Sam and Dean, has any other character appeared in virtually every single episode? Only one: Dean's '67 Chevy Impala, the "Metallicar."*

So why is an ancient, gas-guzzling muscle car such an essential part of the Winchester brothers' journey? Mary Fechter explores the physical, emotional, and metaphorical importance of the Impala in Supernatural's *mythology.*

MARY FECHTER

RIDING DOWN THE HIGHWAY

Why the Impala Is the Third Main Character

She was there for them the night their mother died.

She carried them through their childhood as their father chased his vengeance.

She took them on their quest to find their father.

She saved their lives in an impact with a semi.

She hides their secrets.

She is the Impala.

THE CONNECTION TO THE PAST

The only constant in the lives of the Winchester brothers is Dean's 1967 Impala, a fact made clear from the first act of the pilot episode, where John cradles his sons on the hood of the car as their house burns. In the next act, twenty-two years later, grown-up Dean and Sam walk from Sam's apartment to that same vehicle.

Since childhood, they've known only temporary homes and motel rooms. Whatever belongings that traveled with them had to fit in the Impala or be left behind. Her roomy interior was their playground as their father followed his grim path. Imagine young Sam and Dean on the endless road trip, teasing each other, fighting, wanting to stop to eat or go to the bathroom, likely driving John crazy. The practical jokes shown in "Hell House" (1-17) might have begun on those long-ago drives as the boys entertained themselves.

How long did it take before the Impala wasn't just a means of transportation, but a home in herself? Dean longs so much for a home, and is more attached to the Impala than Sam is, because it is the only home he's known, the only thing he took from the home where his mother died. Sam had a home with Jessica, and he doesn't remember anything about living in Lawrence. Dean does. He's so connected to the vehicle that even when they are on the run from the FBI, he can't give it up, even when keeping it could cost him his freedom. As much as Dean has sacrificed, giving up the car is a last resort.

The Impala as Legacy

John was a mechanic before Mary's death and probably restored the Impala himself. Later, he taught Dean to take care of the vehicle, one of the "normal" activities they did together. Dean craved anything normal and adored his father, so this time together must have been treasured. Imagine young Dean soaking up every minute with his hero, absorbing every word that came out of John's mouth. Perhaps John told him the car would belong to him someday.

Sam and John didn't share the same connection. If they had, if Sam had shown interest in the car—in their work—would his relationship with John have been different? If they'd found more common ground, would John have been able to let Sam go to college without fighting? John understood Sam wanted more than the hunting life.

John's death turned the Impala from merely a connection with their past to a legacy, the only thing, besides his life, that John had left to pass on to his sons. After John's death, Dean was determined to repair the vehicle he loved, the physical tie to his father.

Sam offered to help restore the Impala, partly to be close to Dean in his grief, but also needing to be close to the memory of his father. After seeing his father again, renewing their relationship even if not quite forgiving him, Sam was devastated. Dean refused Sam's help, torn up with guilt over being the reason John died, but also because the love for the car was something he and his dad had shared, something Sam didn't have a part in. Dean guarded his and John's closeness in his grief.

When Sam confronted Dean about his own feelings about John's death, Dean denied his pain. But when Sam walked away, Dean took out his anger and helplessness on the Impala, striking it again and again with a crowbar, destroying all the work he'd put into it. The hunting life had taken that toll on their family—destroying all of them either by taking their lives or coloring their souls so they could never have a normal life. He was angry his father was dead, but also angry at the responsibility, the job, and the secret John had left him.

In season three, Dean had a year to live after bargaining his soul for Sam's life. After he got past the *carpe diem* attitude, he started to think about what he was leaving behind and realized it wasn't much. Meeting Ben, and believing temporarily that Ben might be his son, in "The Kids Are Alright" (3-2), brought this home. His only physical possession is the Impala, and when he tried to talk to Sam about taking care of the car, Sam shut him out. Sam couldn't envision continuing on his own, even though the release of the demons from the Devil's Gate was his responsibility. To Sam, learning about taking care of the Impala meant he was going to have to go forward on his own. Just as Dean didn't want to go forward on his own when he thought Sam had the demon virus in "Croatoan" (2-9), or when Sam died in "All Hell Breaks Loose" (2-21, 2-22), Sam didn't want to do the job alone. But even so, he knew the Impala would be part of the fight, a tangible tie to Dean and his father after they were gone.

THE CONNECTION TO THE JOB

Throughout it all, the Impala ties the Winchesters to their job. She enables them to travel back roads to find the places evil hides. Her trunk, big enough to hide a body, contains their weapons, ammunition, charms, research books, and a dream catcher. Her 427 engine gets them to a case in a hurry, or out of town fast. Her skid plates help protect her when she drives into a haunted house or over a rough country road to escape a haunted truck. Many Americans find freedom on the open roads, but the Winchester brothers don't find freedom from their job even there.

When John passed the Impala to Dean, he showed faith in his son's ability. Giving Dean the Impala meant he was able to send his son out on hunts alone, trusting that Dean knew enough about evil to take care of himself. When this rite of passage happened, though, is not clear.

In the pilot episode, Sam was surprised Dean was doing a job by himself, though Dean was twenty-six. However, when Dean was nineteen, he met Lisa, a.k.a. Gumby Girl, when Sam and John were on a hunt in Florida, so the Impala was probably Dean's at the time. When had John realized his sons would have to carry on the job without him? Had John ever thought they'd be able to stop hunting, or once he knew what was out there, did he intend to keep going, fighting as much evil as he could?

At the end of season one, the brothers didn't know there was a whole community of hunters. As far as they knew, they and Bobby—and Caleb and Pastor Jim—were it. The Winchesters couldn't walk away from this life. In season two, they learned about the Roadhouse and other hunters, but even with this knowledge, they couldn't walk away. Their quest for the Yellow-Eyed Demon wasn't done.

The Impala's trunk, where a secret compartment hid the tools of their trade, was the target of Dean's attack at the end of "Everybody Loves a Clown" (2-2). John had died and left them to do this job on their own, and Dean's anger and frustration and fear and guilt was focused there on the symbol of their work and the sacrifices their job had required them to make.

At the end of "Croatoan," after facing a situation that brought their mortality into sharp focus, Dean said, "I just think we ought to . . . go to the Grand Canyon." When Sam questioned him, he continued. "Yeah, I mean, all this driving back and forth cross country and, you know, I've never been to the Grand Canyon?" Even such a detour, taking time for themselves, would mean people would die because the brothers weren't around to save them from what goes bump in the night.

In season one, Dean loved the job. He didn't think of doing anything else. Everything he learned about being a hunter from his father was black and white. The creatures he encountered, the things people did, were either good or evil. He didn't have choices to make.

In season two, after losing his father to the job and carrying the heavy knowledge that he might have to kill his brother, the job weighed deeper on him. He was starting to see those shades of gray, especially regarding Sam and his uncertain future. Dean had decisions to make, and none of them were easy. The choices and the responsibility were getting to him, and nothing showed this more than his willingness to give the Impala to the survivors of the town in "Croatoan." He confessed how tired he was of the job, and he was willing to die alongside his brother. If he couldn't save these people, maybe the Impala could.

In "Bloodlust" (2-3), with the Impala fixed and cresting the hill to "Back in Black," Dean was putting on an outward show for his brother. He was still grieving for his father, but he was putting on a brave face, and the Impala gleams accordingly. Sam remarked on his good mood and Dean replied, "I got my car, got a case, things are looking up."

Really, Dean couldn't leave the hunter's life any more than he could walk away from the car. When Dean checked the Impala's trunk in "What Is and What Should Never Be" (2-20), the trunk was empty except for some trash and a few copies of *Maxim* magazine. Dean grinned and said, "Who'd've thought, baby? We're civilians." But he seemed to be a bit disappointed in how he turned out, despite how happy as he was to see Mary alive and Sam and Jess together. Dean is GOOD at being a hunter, and in this alternate reality he was a screw-up, as we learned from Sam's stories about Dean's scams and seductions, and the way everyone asked him about whether he'd been drinking. Hunting is his skill, and if he needed proof to go on to fight another day, the fantasy world was it. So he returned to the life he knew and continued the hunt. It holds him together and gives him purpose.

THE CONNECTION TO DEAN

Television shows have long perpetuated the myth that the car defines the man. Starsky and Hutch's Gran Torino showcased the renegade detectives. The Dukes of Hazzard's 1969 Dodge Charger identified them as outlaws. Magnum P.I.'s Ferrari defined the detective as flashy.

What does Dean's 1967 Impala say about him?

The Impala is as much a part of Dean as the leather jacket, the amulet Sam gave him, his boots, and his wisecracks. All the Impala's various meanings come together here in Dean—Dean is a product of a unique past, as much John's legacy to the world as the Impala is John's legacy to Dean, a hunter through and through.

In most of season one, with the exception of the episode "Faith" (1-12), when Dean was dying after being electrocuted during a hunt, the Impala was always gleaming, buffed to where the brothers could see their reflections in her roof during end-of-episode conversations. Dean had everything he wanted—his brother was by his side, they were looking for their dad, and his family would be together again soon. Even in episodes like "Bugs" (1-8), where the weather was rainy, the Impala was shiny. The boys were searching for their father but there was no real urgency. They knew John could take care of himself. At the end of the episodes the Impala would make her triumphant exit into the sunset to the accompaniment of classic rock, job finished, people saved.

The change began in "Provenance" (1-19). The first scene with the Impala showed her lined up next to all the expensive cars at an art auction, and she looked uncharacteristically filthy. The contrast was clear—the Winchesters' life would always be on the fringe of normal society, never a part of it. But more, while the Impala didn't fit in, Sam did. He knew about art history, he charmed the upper-class Sara. Dean hadn't seen this side of Sam. He wasn't around when Sam was falling in love with Jessica, missed out on that part of Sam's life. He regretted not knowing Jess better, not seeing his brother in love. He wanted his brother to be happy, wanted him to have a normal life though he knew that meant Sam would leave him. And while Dean wanted that for his brother, he knew he'd never have it for himself. He'd done too much, seen too much, to turn away from the hunting life. The car's condition reflected this hopelessness.

In "Dead Man's Blood" (1-20), Dean had everything he thought he wanted—the family was working together again. But it wasn't all he remembered. He'd forgotten what it was like to not be in charge, not to be making his own decisions, and he'd forgotten what it was like to be the buffer between John and Sam. Keeping them from each other's throats had become harder now with Sam's sense of independence and John's even deeper focus now that he was hot on the demon's trail. The Impala was dirty and John called Dean on it: "Dean, why don't you touch up your car, before you get rust? I wouldn't have given you the damn thing if I thought you were going to ruin it."

The blow stunned Dean. He valued the trust his father had in him, and if his dad questioned his care of the car, maybe John was doubting his faith in Dean's hunting ability. Sam saw his brother's reaction and bristled at his father, then silently urged his brother to stand up for himself. But Dean remained silent. Perhaps he, who knows John best, understood John's remark was made out of frustration. So much of their lives was out of control—taking care of a vehicle was one thing they could control.

Dean's dreams of family togetherness crumbled further when John revealed their secret weapon, the Colt. Once the demon was dead, what then? John's quest had taken twenty-two years of their lives. What would happen when the hunt was over? Dean's future was uncertain, and the dirty car reflected that turmoil.

By the episode "Devil's Trap" (1-22), when the boys knew the demon had their father, Sam had to wipe dust from the Impala's trunk before he could draw the devil's trap on it with a grease pencil, making it a lockbox to keep the Colt safe. Dean never would have allowed the layer of dust if his mind hadn't been occupied.

Then the Impala was crushed by a semi. Her steel frame protected her men, but she sacrificed herself. When Sam went to help Bobby clean out the trunk before the authorities could find their weapons, he had to convince Bobby not to sell her for scrap in "In My Time of Dying," (2-1). "There's nothing to fix," Bobby told him. "The frame's a pretzel, and the engine's ruined. There's barely any parts worth salvaging." But Sam argued, "Listen to me, Bobby. If there's only one working part, that's enough. We're not just going to give up on . . ." Sam may not have known he was speaking of Dean, but Bobby did. He knew, as we did, that Sam felt that by giving up on the car, he would be giving up on Dean. He refused to give up on either one. He had to believe that Dean would live, so he made the comment that "Dean will kill me" if he allowed the

Impala to get junked.

As season two progressed, the Impala began to look road-weary—particularly in episodes where Dean was worried and anxious, such as "Crossroads Blues" (2-8), where Dean considered trading his soul for his father's return, and "Nightshifter" (2-12), when Dean's face on the news started a manhunt for the Winchesters. On the run, Dean had no time to care for his car or for himself. The secret he carried weighed on him. The ride-into-the-sunset scenes were rare; the boys were encountering tougher cases and failing to find the answers they were looking for.

In season two, Sam never drove the Impala. He was driving the night she was T-boned, and before the car was fixed, John told Dean Sam's secret. Did Dean keep Sam from driving the car because he no longer entirely trusted his brother? It's a stark contrast to season one, when Dean's offer to let Sam drive showed in a very Dean-like way that he was reaching out to his brother, trying to bring Sam back into the hunting life and help him get over Jess's death.

In "Croatoan," when Dean chose staying with Sam, handing over the Impala's keys to the town survivors, Sam understood the depth of his brother's sacrifice. The car was all they had, and with her gone, so was their means of escape, their weapons, their know-how, and their home.

At the beginning of season three, Dean had a year to live. He mistreated the Impala—bouncing her over roads like he was one of the Duke boys instead of a Winchester—even as he abused his own body, eating bacon cheeseburgers for breakfast. But once he found his desire to live, he started tending to his baby again. In "Fresh Blood" (3-7), he began teaching Sam how to take care of the car, symbolically getting Sam ready to fight the war on his own. In the season finale, he told Sam to remember what John and Dean had taught him, and to take care of the car.

Why do the writers use the Impala as an outward sign of Dean's subconscious? Novelists have the luxury of showing their characters' inner turmoil in words. Television writers have to depend on the actors' ability and physical clues. What better physical clue than Dean's most prized possession?

MARY FECHTER has been known to become obsessed every now and again, and one of her favorite obsessions is *Supernatural* (especially Dean, you might have noticed). She writes romance for The Wild Rose Press and Samhain Publishing under the name M.J. Fredrick. Visit her Web site at www.mjfredrick.com or her blog at www.mary-writesromance.blogspot.com.

John Winchester and a demon-killing Colt six-shooter: Supernatural's *own* deus ex machina? *Or do the secretive, seemingly all-knowing, and vaguely mysterious hunter and the magical, seemingly all-killing, and vaguely mysterious weapon parallel each other's journey through the series' narrative?*

Tracy S. Morris explores Daddy Winchester's role within the Supernatural *universe and the weapon that finally brings his mission of vengeance to an end.*

TRACY S. MORRIS

JOHN WINCHESTER AND THE MAGIC BULLET THEORY

> *Back in 1835, When Halley's comet was overhead, same night those men died at the Alamo, they say Samuel Colt made a gun. A special gun. He made it for a hunter. A man like us, only on horseback. Story goes, he made thirteen bullets. This hunter used the gun a half dozen times before he disappeared, the gun along with him. . . . They say . . . they say this gun can kill anything.*
>
> —JOHN WINCHESTER, "Dead Man's Blood" (1-20)

> *There is a fifth character in the play who doesn't appear except in this larger-than-life-sized photograph over the mantle. This is our father, who left us a long time ago.*
>
> —TENNESSEE WILLIAMS, *The Glass Menagerie*

One of the major influences for *Supernatural* as cited by the show's creator, Eric Kripke (if, according to fans, Joss Whedon is God, then surely Kripke is the Little Baby Jesus), is Joseph Campbell's 1949 book

The Hero With a Thousand Faces. As a nod to the book's influence, it was even used as a prop in the first season episode "Wendigo" (1-2).

Most anyone who knows Star Wars or Lord of the Rings is already familiar with the formula that Campbell documented in *The Hero With a Thousand Faces*: the archetypal hero is presented with a call to adventure, undergoes trials, is guided by a wise man, and at some point acquires a mystical and wondrous object to aid his quest.

In *Supernatural*, Sam is obviously the reluctant hero who initially refuses the call to adventure in favor of the safe world of academia and a shiny future in tax law. In the absence of their father, the older brother Dean, who embraced the lifestyle that Sam rejected, plays the role of wise man and guide. (And flirts with the role of the soul mate, in a platonic, manly, and fraternal way. Really. We swear.)

In "Dead Man's Blood," the boys acquire their wondrous object: a gun that can kill anything. This is *Supernatural*'s One Ring of Power, the Holy Grail, the Singing Sword.

Or maybe not.

Fans of the series have had very mixed feelings about the Colt as an item. Like each of the aforementioned plot devices, the very existence of something like the Colt weakens the story because it places too much power in the boys' hands. With a gun that can kill anything, Sam and Dean can—well, kill anything. With it, the boys no longer have to rely on their own skills to solve problems. Every conflict they encounter starts to have a Colt-shaped answer.

According to Super-wiki,[1] a *Supernatural* canon and fandom resource, "the Colt is a singular gun made by Samuel Colt in 1835 for a hunter at the time." The gun is a Texas Patterson 1835, the first cap-and-ball handgun ever made, but this particular version has supernatural powers: "when used with the similarly magic bullets made especially for it, the gun can kill anything."

When the Colt was first introduced, we weren't told specifically how Samuel Colt managed to achieve this marvel of supernatural engineering. John Winchester mentioned that it was created when Halley's Comet was passing near Earth, on the same night as a bloody battle at

[1] http://supernatural.oscillating.net/index.php?title=The_Colt.

the Alamo (according to Super-wiki, it's likely that the battle was the Siege of Béxar, and not the more famous bloody last stand with Jim Bowie, Davy Crockett, and Sam Houston).

Judging by the description that John gave, the Colt's creation presumably required a perfect alignment of magic, noble and willing bloody sacrifice, and a once-in-a-blue-moon astral event. (Or, apparently, a demon who knows how to make magic weapons. But what are the chances that a magic weapon-making demon would be willing to help a hunter? Better in the year 2007 than in 1835, it seems.)

Additionally, the Colt's use was limited to thirteen bullets, the idea obviously being that when they're gone, they're gone. So each bullet had to count. By the time the Colt came into the hands of the family Winchester, there were only five bullets remaining.

Between John, Dean, Sam, and their poignant yet completely screwed-up version of family love, they blew through four of the five bullets in defense of one another—all the while yelling at each other about who wasted which bullet.

From a storytelling perspective the Colt is problematic because it's essentially a *deus ex machina*. The phrase's literal meaning is "God from the machine." The term comes from Greek tragedy, in which an actor playing one of the Greek gods would be lowered to the stage by crane and then right all the wrongs existing in the drama. In modern storytelling, a *deus ex machina* is any kind of unlikely contrivance that solves an otherwise unsolvable problem. When the *deus ex machina* is an object, it usually grants the wielder an almost godlike power. And like the original *deus ex machina*, it makes for a very uninteresting plot—as well as a very short plot.

However, I think the Colt serves an important function outside of its role as *deus ex machina*: as a metaphor for the journey that John Winchester takes throughout the series.

I'll return to John and the Colt in a minute. First I'd like to examine Kripke's interest in the journey itself. From Sam's journey to accepting his place in a world that doesn't fit his definition of *normal* to the Winchester family quest to kill the Yellow-Eyed Demon to the boys' physical trek down the road to the next monster: every aspect of *Supernatural* is about a trip of some type. Though the show is obviously influenced by the hero's journey as laid out in *The Hero With a Thousand Faces*, it also draws on the idea of the great American journey, as expressed through the lure of the open road.

In the past, Kripke said that his influence for this aspect of the show was Jack Kerouac's autobiographical work *On the Road*. In the book, two men set out on a series of trips, searching for something that even they can't define. It's no coincidence that Sam and Dean of *Supernatural* have names remarkably similar to those of Kerouac's main characters, Sal and Dean. Or that Dean Winchester seemed at first a lot like Dean Moriarity: a charismatic drifter, con man, and womanizer who is fixated on finding his father.

And speaking of fathers, while the boys spent most of season one looking for John, he was on his own journey, the same quest he had been on for twenty-two years: to find his wife's killer. John's pursuit was ultimately the boys' pursuit. And while the family motto may be *saving people, hunting things*, it was a diversion at best, something to pass the time while they found information on the demon that killed Mary Winchester.

But what does this have to do with the Colt? To understand how the Colt and John's journey relate, you first need to understand that objects in *Supernatural* take on a deeper meaning. In a show where Sam and Dean are the only characters in each episode, the things that they rely on, such as the Impala, Dean's amulet, John's journal, and the Colt, take on greater significance. For example, many devoted fans have called Dean's classic Impala the third major character.[2] Some fans have compared Dean's emotional state in season one to the condition of the Impala throughout that story arc. And at the end of season one when the car was wrecked, fan outpouring of support to bring it back was greater than some canceled shows get.

If the Impala is affiliated with Dean, then the Colt is an object associated with John's journey through seasons one and two of the series. Neither John nor the Colt were present through much of season one. But John, like Tom's father in Tennessee Williams's *The Glass Menagerie*, was still an important character—one who was never present, yet whose

[2] *Editor's Note*: See essays by Jules Wilkinson and Mary Fechter in this volume.

choices colored everything that Sam and Dean did. While we watched Sam and Dean search for John, John's adventures took place off-screen. The Demon's endgame was starting to play out and John decided to avoid his sons, keeping them ignorant of what was happening, to keep them safe. And while he was getting close to finding the demon, he still had no idea how to kill it. Shortly after John re-enters Sam and Dean's lives, they learn about the Colt. Like the gun, John is wrapped in a little bit of mystery. What was he doing in the year that he separated himself from Sam and Dean? What did he know that wasn't written in the journals? In interviews, Kripke has said that John knew everything that the show has yet to reveal.

The mysteries that surrounded the Colt were just as tantalizing. Who was the hunter that Samuel Colt made it for? Why did he create the gun? Where did the extra bullets go? How did it come into the hands of Daniel Elkins? Why did Elkins hide it from John Winchester?

Even the number of usable bullets left in the gun was significant. By the time the Winchester family obtained the Colt, eight of the original thirteen bullets were gone. Just as there weren't many bullets left in the gun, John's time on the earth was short. From this point on out, every choice he made needed to count as much as each bullet.

Ultimately, in "In My Time of Dying" (2-1), John chose his family over the hunt and vengeance by trading the Colt and his life to the Yellow-Eyed Demon in exchange for Dean's life. But John's journey was far from over (and there was still one bullet left in the absentee Colt). John was down (way, way down in the pit of despair), but as we later learned, he was far from out.

John had given the Colt to the Yellow-Eyed Demon, and we assumed that the Demon would do the smart thing—having been given a gun that can kill anything (except non-corporeal demons, as we saw in baby Rose's bedroom in "Salvation" [1-21]), himself included—and stash it somewhere that it couldn't be picked up by an enemy and fired at him (like, say, the New Mariana Trench). Or at the very least, get rid of the last bullet rather than keeping it loaded in the gun.

Instead, the loaded Colt returned quite unexpectedly at the end of the season as the key to a gate to Hell. (It can kill anything. It's the key to a Hell gate. Does it also make julienne fries?) If the Colt was making an appearance again, could John Winchester be far behind?

Apparently not. In the next episode "All Hell Breaks Loose (Part 2)" (2-22), John, in spectral form, clawed his way out of Hell (which, according to Demon Tammi in "Malleus Maleficarum" [3-9], was a heck of a fight) just in time to tussle with the Yellow-Eyed Demon, save Dean, and buy Dean the time to grab the Colt and kill the demon with the last bullet. Many fans saw John's appearance at the end of this episode as a form of *deus ex machina*, not unlike the Colt—just one more parallel between them.

At the end of season two, John's journey was over and the Colt was reduced to antique status. Of course, that wasn't the end of the gun. But with the conclusion of John's journey, the Colt's function on the show changed. The gun itself even changed: the new and improved version had a seemingly endless supply of bullets. Before this could create another *deus ex machina* problem, however, the writers once again wrote the Colt out of the show.

Will the gun ever be seen again? Will John? In a story where a gun can kill anything and a man can claw his way out of Hell, either seems possible.

TRACY S. MORRIS wants to be as dangerous as possible. She is a black belt in taekwondo and likes to dress in corsetry and poke people with sharp objects—that is to say she has fenced with the SCA. She reports on pop culture, the paranormal, and writing for Firefox News (http://www.firefox.org), and has had an essay appear in the Benbella Books Smart Pop anthology *Alias Assumed: Sex, Lies and SD-6*.

Morris's first novel, *Tranquility*, a southern gonzo whodunnit, was the runner-up for a Darryl Award in 2006. She is currently working on the sequel. You can find her on the Web at http://www.tracysmorris.com.

Gordon Walker: Good bad guy? Bad good guy? Is he a monstrous human being made no more and no less monstrous when turned into a vampire? Or is he an ordinary man who lost a loved one to a supernatural force and was simply doing his best to make sure the same thing didn't happen to anyone else?

That last one would sound familiar to anyone who knows anything about the Winchesters, and yet by the time Gordon was decapitated by, in his view, the greatest threat to the world in existence (namely Sam Winchester), Gordon Walker had become the bad guy everybody loved to hate.

Here, Amy Berner examines Gordon's role in Supernatural, *as a yardstick by which the Winchesters' actions may be judged, and as a warning of what Dean or Sam could so easily become—obsessive, merciless hunters . . . or the supernatural things they hunt.*

AMY BERNER

THE EVILS OF HATING . . . UM, EVIL

What Gordon Walker Did Wrong and Why We Needed Him Anyway

> *"I love this life because it's all black and white. There's no maybe. You find the bad thing, you kill it. Most people spend their lives in shades of gray, but not us."*
>
> —GORDON WALKER, "Bloodlust" (2-3)

Let's say that you have a demon hunter who is dedicated, smart, resourceful, focused, and who makes the world safer for ordinary folks day in and day out. Let's say that this guy will do whatever it takes to rid the world of demons, monsters, and other nasties. Let's say this guy falls at the hands of a traditionally awful sort of creature, a vampire, but although he becomes one himself, he somehow keeps a remnant of himself and tries to carry out one last mission to save the world. Sounds like a great guy, right? Maybe even a hero?

Not if he's Gordon Walker. For a character who only appeared in a whopping four episodes ("Bloodlust," "Hunted" [2-10], "Bad Day at Black Rock" [3-3], and "Fresh Blood" [3-7]), this character developed into one of the most complex that we've seen on the show: a bad guy who honestly believed that his efforts led toward a better, safer world.

Why have a villain who isn't, well, supernatural? Because a character like Gordon is essential, both for establishing who hunters are as a group and for taking a closer look at the Winchesters themselves.

For the structure and mythology of demon hunters to be fully established, the series needed to show what rules hunters follow as they pursue their targets . . . and, more importantly, what rules they *should* follow. And to understand what a hunter should do, we need to know what they shouldn't do. There is no governing body for hunters (as far as we know), so each acts as an independent agent with carte blanche to hunt as they see fit. However, hunters have a brotherhood (and sisterhood) of sorts, and their loose society has a code of conduct. This code isn't enforced, so only social pressure can change behavior . . . at least in the case of hunters who care about the opinion of their fellows. Gordon, of course, didn't care. Above all else, it was the hunt that mattered.

But more importantly, we the viewers needed Gordon so that we could better understand our heroes. The Winchester brothers are different enough from one another—in a complementary way—that there are opportunities for conflict galore every week. However, to fully understand the nature and extent of those differences we need exposure to someone who is the complete opposite of one of them—in this case, Sam. Gordon's presence highlights not only who Sam is (by showing us clearly who he is not), but also where Dean falls in the spectrum between them. Sam and Gordon both became hunters because of the death of a loved one, but they took very different paths afterward, and Dean, well, he's a bit more like Gordon at times than we might like to admit. And he knows it.

> DEAN: (*to Gordon*) I might be like you, and I might not. But you're the one tied up right now. ("Bloodlust")

Thanks to Gordon, we understand both of the brothers better, as hunters and as people. When we see Dean pushing ethical limits in pursuit of the evil of the week, or when we see Sam acting somewhat un-Sam-like after his return from the dead, we have a way to measure how close to the line they are and whether they have crossed it. Without Gordon the ethical barometer isn't quite as easy to read. Gordon is the Winchesters' dark mirror; he shows us what could happen were the Winchesters to travel down the wrong path, a path that both of them approached during the third season thanks to their respective brushes with death.

What drove Gordon down that path? If the details of his background are a bit fuzzy, not to worry, his backstory was fairly straightforward: His sister was captured and turned by vampires when he was eighteen, and his efforts to save her failed. Driven by revenge, he became a hunter, eventually finding both his newly vampiric sister and the vampire that turned her and killing them both. After that, killing vampires and other monsters filled a "hole" within Gordon, a hole ripped out when his sister was turned, and nothing mattered more to him. He became known in hunter circles as a great hunter but, well, I think Ellen said it best:

SAM: I—I thought you said he was a good hunter.
ELLEN: Yeah, and Hannibal Lecter's a good psychiatrist. ("Bloodlust")

In other words, being good at something doesn't at all mean being in any way "good." The other hunters respected Gordon's abilities, certainly, but they were also wary of this member of their loose society. The knowledge and skills that hunters possess give them a sort of power—and Ellen believed that Gordon misused that power, although not to a point that she actively worked against him.

Gordon's hunting philosophy was in stark contrast to Sam's initial style of hunting (although Sam moved closer to the middle as time went by, especially when his brother was in danger), with Dean's falling somewhere in the middle (though he leaned closer to Sam's side as they continued to fight together). Sam was a reluctant hunter rather than one who embraced it like Gordon did, someone who could see shades of grey rather than dealing only in absolutes. Dean understood and bonded with Gordon at their first meeting, but Sam and Gordon were oil and water from the very beginning.

Yes, Gordon did some incredibly awful things while trying to be a good guy: torture, murder, and a near Winchester-cide. But as a hunter, he "embraced the life" ("Bloodlust"). He became single-minded and ruthless, but also incredibly effective at killing vampires and demons. Doesn't he get points for that?

Not really. But do remember that Gordon Walker did try to leave the world a better place every day. He didn't want others to fall victim to his sister's fate. His problem was that his methods weren't what you'd call moral. Just efficient. Eliminating something (not "someone") that was more likely a threat than not and more likely going to kill innocents than not seems, on the surface, like the practical, reasonable thing to do. Walker was a "greater good" sort, the type who is okay with leaving a few bodies in his wake if it means more people are saved in the long run. Problem was, his methods of doing "good" made him as bad as, if not worse than, those naturally predisposed to evil.

But They're GOOD Vampires!

Horror audiences are normally in favor of vampire slayers. After all, conventional wisdom states that monsters are bad and those who hunt monsters are good.

Pitting Gordon against non-evil vampires made for a great character introduction. What happens when the monsters aren't evil and the hunter isn't good? A vampire struggling for redemption isn't a new concept (which is one of the joys of *Supernatural*, how they take familiar concepts and revisit them the Winchester Way. So what if you've seen an idea before on another television show? Horror traditions, legends and folklore are great for storytelling). Such vampires are the reluctant heroes fighting the monsters within themselves every day. But in all of these vampire stories, "good" vampires are the exception to the rule. *Supernatural*, too, has not revealed any way for vampires to become permanently good and productive members of society. No matter what their intentions or how many cows they may snack on, *Supernatural* vampires can slip at any time and kill humans again. To Gordon, someone else's sister could be their next victim. His version of a kindness to a vampire was killing with a well-sharpened weapon, making it "perfectly humane" ("Bloodlust").

Gordon took a hard-line view on the world of demons. Evil was evil. Period. Concepts like redemption, mercy, and compassion didn't enter into the equation. To him, monsters were all creatures of evil bent on death and destruction, and vampires were nothing but "mindless, bloodthirsty animals" ("Fresh Blood"). And 99.9 percent of the time, he was probably right about that. After all, his sister was given no mercy. The guy was bitter due to his history and understandably so. He could not accept shades of gray in his view of the world. A vampire trying to get by as harmlessly as possible could still do harm and therefore must not be allowed to survive.

Of course, going after a poor waiflike vampire named Lenore and her cohorts, who were just trying to get by on a human-free diet, was nothing compared to going up against the Winchesters. Sam defended the cow-drinkers, Dean reluctantly backed him up despite having bonded with his new buddy, and thus Gordon first became their enemy when he fought back. Dean tied Gordon to a chair after the two fought over the issue, even though Dean did and does agree that, when all is said and done, a vampire is still a vampire.

But was Sam right on this count, or were Gordon and Dean? Lenore could have gone back to her old ways at any time. Innocent people could have been killed. Did Lenore deserve to be treated as more than a monster, or was that all she was? To Sam, Lenore proved that she could be more by her actions, just like Ruby proved in the third season. Gordon, however, believed that she would ultimately be true to her nature, and that the danger she posed was too great to risk treating her as anything but what she was. And Dean, without Sam there, probably would have agreed.

> Sam: You didn't kill Lenore.
> Dean: Yeah but every instinct told me to. I was gonna kill her, I was gonna kill them all.
> Sam: Yeah, but Dean, you didn't. That's what matters.
> Dean: Yeah. 'Cause you're a pain in my ass. ("Bloodlust")

Dean, for all of his anti-vampire sentiments, knows where the all-important line is and knows not to cross it. This line (when his brother draws it) has become more and more important as the series has progressed, especially as both brothers have found themselves approaching it—mainly in order to save each other. Thanks to Gordon, they were forced early on to face that line, recognize where it lay. Gordon's actions threw up a red flag that made the brothers evaluate what they believed and why.

The only line that Gordon saw was a finish line, and he'd do whatever it took to get there. He had no moral compass to guide him; Dean, luckily, had his brother. As Dean said, "Come on, man. I know Sam, okay? Better than anyone. He's got more of a conscience than I do. I mean, the guy feels guilty searching the Internet for porn" ("Hunted"). And that conscience does a lot more than cause porn guilt; it makes both brothers better.

Targeting a Winchester Won't Win You Friends

> *Do it. Show your brother the evil killer you really are, Sammy. You're no better than the filthy things you hunt.*
>
> —Gordon Walker, "Hunted"

If you believed that someone was evil and would wreak havoc on all of humanity—the Antichrist, a demon power, whatever—what would you do? Gordon, true to form, took action. Gordon began hunting our boy Sam when he found out that he was a part of the upcoming war. How did he learn this nugget of information? By torturing a possessed teenage girl to death. Dealing with the possessed is tricky ground, to be sure, especially as the human may already be dead. Sam and Dean have had to deal with their share of possessed people, and haven't exactly been pleasant to them by any means, but they seem to save whom they can, using holy water whenever possible and exorcising rather than killing. Gordon apparently didn't consider that option.

He's probably a fan of waterboarding too. But I digress.

When Gordon learned that the human leader of the demon legions would spring from a small group of people, he began eliminating the threat one possibly evil human at a time. Maybe he didn't go quite as far as styling himself a Herod, killing children to prevent the rise of a king, but it's a pretty good comparison. After all, he was trying to kill the Antichrist.

These people were still human, even if some of them (like Ava) chose to use their paranormal powers to become monsters. Unlike the vampires, who were predisposed to evil, all of these humans were able to choose. But Gordon never even considered that they were not required to use their powers for evil. He believed that it should be official hunter policy—if such a thing could exist—that "Sam Winchester must die" ("Bad Day at Black Rock"), and he doubted that Sam was even still human. In Gordon's mind, there was no hope of redemption for Sam; he was already a monster and therefore had to be destroyed.

> GORDON: I'm not a killer, Dean. I'm a hunter. And your brother's fair game. ("Hunted")

Gordon truly believed that the world would be better and safer without Sam in it. In his black and white worldview, Sam was the enemy no matter what, and his actual role in trying to stop the gate from opening was dismissed.

But a quick reminder: John also thought that his youngest son might need to be killed if he became the Antichrist. He even saddled Dean with that responsibility when he died, believing the danger that Sam posed was very real. And Gordon believed that John would have done what Dean refused to do:

> Here's the thing: It would have wrecked him, but your dad, if it really came right down to it, he would have had the stones to do the right thing. You're telling me you're not the man he is? ("Hunted")

The thought that anyone needs to die for the "greater good" is stomach-turning, especially if that particular "anyone" is a character, like Sam, we like. But imagine if the world of the Winchesters was our world instead, and then think about all the innocent people who ended up dying because Gordon was stopped. Had Gordon succeeded in eliminating all of the "special children," Jake the Marine wouldn't have opened the portal to Hell and all of those pesky demons wouldn't have escaped. Think of the innocent folks who died despite never being part of the fight, and then add to them the number of people possessed by demons, their independence and identities ripped away in order to give those demons legs and arms and voices. Then, add on the murders and torment by pint-sized superdemon Lilith, made even worse by Sam's continued status as possible demonic leader because she didn't like the idea of competition.

None of that would have happened had Gordon been allowed to succeed in his task. Knowing all the awful results of opening the gate, all of that pain, that torture, that death, his motivation to kill the lot of them starts to make a little more sense.

Becoming the Monster (For Real)

> *"You got a lot of people fooled, but see, I know the truth. I know what it's like. We're the same now, you and me. I know how it is walking around with something evil inside you. It's just too bad you won't do the right thing and kill yourself. I'm gonna . . . as soon as I'm done with you. Two last good deeds. Killing you and killing myself."*
>
> —Gordon Walker, "Fresh Blood"

Gordon's fate was certainly ironic; after all, he became the creature he hated most. As his actions pushed him further and further from his own humanity, it was fitting that he eventually lost it altogether and became an entirely new kind of hunter. And it was only as a monster, not as a man, that he could be defeated and eliminated by the brothers Winchester.

Yet even as a monster he held on to one thing from his old life: his mission to kill Sam, hunting him with single-minded determination that would make any obsessed vampire proud. Was it that his goal was so monstrous that made it easier to retain so entirely? He was certainly monstrous in his efforts to complete his mission, ripping out the heart of his buddy Kubrick so that he could continue tracking Sam and then kidnapping a girl to serve as Winchester bait.

Or did he believe that his goal was so important to the world that even his new vampire self accepted the mission, willingly allowing it to take precedence over the hunger for new prey? Sam leading a demon army might not bode any better for vampires than for humans.

In *Supernatural*'s world, vampires aren't mindless killing machines. They appear to have free will in addition to their blood hunger. As a vampire, Gordon didn't have to pursue people who knew how to kill his kind. He could have started his life (well, an undead one, anyway) anew, leaving his responsibilities behind. He didn't. He chose the much more dangerous course: to hunt a hunter.

> GORDON: You have to let me do one last thing first.
> KUBRICK: What?
> GORDON: Kill Sam Winchester.
> KUBRICK: Gordon.
> GORDON: It's the only . . . it is the one good thing to come out of this nightmare. I'm stronger, I'm faster. I can finish him. ("Fresh Blood")

Of course, he didn't. And in the end, the only appropriate candidate for killing Vampire Gordon was Sam, his longtime prey. Had Gordon not been turned, the brothers might have let him live yet again, despite their previous attempts to control him (leaving him tied to a chair for a few days and sending him to jail) not having been all that successful. Had Sam killed him as a human, he would have taken a step toward becoming the same sort of monster Gordon was . . . although Sam did seriously consider killing Gordon even before they knew he had been turned, both a testament to how bad Gordon had become and a reflection of how much Sam had changed. Plus, from a pure storytelling perspective, we do like to see the pursued turning the tables on their pursuer, even if Sam did say during his and Gordon's first meeting that "decapitations aren't my idea of a good time" ("Bloodlust").

But Sam has changed. Sam from the first season might not have been able to slowly decapitate anything, let alone someone who used to be a human that he knew; that was a disturbing death even by *Supernatural* standards. In the end, Sam did what he had to do, and we'll never know if he would have done the same had Gordon still been human.

The hunter becoming a monster might have happened most literally to Gordon, but he isn't the only one we have to worry about. In season three, both Winchester brothers were on a slippery slope to monsterhood themselves. As of this writing, we still don't know if Sam is the Antichrist or not, and although his powers are not of his choosing, how he uses them will be. There could be a monster waiting within him, one with the power of our old buddy Yellow Eyes, the one creature that Sam hated most. And Dean has been dragged off to Hell, on the way to becoming a demon himself—exactly what he hates most—thanks to the bargain he made to save his brother. The demonization was a surprise, but Dean probably would have taken the bargain even if he'd known, so long as it saved Sam. Gordon showed us the path, but the brothers walked it all season long.

As for Gordon Walker. . . . He was a guy with morally questionable hunter policies, there's no denying that. But he did try to save the world in his own twisted way. To Gordon, saving a hundred people's sisters was worth the collateral damage his hunting caused, and destroying monsters like the ones that destroyed his life excused his destruction of anyone who stood in his way.

Here's the point that Gordon missed: If you lose your humanity to defend humanity, you're not much better than the vampires and demons that you fight. Becoming a monster for the "right" reasons still makes you a monster. Gordon knew that some of what he did was wrong, but he was a soldier in a war, and he was willing to get his hands dirty in order to serve the greater good. To save humanity, he was willing to lose his own, and losing his humanity, literally, by becoming a vampire, underlined that point. He chose actions that he thought best served the big picture, no matter how each individual action might be judged. But do we know for certain that he was completely wrong?

Freelance columnist **AMY BERNER** is obsessed with television. Although she spends most of her time as an event designer and planner, she pops up in various places with reviews and essays, primarily covering science fiction and fantasy television, film, and novels. She co-authored the book *The Great Snape Debate*, and she has appeared in several Smart Pop anthologies including *Five Seasons of Angel*, *The Anthology at the End of the Universe*, *Alias Assumed*, *Farscape Forever*, *Getting Lost*, and *Neptune Noir*. She lives in San Diego, California.

The Trickster's brand of whimsical justice is the basis of one of season two's funniest episodes, "Tall Tales." But by season three and "Mystery Spot," that whimsy had taken a darker turn with the Trickster returning to teach Sam a valuable lesson that could ultimately save his life—but only by sacrificing Dean's.

Maria Lima examines Trickster lore and the way in which it has been incorporated into Supernatural's *ever-evolving storyline, and how the Winchester boys still haven't learned the lesson the Trickster's been teaching.*

MARIA LIMA

ANOTHER ROADSIDE ATTRACTION

The Role of the Trickster in *Supernatural*

> TRICKSTER: Sam. There's a lesson here that I've been trying to drill into that freakish, Cro-Magnon skull of yours.
> SAM: Lesson? What lesson?
> TRICKSTER: This obsession to save Dean, the way you two keep sacrificing yourselves for each other? Nothing good comes out of it. Just blood, and pain.
>
> —"Mystery Spot" (3-11)

> *What I really dig about the Trickster . . . is that we didn't put a unique spin on him. We were faithful to real characterizations of trickster gods throughout history.*
>
> —ERIC KRIPKE, *Supernatural: The Official Companion Season 2*

MAKING MISCHIEF

As with all of the monsters, demons, and weird occurrences in *Supernatural*, the Trickster, a character who first appeared in "Tall Tales" (2-15), is based on genuine myths and legends from around the world. Every culture has a Trickster figure, whether it's Loki, Anansi, Puck, Br'er Rabbit, Raven, Crow, or Coyote. Modern times have their own manifestations in Captain Jack Sparrow, Wile E. Coyote, Mr. Mxyzptlk, and arguably the most well-known of all: Bugs Bunny. This demigod immortal prankster exists to create chaos, and by doing so, teaches important lessons to those affected. From his introduction as the jokester/mischief-maker in season two's "Tall Tales" to his darker incarnation as the Chaos-bringer in the episode "Mystery Spot," the Trickster plays a seminal role in the mythos of the show.

Though he only appears physically in these two episodes, the Trickster's role goes beyond providing humor to acting as a catalyst, bringing realization through upsetting the norm. As in the many myths and stories, *Supernatural*'s Trickster is a transformative character who by his actions changes the primary characters at an essential level. In a DVD extra for season two ("Tricksters: Lore & Legend"), Dr. Timothy R. Tangherlini, UCLA Professor of Folklore, states, "Tricksters will often target people who are getting too big for their own breeches. [They] . . . look at cultural norms, if someone is trying to pull themselves up, outside the community, at the expense of the community, the Trickster will often recognize that person and in some ways, undermine what it is that they're up to."[1] Both of the Trickster episodes used this conceit as the reason the Trickster showed up in the first place. In "Tall Tales," the Trickster stated, "Those people got what was coming to them. Hoisted on their own petards." In "Mystery Spot," he specifically told Sam that he'd been trying to teach him a lesson.

The key question is, why has he targeted the Winchester brothers? There must be more to his interference than simply serving a comeuppance to the offenders. *Supernatural* isn't solely about the urban legends, nor the scary demons, nor the vampires or succubi or ghosts who populate the episodes, nor is it primarily about the hunt for these creatures: it's also about Dean and Sam Winchester and their relationship as brothers, as family. How does the Trickster fit in to the overall story arc? To find out, let's take a closer look at the way *Supernatural*'s Trickster embodies the historical Trickster legends.

---

[1] Dr. Timothy R. Tangherlini, interviewed in "Tricksters: Lore & Legend," *Supernatural* Season 2 DVD Extra

Tales and Storytelling

In "Tall Tales," those affected by the Trickster were each taught a "lesson" through the pranks: the married Morality and Ethics professor who lusted after a luscious coed fell to his death from a window after taking the girl to his office, echoing a local urban legend; the obnoxious frat-boy who humiliated pledges with hazing rituals got abducted by aliens, probed, and forced to slow dance; the professor who experimented on animals was eaten by an alligator.

The story itself was lighthearted (despite the two deaths), and the Trickster seemed to fulfill the same role as Puck, as Br'er Rabbit, even as *Star Trek: The Next Generation*'s own beloved Trickster character, Q. The tricks remained jokes—amusing, yet also chaotic and insane in a boyish "I'm just having fun" way. In "Tall Tales," the Trickster could easily have been Bugs Bunny, watching the craziness he'd caused, sitting back, chomping on a carrot, saying "What's up, Doc?" This was especially evident in the episode's final confrontation scene, as the brothers burst into the university theater. The setup was so over the top, it was unbelievable (two hot girls in lingerie lounging on a bed under a disco ball, telling Dean they've been waiting for him, Barry White's "Can't Get Enough of Your Love" playing in the background). We got those same ridiculous scenarios throughout the episode (the frat boy slow-dancing with the alien abductor to "Lady in Red"). Bobby, as wise father figure, picked up on this as soon as the brothers explained what had been going on: "And if you two bothered to pull your heads out of your asses, it all would've been pretty clear. . . . You've got a Trickster on your hands."

This Trickster creates illusions straight out of the *Weekly World News*: a huge red flag to the boys, if they were thinking logically and working together, but they weren't. Why? Because although he often plays the Fool, the Trickster *isn't* much of a fool. Not only did he manufacture the silly scenarios on campus, he also messed with Dean and Sam. Sam's laptop was missing, after having been frozen on bustyasianbeauties.com—something Sam thought Dean did. Dean believed Sam let the air out of the Impala's tires. These pranks reduced the brothers to childish bickering (a staple of the show), and they reached the point of actually wrestling with each other like a couple of pre-adolescents. Bobby told them, "These things create chaos and mischief as easy as breathing. And it's got you so turned around and at each other's throats, you can't even think straight. . . . It knows you're onto him. And it's been playing you like fiddles." He was absolutely on target.

By dividing Sam and Dean's attention, the Trickster was free to continue to play his tricks. This foreshadowed what we saw later in the series, and in many folktales—that together, the heroes are greater than the sum of their parts; that divided, they must fall, must fail. It wasn't until they began to work as a team (again) that they could defeat the Trickster . . . or defeat him as much as the Trickster actually allowed. In "Tall Tales," the Trickster's role as mischief-maker, playing tricks and games with Sam and Dean, illustrated that things are not always as they seem, and reminded the brothers that in order to survive, they needed to stick together.

Our Trickster was already on the scene when the brothers arrived at the unnamed university, working in the guise of a janitor (the one holding the physical, as well as metaphorical, keys—in fact, in several scenes, there were close-ups of the Janitor/Trickster's hands scraping the overladen key ring). Throughout the episode, in a narrative structure similar to that of the *X-Files* episode "Bad Blood," the story is told from each brother's point of view. Like in the *X-Files* episode, the details of the story changed depending on who told it, Sam or Dean. Through this conceit, we, the audience, learned about the strange happenings centered around Crawford Hall.

This narrative structure itself can be seen as homage to Anansi, the Spider, a Trickster in the West African folktales of the Ashanti who was transported to the New World along with African slaves. One of Anansi's many roles is that of "King of the Stories," a role that Anansi won due to his trickery and mischief. Ellen Kushner, in her popular NPR radio series *Sound & Spirit*, explains that in the beginning, all stories belonged to the sky god Nyame. Anansi wanted the stories and asked if he could be King of the Stories. The Sky God asked Anansi to bring him Snake. Then, by trickery, Anansi tied up Snake and delivered him, thus gaining mastery over stories.[2] This homage may not have been deliberate on the part of *Supernatural*'s creative team, but considering the care its writers take with research, it's possible that the idea of the unusual storytelling portion of the narrative grew from the legend. During a teleconference about the show,

---

[2] Ellen Kushner, "Tricksters," *Sound & Spirit*, Week of October 21, 2007.

Eric Kripke himself mentions, "The rule in the writer's room, with all our brilliantly talented writers, is no one is allowed to make up anything out of whole cloth. You have to have your references; you have to do your research."[3]

At the end of the episode, it was evident that the Trickster's had played the role of lesson-bringer not just for the episode's victims, but also for Sam and Dean. In her 1995 article about the Trickster, Terri Windling quotes noted fantasy author Alan Garner: "[The Trickster is] the advocate of uncertainty. . . . He draws a boundary for chaos, so that we can make sense of the rest. He is the shadow that shapes the light."[4] In "Tall Tales," the Trickster caused bad things to happen, but in doing so, forced the brothers to realize that together they were stronger than either was individually. By the end of the episode, this lesson was obvious to viewers, if not to Sam and Dean. "Supernatural Woman," a blogger on TVGuide.com, describes this lesson thusly: "One can argue the unhealthy aspects of codependency, but that is better left to psychologists, in the *Supernatural* universe, it's all about love, devotion, loyalty and the consistent thread of 'united they stand, divided they fall.'"[5]

Together, the brothers complement each other. Sam is Dean's grounding force, his conscience and tie to humanity. Dean frees Sammy, liberates him to pursue the hunt, yet enjoy each day as it comes—and in season three, this part of Dean's personality was on full display, given that he only had a year to live. In "Tall Tales," the two POVs illustrated this duality through exaggeration. In Sam's version of the story, Dean was all desire, lust, greed, and impulsiveness taken to the max, letting his base nature skew the investigation. In Dean's account, Sam was a prissy complainer, too anal, too conservative, ignoring the good things in life in favor of facts, figures, and data—a brain with no emotions. An over-the-top rendition? Sure. But an effective, if simple, depiction of the two brothers' personalities. Even at the denouement, when the Trickster con-

[3] Eric Kripke, Teleconference, October, 2006, transcribed on http://www.ramblingsofatvwhore.com/2006/10/05/supernatural-teleconference-transcript/

[4] Terri Windling quoting Alan Garner, *Wile E. Coyote and Other Sly Trickster Tales*, 1995.

[5] Supernatural Woman, "Mystery Spot: 'No, no, no, no, not like this!'" http://tvguide.liveworld.com/blog-entry/Supernatural-Woman/Mystery-Spot-Quotno/800033353&

jured up busty beauties in a red silk bed to entice Dean, the writers continued to reinforce these character traits.

Nugent. Ted Nugent.

In some Native American myths, Coyote Trickster is not necessarily portrayed as an actual animal. His counterpart, the "real" coyote, is seen as a relative. In stories, they often address each other as "elder brother" and "younger brother"—another convention of the legend that parallels the show. Is the reality of the Winchester that they themselves also act as Trickster figures in the overall myth-arc? Certainly, they bring chaos and uncertainty to the demon world, to the world of the "other" that threatens humanity, threatens life as we humans know it. During an appearance on *Sound and Spirit*, Bill Harley, a noted storyteller, explains, "[The] important thing about trickster stories is not where they're going, but how they get there." Could this not also be said about Sam and Dean's own journey?[6]

Federal marshals, FBI agents, priests, cops, reporters from *Weekly World News*, phone company reps—you name it, they've pretended to be it. In their own way, the Winchester brothers are con men, pulling "tricks" on unsuspecting humans so they can accomplish their own: taking out the demons and preternatural creatures. In addition to creating chaos in the demon ranks, they also bring chaos to the lives of those affected by Evil. Across the U.S., every small town that the Winchesters have visited over the past three years has changed in the brothers' wake, usually for the better.

In his essay "Mapping the Characteristics of Mythic Tricksters: A Heuristic Guide," scholar William J. Hynes describes the activities of a Trickster as "usually outlawish, outlandish, outrageous, out of bounds, and out of order"—a description that easily fits both Dean and Sam. By season two, both brothers were living outside mundane law, using whatever trickery they could to accomplish their goals. Like the shapeshifting Trickster, they take on whatever guise suits the occasion. They cross lines and boundaries, and embody the description of the Trickster given

---

[6] Bill Harley, "Tricksters," *Sound & Spirit*, Week of October 21, 2007.

in a Grand Valley University course description: "the trickster is often a traveler, and he often breaks societal rules."[7]

The lesson Sam and Dean teaches never varies—don't mess with humanity. Unlike the traditional Trickster figure, who gives comeuppance to the humans, the Winchesters' lesson is always for the supernatural denizens and those that support them—the demons and evildoers threatening the lives of the innocent. Evil must, and does, pay attention when the Winchester brothers come calling.

It's Not Such a Wonderful Life

Let's take a look then at "Mystery Spot," where our Trickster returned and the game grew considerably darker. Sam lived a Groundhog Day existence, watching his brother die hundreds of times on a Tuesday from Hell. In this episode, the Trickster upset the order of things-as-they-are in a sort of reverse *It's a Wonderful Life*. By doing so, he made Sam—or at least those of us watching—realize two crucial things: Dean is Sam's ultimate weakness (just as Sam is Dean's), and that of the two brothers, Sam is more like their father—a relentless, single-minded hunter with a Purpose. The chaos here no longer lay in jokes played on others, aside for the off-screen comeuppance to the missing man, a professor who spent his life debunking urban legends (how's that for meta!). The joke instead is on Sam Winchester. The gruesome and often hilarious deaths experienced by Dean became meaningless in themselves, a parody of horror, highlighting the randomness and quirkiness of the universe. Dean never died as a hero, but instead got shot accidentally, choked on a sausage, was electrocuted, etc. At no point in any of these deaths did his demise find meaning.

This is the Trickster who is Raven, Crow, Coyote, his jokes and tricks taking on a more sinister cast. No longer the amusing Bugs Bunny, Captain Jack Sparrow, or Q, nor the more innocent Fool figure, the Trickster becomes a harsh lesson-giver (the ridiculous nature of Dean's deaths notwithstanding). During the episode, Sam had to explain the

[7] William J. Hynes. "Mapping the Characteristics of Mythic Tricksters: A Heuristic Guide." *Mythical Trickster Figures: Contours, Contexts, and Criticisms*. Tuscaloosa: University of Alabama Press, 1993.

time loop to Dean over and over again, and finally, when Dean clued in, he reinforced the strength of his belief in his Sam—completely contrary to the lesson the Trickster was trying to teach. "If you and I decide that I'm not going to die, then I'm not going to die," Dean said—just before choking on a breakfast sausage. This was the crux of the matter: not the Trickster-induced deaths, but Dean's absolute belief that Sam would win out in the end and Dean's deal with the demon would be broken (a message unstated, but nevertheless understood). Dean's conviction seemed to give Sam strength, to make him try harder to discover how to stop the loop. Once Sam cottoned on to the fact that the time loop was indeed the work of a Trickster, the brothers found and confronted him before Dean could die again. To their surprise, it was the same Trickster from "Tall Tales," evidently not as easy to kill as they'd thought.

> SAM: So this is fun for you? Killing Dean over and over again?
> TRICKSTER: One: Yes, it's fun. Two: This is not about killing Dean. This joke? Is on you, Sam. Watching your brother die, every day, forever. . . . How long will it take you to realize? You can't save your brother . . . no matter what.

Once again, we were back to the Trickster as jokester, but this time, the lesson was cruel. Sam discovered just how cruel when, after the confrontation, Tuesday finally became Wednesday and the time loop was over. Except, to Sam's surprise and agony, the lesson wasn't. Dean walked out into the parking lot and was shot by a thief; this time his death was permanent. There was no coming back, because Dean was truly dead. As a result, Sam became an echo of his father John. We saw the future, in a parallel to George Bailey's experience with his own Trickster, Clarence. Sam without Dean was a man on a mission: dark, uncaring, unfeeling. He was Justice personified, untempered by compassion or love. His only goal: revenge—finding the Trickster and getting Dean back. It was an obsession that controlled him, burned inside of him, and fueled his every action. This was Dark!Sam, all humanity, everything that made him a person, seared away by the fires of obsession, just as the fires of Hell burn away all that is human, creating demons from those unfortunate enough to land there. What we knew of

Sam was gone, replaced by someone whose life had only one direction, one purpose.

But it was not until Bobby tricked (there's that word again) Sam into coming to visit that we saw how far Sam Winchester had fallen. Supernatural Woman observed, "Sam has been Dean's voice of conscience because Sam has been the champion of humanity and avoiding having to kill a human, but we've never considered what a world without Dean would be for Sam. We've assumed that Dean's been the constant needy one. Oh and how this DeanGirl loves the idea that Dean, too, has been a voice for Sam, keeping him on track somehow, maybe not so much about sparing humanity, but more the presence that has never left him for most of his life, except when he left for Stanford"—a chilling prophecy for, and a likely foreshadowing of, season four. True to the lesson, no matter how hard they tried, Sam couldn't save Dean, couldn't break the contract with Lilith, and ended up losing him.

> SAM: Look. . . . Dean, you're leaving, right? And I gotta stay here in this crap hole of a world. Alone. So the way I see it, if I'm gonna make it, if I'm gonna fight this war when you're gone . . . then I gotta change.
>
> DEAN: Change into what?
>
> SAM: Into you. I've gotta be more like you. ("Malleus Maleficarum," 3-9)

From the pilot, where Dean sought Sam out at Stanford, through season two and beyond, we saw Dean's need for his brother, the imbalance never so obvious as in the episodes where Sam took off on his own, momentarily disgusted with the nature of their lives. Dean's entire *raison d'être* was to "Take care of Sammy," an edict uttered by John Winchester as Dean grew up. Never, until "Mystery Spot," did we see the reverse. Careful, confident, conservative Sam became an amalgam of his father and brother, blood vengeance his goal. He had to bring Dean back; he had to reverse the Trickster's trick. In order to do so, he would do whatever it took, without remorse.

Like Mary's death changed John, like Jessica's death in the pilot changed Sam, like their father's death changed Sam and Dean, Dean's death, we saw, changed Sam—forced Sam to become the opposite of what he desired so much in the pilot. Instead of becoming a lawyer, an upright *normal* citizen, Sam transformed into an obsessive Hunter, determined to either wreak vengeance or find a way to get Dean back. It's a transformation that on the surface seems surprising, but the foreshadowing had been there from the beginning:

> DEAN: Since when are you all shoot first and ask questions later?
> SAM: Since now. ("Wendigo," 1-2)

> SAM: Dean, no. I gotta find Dad. I gotta find Jessica's killer. It's the only thing I can think about. ("Wendigo")

The Sam of the latter third of "Mystery Spot" was focused, determined, ruthless, his need to find the Trickster obscuring his humanity and compassion—the parts of him that balanced out Dean's focus on hunting and killing evil. Like John, who abandoned his life as a mechanic to go after Mary's killer, Sam sloughed off the veneer of normality he so frantically tried to keep in the first season. Like Clark Kent's pretense of a normal human life is sheared away when he strips off his mundane glasses and suit, Sam Winchester's own façade peeled off after Dean's true death. Sam lived, as Dean did, for the moment, knowing that nothing mattered but the goal. In a parallel to John's path in season one, Sam's obsession lead to what ultimately was the Trickster's final test: Would Sam sacrifice everything, including people he loved?

Bobby told Sam that in order to summon the Trickster, they needed about a gallon of blood—fresh blood. Sam didn't falter, didn't hesitate. He knew what it meant. Sam had to sacrifice an innocent to bring Dean back. Would he do it? Sam had to make a sacrifice, just as Dean had to in "All Hell Breaks Loose (Part 2)" (2-22). And in the world of this Sam Winchester, no sacrifice was too large. Bobby then offered himself, protesting that if it were going to be done, 'twere best done by family, and quickly. Sam obliged, but at this point, he knew—so he thought—that "Bobby" was actually the Trickster. A beat, two, three later, and for a gut-wrenching moment, Sam Winchester appeared to have lost everything.

Bobby lay still, his life seeping away. Then, as Sam's doubt (and that of the viewers), reached the inevitable conclusion, there was a metaphorical "tah-dah" as the Trickster's form replaced Bobby's. Getting up, the Trickster immediately commented, "Whoever said Dean was the dysfunctional one? Has never seen you with a sharp object in your hands."

Finally Sammy learned the truth of the matter. It wasn't about Dean at all. It was all about *Sam.* "Dean's your weakness," the Trickster explained. "The bad guys know it, too. It's going to be the death of you, Sam. Sometimes, you just gotta let people go." Sam is less willing to accept death, less comfortable with the truth of what they do, then Dean, who is old friends with the reaper—both metaphorically and actually. His own near death and his father's sacrifice in "In My Time of Dying" (2-1) only served to underscore that connection. Dean was old enough to remember his mother, and grew up mourning her death. So letting people go is a lesson Dean should already know—but when it comes to Sam, Dean hasn't really learned it. His need to keep Sam safe has led him to his own dark places, and resulted in the Crossroads deal. So is it really surprising that Sam's reaction to losing Dean is as extreme? Sam has only had to cope with loss over the past couple of years, since he was an infant when his mother died. First, he lost Jess, then reconnected with Dean and their father only to lose John just when they'd begun mending their differences. Over the several episodes just prior to "Mystery Spot," Sam had to face some rough truths, including the fact that sometimes, they (as the heroes) and we (as the viewers) *don't* always win.

Richard Pulfer, on popsyndicate.com's review of the episode, describes "Mystery Spot" thusly: "Quintessential with a capital 'Q,' the Trickster has managed to re-affirm Sam Winchester much in the same way dream-walking did for Dean in the last episode."[8] In "Dream a Little Dream of Me" (3-10), Dean was confronted by a Demon!Dean doppelganger, forcing him to acknowledge that his acceptance of the inevitable had only been a cover. In reality, Dean Winchester didn't want to go to Hell and didn't want to accept the terms of the contract. He wanted to be saved. The Trickster served the same role in "Mystery Spot" for Sam, confirming Sam's need to be Dean's

---

[8] Richard Pulfer, *Supernatural (3.11)-Mystery Spot*, http://www.popsyndicate.com/archive/story/supernatural_311_mystery_spot

savior—something Sam had, granted, been more open with about all along. What "Mystery Spot" did was show us how far Sam was willing to go.

The events set into motion by the Trickster revealed the core essence of each of the brothers. But would the Trickster's lesson, at last, be learned? Dean has lived with death all his life, Sam, only recently, but at the center of it all is their mutual need to keep the other safe, at the expense of their own lives—exactly contrary to what the Trickster keeps trying to pound into their heads.

What's Up Next, Doc?

Although we didn't see the Trickster again in season three, the lesson he taught informed everything that followed . . . yet, it hadn't actually been learned. Three episodes later, Sam was still just as set on saving Dean, and Dean was just as willing to let him:

> DEAN: I can't expect Dad to show up with some miracle last minute. I can't expect anybody to. The only person going to get me out of this is me.
> SAM: And me. ("Long Distance Call," 3-14)

And in the final episode of season three, despite Dean's protestations that they couldn't keep sacrificing themselves for each other, both boys are still fighting, still trying to find a way to win. Yet despite all their efforts, in the final scene of the final episode, Dean was left hanging on meat hooks, calling out for Sam, and Sam was alone, stunned by the fact that Lilith, über-demon and holder of Dean's contract (and all other contracts, according to Ruby), couldn't kill him. In his "Peat and Repeat" article in *Trickster's Way*, noted Trickster scholar C.W. Spinks tells us, "the fracturing edge of Trickster cleft will move us in directions we yet do not understand."[9] At the time of this writing, at the end of the third season, Sam Winchester's path is about to head in those murky directions.

We've already seen how Sam deals with the death of his brother, and the emergence of his preternatural powers may very well be what lets

---

[9] C. W. Spinks, "Duck Watch: Peat and Repeat," *Trickster's Way, Volume 2, Issue 1*, http://www.trinity.edu/org/tricksters/TrixWay/

him figure out a way to bring Dean out of Hell. But at what cost? I believe that Sam's transformation is as inevitable as Dean being dragged off to Hell, both outcomes foreshadowed again and again throughout the series, and given voice in the Trickster lessons. The sacrifices Dean and Sam have made for each other will change them, will be the "death" of them . . . the death of who they thought they were.

In a fan Q&A at the convention *Salute to Supernatural*, Eric Kripke stated, "They keep presenting themselves as targets because they are so obsessed about saving each other; they take self-sacrifice to this pathological level. It actually serves as a character flaw. What they are willing to do for each other is both a strength and a character flaw. And with each occurrence they keep turning further and further against nature."[10] Kripke continues this thought in a TVGuide.com interview, talking about season two: "Sam promised Dean right before Dean [almost] died [in "In My Time of Dying"] that he wasn't going to pursue any of his powers in terms of discovering his potential. Upon Dean's return, Sam tells him, 'I promised I wouldn't head down that road because you made me promise,' but we begin to wonder if indeed that is the truth."[11] How then is this situation any different? It's been two years and now Dean, although not exactly dead, is in Hell. And a return from Hell will no doubt require an even stronger sacrifice than before. Sam must indeed turn to the dark side—or at least away from the side of light—in order to go after his brother: a modern-day Orpheus and Eurydice. Let's just hope that Sam can avoid looking behind him.

---

[10] Eric Kripke, Q&A Transcript by Anna Beck, *Supernatural Creator Eric Kripke Answers Fan's Questions-Part III*, http://eclipsemagazine.com/hollywood-insider/supernatural-creator-eric-kripke-answers-fan%E2%80%99s-questions-%E2%80%93-part-iii/5639/

[11] Eric Kripke, Interivew with Ileane Rudolph, TVGuide.com, *Supernatural Creator Eric Kripke: "Dean Lives!"*, http://www.tvguide.com/news/supernatural-eric-kripke/080529-01

Maria Lima writes dead people . . . no, really. Author of *Matters of the Blood* and *Blood Bargain* (Juno Books), and an Agatha-nominated short story, "The Butler Didn't Do It" (Chesapeake Crimes), Maria keeps one foot in the real world and the other in make-believe. Her role models include Tanya Huff, Joss Whedon, Christopher Golden, and Russell T. Davies. She has a soft spot for both the Trickster and Dean and Sam Winchester. Like Jensen Ackles and Jared Padalecki, Maria also hails from Texas, but now lives elsewhere. Visit her at www.thelima.com.

Urban legends, campfire stories, myths, fairy tales—these are the bedrock of Supernatural's *storytelling, and Eric Kripke's original inspiration for the show. The Trickster, Bloody Mary, the Hook Man, the Woman in White—all of these and more have been given the* Supernatural *treatment, demonstrating how each of these tales or legends has stood the test of time, lending themselves to successful reinterpretation for a new generation.*

Here, Shanna Swendson examines the origins of many of Supernatural's *myths and legends, and demonstrates how the unique spin the show has put on each ensures the moral of the story remains relevant to a modern audience.*

SHANNA SWENDSON

KEEPERS OF THE LORE

Once upon a time, before the advent of television or radio, before electric lighting made it possible to get things done after the sun went down, people had to create their own entertainment, and so they told stories. They sat by the fire and told tales meant to amuse, entertain, frighten, inform, and explain the world around them. A wealth of valuable advice is hidden in those stories: be kind to old beggar women and small forest creatures (you never know when you might need their help), don't take apples from strange women, think about the exact wording of an offer before you agree to it, stealing from giants can get you in trouble, there are dangerous things lurking in the woods, and the king won't be thrilled about his daughter marrying the foolish youngest son of a woodsman, so be prepared for treachery on the eve of the wedding.

We may not sit around the fire when we tell stories today, except perhaps at camp or during a blackout when there's nothing else to do for fun, but we do still tell stories. They're just more likely to be passed around the

Internet as events that happened to a friend's mother's cousin. And there is that flickering box we sit around that tells us stories.

Some of the stories on that flickering box are about two brothers who travel the country. They're the keepers of the lore, the ones who remember what others have forgotten or who believe in what others scoff at as old wives' tales or urban legends. The Brothers Grimm nearly two centuries ago collected the old tales before the oral tradition died out; the Brothers Winchester face the truth behind tales that many of us have forgotten. Because they remember the lore and believe, they can take action against things the rest of us don't suspect, because the fantastic doesn't fit in our modern worldview or else because we've grown too cynical to believe a story that sounds too weird to be true.

Sam and Dean are just as likely to run into the truth behind a story spread by the Internet as they are to run into ancient legends, and often the ancient and the modern mingle. There are the traditional horror story subjects like ghosts, vampires, and werewolves, and then there are the stranger things that go bump in the night.

The pilot episode kicked off the mingling of old and new stories by blending the "woman in white" myth (or La Llorona—the weeping woman) with the "phantom hitchhiker" urban legend. La Llorona is a Spanish myth and figure of South American folklore who functions much like the banshee from Celtic cultures in that she weeps and wails loudly, and those who see her are considered marked for death. She's a woman wearing white, usually seen near bodies of water. According to various versions of the legend, she drowned her children—often because her lover demanded it as a test of her love and loyalty or because her lover from a higher social class abandoned her—then realized the error of her ways and drowned herself.

The *Supernatural* pilot merged this legend with the urban legend of the phantom hitchhiker. In this story—the kind of thing that always seems to happen to someone a friend knows—a person driving late at night stops to pick up a woman standing by the side of the road. She asks for a ride home and gives an address, but when the driver reaches that address, she's disappeared. The driver asks the people at the address about her and learns that she died in an accident at the spot where the driver found her, and that the incident usually happens on the anniversary of her death. In some versions of the story, she makes some prophecy to the driver. In others, she seems cold and the driver puts his coat or sweater around her; he later finds the coat or sweater neatly folded at her grave when he goes to check out the story about her death.

Although this story is classified as an urban legend, it has very old roots. There were similar stories told at least as far back as the 1600s, and Washington Irving used the legend in one of his stories. Of course, the drivers in those versions were traveling in something other than automobiles. There are also localized versions, including a well-known one in Chicago and the Lady of the Lake in Dallas, where (naturally) the mysterious passenger is identified by her clothing from Neiman Marcus.

In the *Supernatural* universe, these two stories add up to create one very ticked-off ghost, one who isn't content to merely vanish from the back seat. She's sad for herself and for her dead children and lashes out at men, creating a trail of deaths and disappearances. This woman in white also sets the *Supernatural* precedent that anyone in a white nightgown is either doomed or to be feared—including Mary Winchester, Sam's girlfriend Jessica, and a host of irate female spirits.

The series revisited the phantom hitchhiker story in the second season in the episode "Roadkill" (2-16), this time telling the story from the point of view of the phantom hitchhiker, who doesn't realize she's a ghost and who is still trying to get help or a ride home so she can find her husband. This episode addressed another aspect of the myth, the supposedly haunted stretch of highway where accidents often happen, because the ghost causes them or because the driver sees the ghost and either overreacts or isn't paying attention to the road. In the episode, as in the original myth, the phantom hitchhiker appears on the anniversary of the accident that killed her, but in the *Supernatural* universe, the stakes are even higher because the hitchhiker is tortured every year by yet another phantom, the man she accidentally killed in the car wreck. She finds peace at last when she's picked up by the Winchesters, who know all about phantom hitchhikers and how to help them.

Another old legend the Winchesters investigate is the shtriga, in the season one episode "Something Wicked" (1-18). The shtriga is an Albanian vampiric witch who sucks either blood or life force from children and infants. This is one of many folkloric explanations for crib death or sudden illness among children, much like the Celtic changeling lore. If a child died suddenly in the night, or sickened and began to fade, then obviously it was swapped for an unhealthy fairy child or had its life force sucked out by a witch—and come to think of it, it was probably that crazy old childless woman in the village who did it. Stories like these gave grieving parents a focus for their anger and someone to blame for the unexplainable death.

Today, we have our own kind of "folklore" to explain seemingly healthy infants dying unexpectedly during the night. We may not blame a mysterious witch or point fingers at the neighborhood crone with a suspiciously lush herb garden, but we do have a name—Sudden Infant Death Syndrome. SIDS sounds a lot more scientific than blaming a shtriga, but it really only means nothing more than that infants die suddenly for no good reason. We aren't entirely sure what causes SIDS, but we have our own rituals for preventing it. Putting infants to sleep on their backs has resulted in a dramatic decline in SIDS cases, but doctors still don't know exactly why it works. They think it might keep infants from smothering in bedding, but all they can really do is offer parents hope that if they do this one little thing, they can protect their children. It's not too far removed from garlic over the window or a crucifix over the door.

"Something Wicked" reminds us of the potential dangers of complacency and forgetting the stories. If you don't know what's happening, you can't fight it. With their more modern, scientific viewpoint, the people in this episode saw only a disease that didn't respond to treatment, so they were incapable of really protecting their children from the true threat. Stories like "Something Wicked" provide us with a certain kind of comfort: they give a body and a physical presence to a threat, which means we can vanquish it. We can't attack and destroy SIDS, but Sam and Dean can shoot a shtriga with consecrated iron bullets and save the children of the town.

The Trickster is a classic archetype in folklore, existing to poke fun at the status quo, expose hypocrisy, demonstrate the need for change using absurd situations, and cut the hero down to size. The Norse had Loki, the Native Americans have Coyote, the West Africans have Anansi, rural African-American Southerners had Br'er Rabbit, and even our armed forces had the gremlins that plagued military equipment during World War II. Trickster characters are our way of explaining the unexplainable, scapegoats for everything that mysteriously breaks or goes missing. The Trickster showed up to mess with the Winchesters in the episode "Tall Tales" (2-15), but he did so in a thoroughly modern way: by using a form of modern folklore, the supermarket tabloid.

This creature of ancient legend meted out his usual poetic justice, using people's weaknesses against them by way of modern legends like alien abduction and alligators in the sewers. Since the Trickster made another appearance in season three, it's likely we haven't seen the last of him. He's probably trolling snopes.com for urban legends he can use against the Winchesters, and I wouldn't be surprised if he was behind half the "Virus alert! Forward this to everyone!" e-mails going around the Internet today. If you got a virus from blindly following the virus alert warning, you know whom to blame. We can only hope that Sam and Dean eventually take care of this guy for good. I wouldn't be too optimistic, though. The Trickster is too pervasive, and I don't know that there's been a story yet where he was permanently defeated.

Dean himself often fits the trickster archetype as well. Dean's life mission seems to be to upset the status quo and make the powerful look foolish while thumbing his nose at the people in charge. He has little respect for authority, whether it's the police, the FBI, the legions of Hell, or even death itself. Like the Trickster, he takes on multiple identities to blend into situations, changing his name (often to something involving a sly inside joke or reference), making up roles to play, and sometimes even putting on costumes or uniforms to get him into places where he needs to be accepted. Dean makes his living on fraud and scams, gambling and committing credit card fraud to fund his demon-fighting adventures. Both Dean and the Trickster have strong hedonistic tendencies. The Trickster's lifestyle in "Tall Tales" was right out of Dean's fantasies: lots of food (especially sweets) and hot chicks. Both Dean and the Trickster also target Sam as a victim. Dean delights in undermining his brother's formal education with the information he's learned from his own education at the school of hard knocks; he plagues his brother with practical jokes, teases him about his sex life (or lack thereof), and generally tries to get Sam to loosen up, playing the trickster role of keeping others from taking life too seriously. The Trickster's elaborate prank on Sam in the third-season episode "Mystery Spot" (3-11) was far darker, but just as relentless. If Dean and the Trickster character had a common goal and a common enemy . . .well, they'd either be really effective or go totally out of control.[1]

The Winchesters took on more modern urban legends in "Bloody Mary" (1-5) when they investigated the popular slumber party story. The Bloody Mary game is a typical girlish game in which one girl is dared to look in a mirror in a darkened room and say "Bloody Mary" multiple times, usually from three to thirteen (they went with three in the episode, probably because watching someone say "Bloody Mary" thirteen times isn't exactly enthralling television). Supposedly, Mary herself will then appear and do something awful, but the stories of what exactly Mary will do probably vary with each slumber party. On the mild end she only appears in the mirror, but some stories tell of her clawing her victims' eyes out, and on the extreme end she comes through the mirror to kill.

I know this story was going strong in the mid-1970s during my peak slumber-party years. It was a favorite way for our neighborhood queen bee to pick on the weak members of the group. If you refused to take the Bloody Mary dare, you were chicken, and if you took the dare and did it but nothing happened, then you did it wrong, or else you weren't worthy. I was nerd enough to look up Bloody Mary in the encyclopedia, which led me to learning about Mary Tudor (who is not believed to be

[1] *Editor's Note*: See Maria Lima's "Another Roadside Attraction" for more on the Trickster's role in *Supernatural*.

the Bloody Mary associated with this myth) and then boring even the neighborhood queen bee with a historical discourse at the next slumber party. That put an end to that game.

Some versions of the story involve a woman who lost her baby, and the game includes a taunt about knowing where her baby is. In some versions, she's known as Mary Worth (though, apparently, not the Mary Worth from the old comic strip). *Supernatural* called her Mary Worthington, and as in most *Supernatural* treatments of folklore, she was a lot bloodier and more violent than in the legend itself—whenever she was summoned she went after people who felt responsible for someone's death and kept it a secret. This was a vengeful spirit rather than the grieving mother of legend. There are no reports of anyone actually being killed or harmed by a Bloody Mary appearance, but *Supernatural*'s Mary Worthington racked up quite a body count and nearly killed Sam.

As research guru Sam noted in the episode, this legend may be related to folklore about mirrors and the belief that mirrors could capture a person's soul. That's why breaking a mirror is bad luck and why it once was common to cover mirrors during sleep or illness, when the soul might not be as firmly connected to the body, as well as after death, to make sure the soul moved on instead of getting caught in a mirror. In *Supernatural*'s take on the legend, the mirror not only captured Mary's soul, but allowed her to move from mirror to mirror as she was summoned.

The game is often played as part of "truth or dare," as seen in the episode. Summoning Bloody Mary is taken as a dare to avoid having to tell a truth. With the *Supernatural* twist of Mary punishing her victims for their secret sins, the episode's dare ended up revealing even more truth, and not just for the person summoning Mary. Anyone nearby with a secret was in danger. The person didn't even have to actually be responsible for a death as long as they felt responsible; it was the secret itself that was deadly.

One possible source of the Bloody Mary slumber party game was a divining game, popular among teenaged girls and young women in the early twentieth century, in which a girl would perform a ritual in front of a mirror to see the reflection of the man she would marry. Anyone who's spent much time with pre-teen girls can see how that could quickly turn into horrifying taunts and cruel games, with the suggestion first of an ugly man in the mirror and then later a vindictive, child-murdering witch. This element of cruelty played out in the *Supernatural* episode, with the slumber-party girls using the game to taunt a friend, then the older girls using it as a prank or to prove they didn't believe, even after there had been deaths. Perhaps what Bloody Mary really represents is an adolescent mean streak, where the person you really have to fear is the friend who pushes you to do something scary, and in whose hands a secret can become a deadly weapon.

The old folklore often contained instructional or moral messages, and urban legends are no different. There's frequently a cautionary tale involved, with the wicked being punished for transgressing society's norms and the good escaping unharmed because of their virtues. In fairy tales, the greedy, selfish, cold older brothers refuse to help the beggar woman and pay the price, while the goodhearted youngest brother helps her and ends up marrying a princess because the old woman turns out to be powerful and repays his kindness. In urban legends, the good girl who protects her virtue survives while the sex-crazed boy and the girl who gives into him are punished. That's what happens in the three urban legends that are woven together in the episode "Hook Man" (1-7).

The "hook man" and "dead boyfriend" stories involve Lover's Lane scenarios, while the "dead roommate" legend generally involves a college dormitory. The "hook man" story, which dates back at least to the 1950s, tells of a murderous madman with a hook for a hand who has escaped from a prison for the criminally insane. A young couple parked on a remote lane for a make-out session hear the bulletin about the escaped madman on their car radio. The girl wants to go home immediately, but the boy wants to stay because he has high hopes for the evening. The girl stands her ground and insists that they leave, and won't let the boy touch her until they go. He finally gets fed up and agrees, gunning the car and pulling away quickly. When he gets to his girlfriend's home, he finds a hook stuck in the car door handle. Only the girlfriend's virtue saved them both from a grisly death.

The "dead boyfriend" story also involves a make-out session gone wrong. Depending on the version, the car breaks down and the boyfriend has to walk to get gas or get help, or else he hears a noise and has to go investigate it. The girlfriend stays in the car, growing increasingly irritated by his long absence. In some versions of the story, she hears a scratching noise on the car roof and gets out to see what's happening, only to find her boyfriend dead and hanging upside down above the car; the noise she heard was his fingernails scraping the car. In other versions, she's rescued by the police, who tell her not to look back at the car as they take her away. She does anyway and sees her boyfriend dead. Sometimes, her hair turns white at the sight, echoing the Bible story about Lot's wife being turned into a pillar of salt because she looked back as they fled the destruction of Sodom. The lesson here is that taking a girl to a remote area to go "parking" can be hazardous to your health.

However, that isn't entirely an urban legend. People have been killed in areas known for being places to park and make out. In the 1940s, the Texarkana area was terrorized by a killer known as "the Phantom," who killed couples (after sexually assaulting the women) on country lanes and in other remote areas. This killer was as terrifying and mysterious as the Hook Man of legend, and the killings were never solved. They did seem to stop after a man was arrested for something else and put in prison; his wife confessed that he committed the crimes but refused to testify against him in court, so he was never tried for the killings and the case remains officially unsolved. The popularity of Lover's Lane urban legends in the 1950s may have stemmed from these murders, as well as the increasing number of teens who had access to cars for extracurricular activities and who therefore needed a good scare to steer them away from immoral behavior.

The "dead roommate" story has less of a moral component, functioning more as a general scare or cautionary tale. In some versions, a college student gets back to the dorm room late at night and gets ready for bed without turning on a light so she won't disturb her roommate. When she wakes up in the morning, she finds her roommate dead, and written on the wall in blood is the taunt, "Aren't you glad you didn't turn on the light?" There are other versions in which she just wakes during the night when she hears a noise, but is reassured when her faithful dog lying beside the bed licks her hand. In the morning, she finds her dog and/or her roommate dead, and this time the taunt reads, "Humans can lick, too." This myth feeds into fears about being away from home and living among strangers in college dorms, and it's still being spread by e-mail today.

Supernatural adds to the moral judgment (or "sex is bad, okay?") theme by making the Hook Man the ghost of a deranged, judgmental preacher and having him commit the "dead boyfriend" and "dead roommate" murders. A preacher's daughter, a good girl being pressured to live a little, inadvertently summoned him through her own moral conflict, via a cross made with metal from his hook. She wasn't entirely comfortable with her boyfriend's desire to get more physical or her roommate's urging to loosen up; the boyfriend got strung up after he grew frustrated with her trying to maintain her boundaries in a necking session, and her roommate died after encouraging her to dress sluttier and skip her usual time with her father for a girls' night in. Their deaths meant she could remain uncorrupted. Her father—who gave her the cross in the first place—nearly became yet another victim when she learned that he was having an affair with a married church member, because she was disappointed he was going against the morals he had taught her.

The link between sex and death is a common one in horror, going back to the psycho-sexual implications of vampire lore, and is still going strong in the modern horror movie, where people who have sex might as well have signed their own death warrants, and it's those who are pure who stand a chance of survival. And in the *Supernatural* universe, having sex with Sam Winchester is a good way to commit suicide, since you're sure to die horribly afterward for maximum Sam angst.

As guardians of lore both ancient and modern, Sam and Dean protect people from things they've forgotten or don't want to believe in—the stuff of folklore. There are countless tales buried in our cultural memory capable of rising again to cause trouble among those who've forgotten the danger, and even more tales in the present that we've become too jaded to believe. Could there still be fairy changelings or people missing for hundreds of years because they got trapped in the world of the fey? And what about those people waking up in bathtubs of ice without their kidneys? There's bound to be an even gorier explanation than black market organ harvesting, and Sam and Dean are just the men to track down the culprits.

Meanwhile, along the way they're weaving their own lore as they battle ghosts, demons, and bratty thieves of arcane objects. Will people someday tell stories about the Winchester brothers around a campfire deep in the woods, late at night, where a hook man could lurk just out of sight?

SHANNA SWENDSON puts her own twist on folklore and fairy tales in her contemporary fantasy novels, which include *Enchanted, Inc.*, *Once Upon Stilettos*, *Damsel Under Stress*, and *Don't Hex with Texas*. She's also contributed to *Flirting with Pride & Prejudice*, *Welcome to Wisteria Lane*, *So Say We All*, *Perfectly Plum*, *Serenity Found*, and *House Unauthorized*. Visit her Web site at www.shannaswendson.com.

When Eric Kripke set out to produce a "horror movie every week" based on myths, folktales and urban legends, he knew a gold mine of source material already existed just waiting to be tapped. But for every Hook Man, every Bloody Mary, every Wendigo or rakshasa, there has to be an origin, a first story, a place where the myth began.

Here, London Brickley examines the origins of Supernatural's *tall tales and how today's modern sources of information—the Internet, blogs, tabloid newspapers—have altered not only our perceptions of these stories but also, perhaps, the stories themselves.*

LONDON E. BRICKLEY

GHOULS IN CYBERSPACE

Supernatural Sources in the Modern, Demon-Blogging World

Open on *Supernatural* season three: Dean's made a deal with the Devil, he has a year to live, and his time is decaying fast. Sam sits in the Impala, finger-scanning over the text that he hopes might hold the answer to saving his elder brother's Hell-bound soul. His eyes squint, the camera pans up, and we see that "The Book" that might just hold the answers to reclaiming Dean's life from the demon he contracted it out to is . . . a copy of *Dr. Faustus*? *(Wait—didn't we have to read that in high school?)* Sure, the book wrapped in worn leather and ink-block prints of the devil *looks* like it could resurrect the dead, but then again, while the text may not be the week's bestseller, it's still rather accessible for a book that could hold the key to finding Dean a get-out-of-Hell-free card. And really, when faced with such a dire predicament, seeking a soul-saving loophole from something available in SparkNotes seems up there with *Your Pathway to Hell Gone Wrong* and *The Idiot's Guide To Selling Your Soul* as a rather dubious choice. It's a fairly recent text as far as demonic manuscripts go, and aside from suspiciously resembling a filched library book, there is nothing to suggest that the particular copy Sam has clutched in his fist is any different from the rest.

Yet Sam is a Winchester, and by this point we have learned to believe that if Sam and Dean need information then they (or at least Bobby) know where to get it. And as we learned the very first time we saw the boys in a motel room lined with news clippings, old torn-out encyclopedia pages, and Scotch tape, the aid and answers they seek usually reside, rather surprisingly, in newspapers, Web sites, and folktale anthologies. In other words, the lowest rungs on the un-credible source list. Sources which, despite their reputations in an academic or mainstream setting, again and again prove to contain secrets not only vital to the success of the hunt, but also the Winchester boys' personal ongoing battles to survive.

Over the last fifty-six episodes that have become the crazy and heartbreaking adventures of the father and sons Winchester, we have seen the boys fight a lot of various forms of manifested lore. Seeing these ghosts and demons believably projected in the "real world" could come as a bit of a shock to the viewer, and yet none of them is as surprising as the sources that help the Winchesters deal with them. Particularly apparent in the show's first season, whenever the Winchesters needed a new hunt or answers for the one currently underway, there Sam would be, half-caf vanilla latte in hand, browsing the *dingoes ate my baby* tabloid articles, blood-drinkers anonymous classified ads, news clippings from the local paper (page 12), and demonology.com Web sites—each and every one zones of information that we as a society and culture tend to ignore (and often scoff at).

Now I know that what the boys consult in order to do a little demon research may initially strike some as an issue *that is as marginal as the sources themselves. (What does it matter where the Winchesters turn? They have to get their information from somewhere, right?)* But sources are important. And if closer consideration/study of mythology tells us anything it is that everything has a source. Every mythology begins with the "origin." Where they say the world is going is a bit more ambiguous and cross-culturally varied, but they all agree that life and death (and all the supernatural shades in between) had a moment of conception—they came from *somewhere*.

However, myths aren't static. After their births, they have lives—*still* have lives now. As time has gone on, the early legends have been spun into more intricate tales, or been deconstructed into simple parables. New tales have crept in around the edges—stories of bloodshed over campfires, flesh feasts in the forests, and haunted pretty things that press out from behind the mirror's glass—each and every one coiled around the culture that conceived it, waiting to strike out at the next audience to come along before it is captured and reshaped into something ever more potent or domesticated. Some of these tales have undoubtedly been lost along the way, but those that survive for our current consideration have done so thanks to the various forms of documentation that have carried them through the time and cultures.

We call these remnants "stories," but they have always been, and still remain, just outside classification as "fiction." Sure, there will always be your skeptics, but start spouting off about ghosts, out-of-body experiences, haunted places, or cursed objects, and you are bound to find a few people who believe you. This is a major theme explored on (and by the very existence of) the show.

On occasion it becomes inevitable that Sam and Dean reveal who they truly are—not FBI agents, or priests, or undercover reporters for the *Chicago Tribune*, but hunters of supernatural forces (one or several of which are after that particular person *now*). However, getting the victim of the week to accept the paranormal threat is met, realistically, with varying levels of success. It may take *a bit* of convincing, otherwise known as getting hit by the proverbial demon-driven truck (Agent Henriksen, "Jus in Bello," [3-12]), or they might be a little more open to the supernatural realm and go along with it (Sarah, "Provenance" [1-19]). Some have even already reached that level of belief all on their own (the "Ghostbuster" hunters, "Hell House" [1-17]).

Pulling back to the external world, the fact that there is an audience base for *Supernatural* in the first place demonstrates a certain prevalence of interest in paranormal activity. It is simply human nature. We are drawn to the unknown, and what the darkness tries to cover as we sleep. And yet, even the paranormalphiles often draw a line somewhere. Telling people ghosts are real is one thing; telling people paperback books and Internet Web sites hold the truth or key to these mysteries is another. (And in googling "batboy lives" it maybe isn't hard to see why.)

One of the primary reasons Internet sites have earned their "unreliable" reputation is on account of the mass accessibility of the Web. Anyone can set up and operate a Web site, keep a blog, or post tales and images for their fellow 'net surfers to come across. This information cannot be regulated. On occasion it can be taken down, but it really becomes too late the second the information is released.

I had a friend during my freshman year of college who added to the trivia section of a particular musician on Wikipedia that he had an affection for plastic model horses and small gaming fowl. Though her addition was eventually reviewed and removed, any surfer that accessed the site during the several weeks the information was posted would have seen the "fact" and absorbed it. They might have thought it was weird but plausible all the same, and continued through life assuming it to be true. Or perhaps they might simply hear the opening chords to a song filtering through the radio and get hit with a wave of nostalgia for *My Little Pony* and an inexplicable craving for braised pheasant. Either way, that information has infiltrated the culture as a special form of truth that exists solely because people believe it. On the off chance that someone who read the Wikipedia trivia section is now reading this essay, suddenly what they knew as truth *seems* completely disproven and becomes an outright fallacy. But then again, I am no authority on the matter. The man might very well indeed have a collection of toy horses that I and the Wikipediaists do not know about. What "truth" comes down to is how many people latch on to an idea and believe in it. If no one believes it, then it fails to have any true impact on the culture. If the majority of the culture believes it, regardless of whether it's been officially proven, it becomes impossible to expunge.

The *Supernatural* episode "Hell House" examined this phenomenon beautifully. The mold-infested, rotting wood house appeared classic enough grounds for a haunting, and yet the spirit was anything but. We were reminded that usually hauntings have patterns; ghosts are annoying but consistent. Yet old Hell House kept changing. As it turned out, the female-lynching, *no*, child-killing, *no*, non-discriminate gun-fearing homicidal spirit was not the ghost of a man after all, but the manifested shadow of a mass-supported idea that began in a local boy's imagination and ended up as a blog-based Web site frequented by thousands. Add to that house's decayed wall a harmless little symbol that allows things that are believed in strongly enough to come to fruition alongside some Blue Oyster Cult paraphernalia and symbols declared satanic by twentieth-century Hollywood, and the ability for you to participate in the conjuring up of some demons and the slaughter of a few townies is just a Google step away. The crux: ideas and beliefs can be powerful things. All right, but when Sam turned to Dean and asks, "How do you kill an idea?", the answer, it seemed, is that you can't; but you can change it.

The boys, however, could not change it all on their own. Dean just deciding that a gun can kill the spirit wasn't going to cut it. As the server crashed, the site was no longer accessible, so the potential viewers couldn't access and believe the change in the tale. The myth couldn't change until people changed it, and Sam was left questioning, "Out of all the things we've hunted, how many existed just because people believed in them?" ("Hell House").

The question rings with a resounding truth, and yet still, for some reason, the fact that tales like Hell House and others told on the Web set "much older" myths within a modern context opens them up to public scrutiny. To the modern mindset, necromancy and alchemy may sound romantic and even potentially plausible to attempt, so long as that attempt is set in the fourteenth century. Respectable practical application of such ideas in today's world, however, better have a whole lot more scientific jargon attached—say, "cell rejuvenation" and "particle reassignment/stabilization." In other words, ideas and concepts from the past often carry over into the present, concealed in language that is more acceptable to the current culture. But when those ideas and concepts appear in the present in their original manifestation, they seem like alien or distant myths.

Most modern upgraded sources that maintain mythical language (spirits, shapeshifters, ritual magic, augury, etc.) stick-out as mythical subjects and are not taken too seriously. Although the ideas are interesting to the modern audience, that fascination is accompanied by a general underlying cultural superiority: "*but we know* now *that isn't how it really works.*" As a result, a common, tempting solution to such potential source skepticism (for, let's say, a television show wishing to create an environment where the audience will accept the plausibility of fantastic tales in their original, fantastic terms) is to remove or displace the source material from the modern world. Current tabloids and Web sites are overlooked and left as the space for crazies and the paranoid. Instead, as if somehow the age of the text automatically allots it a certain level of credibility (a credibility that it most likely did *not* have back in its own time), rituals, incantations, symbols, and prophecies become lost elements of the distant past that are then "rediscovered" in the present through ancient buried scrolls, scribbled out in long-forgotten tongues. The problem lies not in the decision to use ancient sources, but in scenarios where the sources are *exclusively* ancient, as it suggests the potential relevance of a certain point in the past on contemporary culture, but fails to address the importance of the time stretching between that point and the present as well as the time that will come after.

Thus, what makes *Supernatural* particularly unique in comparison with many of its sci-fi/fantasy-labeled counterparts is the way in which the show acknowledges the importance of contemporary culture's contributions in the shaping of folklore. Mythology, legend, and lore are not a neatly contained package from the past with no other use than to be opened and explored today for entertainment purposes. Myth is a continuum and it is shifting and evolving *right now*. Today's Internet Web sites are yesterday's peasant folksongs, tomorrow's paranormal journal articles the modern version of villagers whispering what they saw in the woods. The difference is that in today's media-accelerated world information moves more quickly and on a more massive scale, reaching a larger audience. Where such mass exposure and easy accessibility might de-romanticize these sources, making them seemingly less desirable to draw from in researching rusalkas and banshees, it actually allows them to hold more power. As they reflect sources created by the current population, they are the ideas, interests, values, and beliefs of the modern audience—in other words, mythology at its most up-to-date. Undeniably, the things these sources contain are enticing to people today, as their audience is the same people who are documenting and discussing them.

The best way to truly make the audience feel a part of the

Supernatural world is to make that world as relatable for the audience as possible. And there is hardly a better way to do that than by utilizing the blueprint cosmology from the audience's actual world. And so usually when the Winchesters need to research, the materials are not ancient texts that have been lost for centuries, or one of three copies that still survives, useful only if you can read the second-century B.C. tribal dialect. They are accessible sources to anyone with an Ethernet cord or library card. The message here is that the *Supernatural* world is our world. We all have access to the same sources, we just do not see or realize the truth of the information that these sources hold.

That is not to say that ancient things don't come out to play. Things like old Latin incantations often fulfill their own vital roles in the battle. However, these too, can be—and often are—interfaced with the modern age. In "Jus in Bello," we were graced with an exorcism (preformed with a rather good pronunciation of the language, might I add) that, though often effective the good, old-fashioned, tie-the-demon-to-the-chair-and-read way, here worked on a much larger and more efficient scale when recorded and then broadcast over the speakers. In "Hollywood Babylon" (2-18), the true danger behind the theater and production ghosts was simply a well-researched script, showing that if we collect the tools and know how to use them, the old, when translated into a new-age media form such as film, the Web, or MP3 files, can still retain its power. The mystery, significance, and potency of the old legends and lore need not be lost in the digital age. Instead, they can be accessed more quickly. *Supernatural*'s acknowledgement and exploration of the potential strength of today's available resources inevitably binds the show to the present time and culture, and once there, *Supernatural* refreshingly does not shy away from the world it is in—a world that holds both thousand-year-old demons and a good WiFi connection.

Looking back, we find that *Supernatural* has always been deeply rooted in "the source." Kripke's original idea—a tabloid writer and the journal articles that he jots down during his paranormal-laced trip across America—shows a certain interest in or emphasis on sources of information and communication from the very beginning—particularly *marginalized* forms of information and communication.

The tabloid article, as it stands in the modern context, bears a strong resemblance to its "Hell House" ghost cousin. What starts out a fictitious rumor or truck-stop story, with enough circulation and enough people to believe, eventually crosses the line into believability, becoming potentially true, then accepted, and then absolute *truth* within certain communities. The result is mainstream backlash. Whereas most fiction novels or films are viewed as sources of entertainment, uncensored sources, from rune singing and spell-etched coins of the past to tabloid articles and Internet Web sites, when marketed as holding even a *spot* of potential truth are easily scorned. They become not just fiction, but *negative* forms of fiction.

Thus anyone who even begins to believe in "such things" becomes vulnerable to being seen as crazy. If you happen to be a big fan of a recent bestseller, or a more classic work of literature, there are book circles or clubs available where you can get together and talk about them and their relevance to your own life. We have college courses that look at everything from Jane Austen to (more recently) science fiction and fantasy novels, which deconstruct the stories in terms of what they mean to us and our society. But you certainly would never find groups that discuss tabloid articles in an academic setting (yet) or that talk about paranormal activity without suffering certain social stigmas. "Those kinds of people" are usually pushed off into separate, marginalized societies and must resort to communication through the Internet or other, equally marginalized channels.

Despite the fact that myth, lore, and legend form the fundamental core of our culture, the exchange of ideas about them from an *intrapersonal* perspective—what we may really think, feel, and believe about certain supernatural events, paranormal stories, and superstitions—remains a controversial form of communication. And yet here, in the earlier conception of *Supernatural*, we have a show that projects such ideas as definite truths. Watching it, we would have seen unnatural things happening in our world—or at least a version of our world. Then, as we observed the articles being written up, we would know they were true. And once those articles were released, we would then have seen how society reacted to them as sources of "information."

So even before the Winchesters, *Supernatural* was already about legitimizing the marginal source. In the final reworking of the show as two brothers on the road, fighting the truth behind the stories, we see them actually turning to the same types of articles that the journalist would have written. And okay, not all of them are *True*. Every now and again the show reminds that not every Web maintainer knows what to do with a kelpie or disgruntled pagan god when they meet one. (But who knows? If enough people like what they read, that might just change.) But as seen in the episodes utilizing everyone's favorite Trickster since Loki was chained to a cave wall, though some things may not be true in the way the sources say they are, even the most outlandish source can hold a degree of truth. And just because there is a reasonable explanation for that truth, that doesn't make it any less supernatural.

As the show creates a reality in which the ideas offered by modern sources are true and the modern sources themselves are legitimate, it provides grounds for the audience to believe in a world where the source text could be real. And as the sources that the Winchesters turn to are familiar access points of information to any modern-day audience, they become a unique, interconnecting link between the present real world and the world of *Supernatural*. The Winchesters' sources are *Supernatural*'s writers' sources. The writers' sources are the Winchesters' sources. The people wrote the sources, and the people watch the show.

I believe that this is a large part of the success of *Supernatural* as a whole, as there are a lot of us out there who find a degree of truth or relevance in some of the show's sources. And yet, while we can go out and access them—visit the Web sites, read an old book, or study incantations in Latin on our own—the thing that we cannot do on our own is develop a sense of community, the feeling that there are other people out there who read these sources in that same way, or at least enjoy reading them in the same way whether they believe in them or not. The continuing emergence of the *Supernatural* community—the collaborative network of the show's writers, cast, crew, audience, fans, and interfaced media—creates a safe space in which to explore the fringes of our world together through new perspectives, to use the information that we all access every day while allotting it a greater sense of relevance and importance.

We can feel comfortable about being interested in Internet Web sites that have popped up in the last seventy-two hours, or intrigued by a guidebook on the "Thirty Most Haunted Places in New England"—sources that may not be accepted in a mainstream or academic setting, but are still valuable reflections of current mythologies, and as such, worthy of consideration.

As we have seen through episodes like "Hell House," the way truth in myth develops is through communities, through people and their participation within a given culture or restricted zone. So when culture-conscious and media-linked creations, like *Supernatural*, provide those boundaries of community in which such truths can be explained, it becomes a way for us to observe culture as it shifts. It allows us to watch the development of folklore—a process that in the past would have taken years or even generations. Now, however, with the fast-paced environment of rapid information exchange, we have the opportunity to gaze upon ourselves and reflect on the development of our culture as it is happening. The Web sites, the tabloids, the networking and convergence of groups through the media, these are all reflections of how we see the world—and what we believe to be in it—today. Some of these sources may be "wrong," but with folklore they really do not necessarily need to be accurate—just popular or supported enough to catch on and make an impact.

By interacting and drawing from the modern culture, *Supernatural* becomes an exercise in all of this. It works to show that mythology is not dead and never was.

Supernatural is the convergence of myth as it stands in our culture today. And as more people access, watch, and embrace the show, absorbing its contributions to the morphology of myth—faster than one might think—*Supernatural* itself may soon become a source. In fact, it probably has already.

LONDON E. BRICKLEY is an undergraduate of English and Classics at the University of Rochester. Having spent the better part of the year studying abroad in the Arctic with nothing but ice, limited light, an iPod stuffed with *Supernatural* episodes, and a BlackBerry with satellite Internet, she has had rather ample time to marvel at the scope of networking through global media, acquire a secret crush on Ash, and ponder significant questions like "Do ghosts freeze?" She is gratefully indebted to the entire *Supernatural* team (and fellow fans) for providing limitless, riveting entertainment and for making Latin verb conjugation sexy.

Acknowledgments

Special thanks are due to Sharron Hather (irismay42) for her invaluable assistance with the book's essay introductions.

The publisher would like to thank the following for their assistance with the manuscript:

Christine of Team Winchester (www.teamwinchester.com)
Claire/Wenchpixie of Spnfencentral (spnfencentral.livejournal.com)
Deannie Warner of spn_heavymeta (spn_heavymeta.livejournal.com)

Congratulations to our Supernatural.tv/Smart Pop *Supernatural* Essay Contest finalists:

Mary F. Dominiak (Bardicvoice)
Amanda R. Hauck
Lee C. Hillman (Gwendolyn Grace)
Laura Kilmartin
Samara Jensen
K. Hanna Korossy
Onuma (Anna) Lakamchua
Dawn Nyberg
B.J. Peterson (bjxmas)
Michelle Shavlik
Diana Taleski
Shannon Zufer

And of course, congratulations to our contest winners—London E. Brickley, Avril Hannah-Jones, and Sheryl A. Rakowski—whose essays appear in this book!